NORMANDY
Landscape with Figures

by

PETER GUNN

LONDON
VICTOR GOLLANCZ LTD
1975

© Peter Gunn 1975

ISBN 0 575 01962 x

Printed in Great Britain by
The Camelot Press Ltd, Southampton

To
Lucy M. Boston

But you never saw anything yet in France so lovely as
this Normandy . . .
John Ruskin, August 1848

CONTENTS

LIST OF ILLUSTRATIONS

The illustrations listed below are reproduced by kind permission of the French Government Tourist Office, unless otherwise specified.

PREFACE

To WRITE A readable, and at the same time comprehensive, guide-book on Normandy is perhaps an impossibility; the nature of the country does not lend itself to the kind of formal treatment our natural expectations demand of a guide. Between the polar extremes of the encyclopaedic and the too arbitrarily cursory, the all or nothing, there is no generally acceptable middle term. It is very different from writing a guide, say, to Umbria, where the people in their history have crystal-lised into so many urban nuclei (Perugia, Assisi, Foligno, Orvieto, Spoleto, and so on) like a string of rosary beads, each of which forms successively a centre for our interest and can thus be described seriatim.

The ancient Duchy of Normandy has a well-defined homogeneity, an identity, the result rather of the actions of men, its history, than of the physical configuration, its geography. But our interest is by no means predominantly absorbed by its larger cities and towns—by Rouen, Caen, Bayeux, Alençon and others—to the relative exclusion of its countryside. Further, the ground to be covered is so wide; with a surface of some 11,800 square miles, Normandy has an area nearly a quarter of that of England. A glance at the Michelin map will show, like an astral chart of the northern skies, that this surface is pinpointed with towns, villages, hamlets, châteaux, historical monuments. . . . Off the main roads it is quite impossible for one person both to drive a car and to find his way by map and signpost among those enchanting byways and deep shaded lanes which are so characteristic of the Norman countryside. The composition of an all-inclusive guide is (I repeat) well-nigh impossible. Alan Houghton Broderick, in his in-dispensable book on Normandy in 'The People's Frances' series, has sought to overcome the difficulty of presentation by listing alpha-betically the places worthy of visiting, a traveller's gazetteer. He is not altogether successful, for the subject matter is too intractable; yet his book remains invaluable for its erudition, charm and unflagging interest.

In writing another book on Normandy I have kept before me the aim, or at least the intention—presumption is perhaps the juster word—of attempting something different from what is usually meant by a guide, of producing what might be best described as—failing a better term—a meta-guide. A guide to guides on Normandy; a pointer to where signposts (when they are lacking, as only too often they are) should point. I have tried to present the Norman landscape, peopled with Norman figures; an admixture of the general and the particular, of broad brush strokes and the suggestion of stippling. I wanted—how far short is the wish from the fulfilment—to achieve the kind of travel book that stimulates as a foretaste, an overture, to travel; that serves as a congenial companion to the traveller while in the country ('In thy most need to go by thy side'); and that read in retrospect revives and prolongs past enjoyment. Hell is paved with such intentions.

The first chapter is to an extent descriptive of the countryside, of the regions which geography and history have imposed on Normandy; and this is followed by a series of self-contained essays, arbitrary perhaps in the choice of subject but designed to depict something of the most characteristic aspects of Normandy and the Normans.

Over the centuries a distinction has arisen between High and Low Normandy (*Haute-Normandie* and *Basse-Normandie*), with their capitals respectively at Rouen and Caen, terms which are used still, but which do not correspond to any real or apparent geographical difference, but rather perhaps to the prominence of these two regional capitals. Roughly, High Normandy is the area to the east and north-east of the River Touques, but excluding, to the south, the Norman Perche; all the country to the west of the Touques, with the addition of the Perche, is regarded as Low Normandy. Somewhat paradoxically, in a chiefly undulating countryside, with few hills of more than six hundred feet, Low Normandy includes two of the highest points in the province, the Signal de la Forêt d'Ecouves and the Mont des Avaloirs, the altitude of both being some thirteen hundred feet.

Since Normandy is an ancient province and its inhabitants wedded to tradition, the old names continue to be widely employed to mark off particular districts or regions. At the time of the Revolution, however, the central authorities, with an arbitrariness which is the mark of bureaucrats, decided that the historical province should be obliterated, parcelled into five departments to which rather unimaginative labels were attached: Seine-Inférieure (changed to Seine-Maritime after the Second World War), Eure, Calvados, Orne and Manche. Seine, Eure and Orne are, of course, named after the rivers; Manche is simply 'Channel'. Calvados alone has some historical reverberation, being taken from the designation of the coastal district between Arromanches and Landgrune-sur-Mer, off which lie dangerous reefs, visible at low water, and marked on old English charts with this name, derived from the wreck of the *San Salvador*, a galleon of the Invincible Armada. This is the usual view of the etymology of 'Calvados', but La Varende favours another, an older, origin for the word, arising from the legend that in the year 1001 a wooden figure of Christ was washed ashore near Dives-sur-Mer. The figure—known as the Sanctus Salvator—becoming an object of veneration to thousands of pilgrims, gave the old name of St-Sauver to Dives-sur-Mer and in its corrupted form to this stretch of coast. For the convenience of the reader we have shown these historical and still-used district names on our map—names like the Pays d'Auge, the Perche, the Norman Vexin, etc.

The maps most useful to the visitor to Normandy are the Michelin series (one centimetre to two kilometres), numbers 52, 54, 55, 59 and 60; and those contained in the Michelin *Guide Vert* series, *Normandie* (also published in English, an excellent practical guide).

Those who have helped me with their knowledge and advice are too many to thank individually. However, I am particularly indebted to Philip Hope-Wallace, and to M. l'Abbé Q. Montgomery Wright of Le Chamblac, Eure, whose willingness to put himself at the disposal of others extends far beyond the confines of his Norman parish. He has my warmest thanks for his assistance, hospitality and many acts of kindness. I wish finally to acknowledge my deep sense of gratitude to M. le Commandant J.-F. Dupont-Danican of Le Havre, Président de la Société Pays de Caux, a Norman possessed of a remarkable erudition in all matters of his native province, its history and people, who has helped me in ways too diverse to enumerate. The book is so much better for his having read it; that it is not better still is no fault of his; that must fall squarely on me.

SWALEDALE, YORKSHIRE   PETER GUNN
AUGUST 1974

CHAPTER I

The Lie of the Land

TO THE ENGLISH visitor, who first arrives by sea at the port of Dieppe, Le Havre or Cherbourg and proceeds south, the landscape of Normandy presents an unexpected familiarity, so striking in its likeness—its identity even—to the rich Hampshire countryside or to the rolling Sussex Weald that he senses, with some initial surprise, no shock of foreignness—he feels immediately at home. This feeling must have been shared by the Norman invaders, when nine hundred years ago, after a night's uneasy tossing on the waters of the Channel, they stood on the shore at Pevensey and looked on the land that so soon was to be theirs. This first view of Normandy is not a false one; it is true of much of the ancient province. It will represent the typical Norman landscape in the mind's eye, rather than the much more diversified configuration that is the actual Normandy.

For an understanding of the physiognomy of the country, the lie of the land, something should be said, however summarily, of its geological structure, since this is the key to local variations in the Norman landscape. For ease of representation we may imagine a line drawn from about Cherbourg in the Cotentin peninsula to a little to the west of Alençon in the south. Westwards of this line we are in a region which is a continuation of the ancient Armorican massif, with the schists, hard sandstone and outcrops of granite similar to those of Brittany, and here much modified by the effects of erosion. The rocky nature of the terrain is most noticeable in the north-west of the Cotentin, in the cliffs of the Nez de Jobourg and the Cap de la Hague; but it is also evident in the south of the province, in the range of high ground which runs east from the Bay of Mont-St-Michel through Mortain, Domfront, the environs of Bagnoles-de-l'Orne, and peters out in the hills of the Perche; and it appears also in the parallel lines of hills which cut across the Bocage, and, traversing the upper reaches of the River Vire, extend to the neighbourhood of Argentan.

To the east of this line we find the countryside most usually associated with Normandy, the familiar landscape of smiling, fat meadows covered with lush pasture, of broad, rich cornfields, of gay apple orchards and of magnificent forests of oak and beech. North from the rolling wooded hills of the Perche, which can be regarded as the rim of the Parisian basin, are the upland limestone plateaux, which average some four hundred feet in altitude, cut through by river valleys, that of the Seine being by far the most pronounced, but also by many others—those of the Bresle, Béthune, Epte, Andelle, Eure, Avre, Risle, Charentonne, Touques, Dives and Orne, to name the more important. Among the prevailing chalk and the deposits of alluvial soil, disturbances of the land surface at early periods have revealed outcrops of clay and of clay mixed with flint, the results of erosion at a time when the climate was hotter and wetter than it is now. Two such regions provide some of the very richest pasture land in Normandy, the Pays d'Auge and the Pays de Bray.

The Valley of the Seine

On a map, and indeed on the ground, the most striking topographical feature in Normandy is undoubtedly the valley through which the River Seine meanders, coiling like some mediaeval sea monster. And despite the ugly industrial growth on its banks, particularly the oil refineries towards Le Havre, the river valley is of a singular beauty. The Seine enters Normandy from the Ile de France at its confluence with the Epte, just near Vernon and the village of Giverny, where Claude Monet's water-garden with its lilies (*Nymphéas*) still hides behind its barrier of white wistaria and even whiter roses. In performing its contorted loops, the Seine has in places cut into the high plateau on its banks, exposing the crumbling chalk cliffs, topped by the majesty of its beech woods. It is the magnificence of this almost unbroken woodland that gives the skyline its lofty silhouette, and that closes in the valley with freshness and verdant charm—the forests of Bizy, Vernon, les Andelys, la Tremblaie, Côte-des-Deux-Amants, Louviers, Bord, Rouvray, Verte, Roumare, la Londe, Mauny, le Trait, Brotonne, St Arnoult . . . an exquisite litany of place names. It is through such sylvan scenery that processions of river craft pass (up and downstream) between Paris and Le Havre, gaily painted barges, with their pots of geraniums and fuchsias by the living quarters in the stern and the family washing hanging on the line, more colourful than any herbaceous border. And then the attractiveness of these riverside towns —les Andelys, beneath the shadow of Richard Cœur de Lion's Château-Gaillard; La Bouille, famed for its restaurants right on the river, patronised by the Rouennais; Duclair; Caudebec-en-Caux, with its jewel-like church of Our Lady; or Villequier, where on the river bank stands the Musée Victor Hugo, arranged in the old family house of his ill-fated son-in-law, Charles Vacquerie. Vacquerie and his young wife Léopoldine Hugo were drowned on 4 September 1843, when their boat was upset by the tidal wave, the *mascaret*, which in those days was much fiercer than now. At spring tides, particularly those at the equinoxes, the marine water mounts up against the flow of the Seine; then suddenly its massive build-up is released, and it advances as a barrier of water, moving at the speed of a gallop, dangerous to the unwary. The Vacquerie couple, together with Mme Hugo, are buried in Villequier cemetery.

The whole valley is thickly studded with places that demand a leisured visit: sleepy towns and villages, with their framed houses and carved façades and high slated roofs, and parish churches among the immemorial yews of their churchyards. And, standing between the woods in their pleasant parks, are innumerable châteaux: Bizy, with its rearing horses frozen in stone, the renaissance Gaillon, the decayed manor at Mesnil-sous-Jumièges (where the beautiful Agnès Sorel died in the arms of Charles VII), Tancarville. . . . A valley famous for its ancient abbeys: Fontaine-Guérard, St-Georges-de-Boscherville, Jumièges and St-Wandrille, the last with its very early chapel of St-Saturnin. At Lillebonne, the antique Juliobona, are the remains of the Roman amphitheatre, and above it on the rising ground the ruins of Duke William's castle, where he used his best diplomacy to persuade his Norman barons to join him on his conquest of England. Harfleur, encroached on by Le Havre, retains its mediaeval nucleus round its church with the beautifully tapering spire. At Croisset, on the outskirts of Rouen, only the pavilion in the garden, in which Flaubert wrote most of his works, including *Madame Bovary*, is left of the Louis XV house, once an appendage of the abbey of Jumièges, where (some claim) the Abbé Prévost wrote *Manon Lescaut*. But it is the burly figure of the great Flaubert which still haunts this spot, which he once described typically in a letter to a friend: '. . . the trees, the river-bank and the garden—everything is splendid. Yesterday my lungs were tired from smelling lilacs, and tonight in the river the fish are cutting incredible capers like bourgeois invited to tea at the Préfecture.' And astride the river, and dominating it with its endless rows of docks, is the ancient city of Rouen, the capital of Normandy, seated in an amphitheatre upholstered in green plush.

Maupassant describes in *Bel-Ami* the scene from 'the place famous for its view' on the hill top of Canteleu above Rouen:

> It looked out over the great valley, a long broad chasm through which the shining river wound its way from end to end. It could be seen approaching from far away, dotted with numerous islets, and describing a curve before traversing Rouen. Then the city appeared on the right bank, dimmed by the morning mist, with gleams of sunlight on her roofs and her array of steeples, some pointed and some squat, pierced and wrought like giant jewels, her towers, square or round, topped with heraldic crowns, her belfries and bell-turrets, the entire gothic population of church roofs dominated by the slender spire of the cathedral, that astonishing pinnacle of bronze, ugly, odd, immense, the tallest on earth. . . .

The Pays de Caux and the Pays de Bray

To the north of the Seine lies the Pays de Caux, wedge-like in shape, with its apex at Le Havre. Its centre, properly speaking, would be in the proximity of the market town of Yvetot—or better, Fauville; but, because of the similarity of the countryside to the east of the River Béthune, the name of Pays de Caux has been conveniently extended to include the coastal plain to the north of the Pays de Bray—indeed, right to the boundary of Normandy with Picardy, which is here formed by the River Bresle. It consists of an upland limestone plain, the 'Cauchois plateau', rising gently from south to north, and meeting the Channel in an abrupt jagged face of white chalk cliffs some three hundred feet above the sea. The Pays de Caux is watered by a number of placid streams, the delight of trout fishermen: the Bresle, Yères, Eaulne and Varenne (these last three joining and flowing into the sea at Dieppe as the Arques), the Scie, Saâne, Dun, Durdent, and finally the Lézarde, which, unlike the others, flows south and enters the Seine at Harfleur. The angry seas of the Channel, whipped into fury by Atlantic gales, have clawed deep into the Norman cliffs, subjecting them to a remorseless erosion, and leaving at their feet a shelf, covered with some sand at low tide, but mostly with a noisy shingle of water-smoothed pebbles. The rivers have gouged out valleys in the softish limestone, and it is at their mouths that have been established the fishing ports, like Le Tréport, Dieppe and Fécamp. Other streams have not had the force to achieve this level junction with the Channel, and the steady erosion of the coast has, as it were, left them suspended, forming the distinctive '*valleuses*', hanging coombs or steep clefts in the cliffs, by which one can descend to the beach—such as those at Mesnil-Val, Bruneval or Varengeville.

This landscape of the Pays de Caux, so benign in certain seasons, can be at the mercy of the sea, when gales blow in from the west, with low scudding cloud and driving rain, lashing the trees and leaving them leafless, permanently bent; and hurling the waves at the foot of the cliffs, so that the sea's surface is frothy and churned up like boiling milk. On certain days, or at times of the day, in these flat arable lands, almost barren of trees save for what from the distance appears as an occasional copse, but which in reality marks the presence of an isolated farm—at certain times there is something inexorably melancholy in the Cauchois plain, something of an uneerie desolation. It seems almost as if the Norman painter Millet was not so much depicting his own native Cotentin, but rather that his peasant figures, lonely in the infinite space of plain and sky, were listening to the distant angelus on a sombre evening in the Pays de Caux. But this is only one side of the picture, one aspect of the landscape. There are others, notably the splendid woodland scenery: woods of beeches, through which the sunlight filters, the colour of amber; and of oaks, rosy russet in autumn, when the bracken turns gold beneath them—the Forest of Eu, cool like a cathedral in the summer heats, high above the left bank of the River Bresle; the Forest of Eawy, south of Dieppe, where Sickert delighted to wander; and the magnificent beech woods which border the right bank of the Seine. The smaller woods, sometimes but spinneys and copses, in the hollows which so frequently are found breaking the monotony of the plain, have often hazel and ash as well (supports for thick hanging webs of old man's beard), and at times wild cherry on their edges, and slender silver birches. The roads and drives to châteaux become avenues of chestnuts and limes; the lanes, bordered by tangled thickets of the vegetation of English hedgerows, form dim arboreal tunnels. And then there are the many river valleys, the rich emerald meadows, where cattle comfortably graze by slow meandering streams, that bubble idly over weirs and glide by poplars and pollarded willows, which the blue sky silhouettes, mirrored in the limpid surface of their enamelled waters. These are the streams that Monet loved to paint, with their reflected colours—rivulets, rather than the larger wind-flecked surfaces of Sisley's rivers.

The Cauchois farmhouse, especially in those places exposed to the westerly winds, is as a rule surrounded by high banks lined with rows of trees—elms, oaks, beech and poplars—enclosing the green-carpeted orchard, where the more domestic animals wander at large under the apple-trees, the *cour-masure*, as it is known in these parts of Normandy. Sometimes the farm enclosure is approached through an orchard gateway. Set back and often obscured by the whitewashed boles and the leaves of the fruit trees stands the low farmhouse, flanked by the farm offices, facing a pond and the midden and dung heap. Any wall space is used to support espaliered fruit trees and climbing roses, of which Gloire de Dijon seems still to be a favourite. The well-cared-for garden appears, as is frequently found in Normandy, a delightful mixture of fruit bushes, vegetables and flowers, as if to prove that there no preference is given to any particular branch of horticulture. The house itself, in this part of the country where building stone is scarce, is more often than not built with a timbered frame filled in with local brick, turned rosy-red with the passage of time, or with roughcast finished in a pale colour-wash, or even with 'torchis' (a mixture of clay, straw and horsehair) in some of the oldest. This construction, reaching back to the Gallo-Roman times, is still widely used today, even for more expensive private houses; and so traditional, and socially regarded, is the frame, that I have seen the newly plastered wall of a house in Etretat having the brown woodwork painted on the bare façade.

In modern times, the pace accelerated in recent years, arable land is giving way to pasture all over Normandy, but especially so in these time-honoured cornlands of the Pays de Caux. However, from the middle of last century the inhabitants of the Channel coast have taken to the sea again (following the fashion set by the Duchess of Berry at Dieppe) and have turned to the tourist trade to supplement their economy, lacking as it does any great industrial resources. Apart from the oil-refining and the ancillary processes, and some engineering works at Le Havre, there is little industry in the region, unless we include in it the Pays de Bray, with its huge production of soft cheeses at the Gervais factory in Ferrières-en-Bray. A long chaplet of seaside resorts has grown up from Le Tréport in the north, with its plebeian weekend crowds of hot Parisians pouring from excursion trains: Criel-Plage, Biville-sur-Mer, Berneval-sur-Mer, Puys (made popular by Dumas *fils*), and the fascinating Dieppe. Then westward follow Pourville, Varengeville (with its beautifully placed cliff-top church, where Georges Braque painted a window, and lies buried in the churchyard), Sotteville, Veules-les-Roses, St-Valéry-en-Caux, Veulettes, the two Dalles, Fécamp, Yport, Etretat (brought into fashion by the painter

Isabey, the journalist Alphonse Karr, and by Guy de Maupassant, whose pavilion and garden still stand in the main street) and finally the residential suburb of Le Havre at Ste-Adresse. Most of these are small, intimate resorts, where families return each summer, some having done so for three or four generations; and everyone will have his favourite.

To the east of this plateau of chalk a strange geological quirk of the tertiary period, a displacement of the earth's crust, has resulted in the formation of a depression, known as the 'buttonhole' (*boutonnière*) of the Pays de Bray. Erosion has done its work, and here the rich black clay, which originally lay under the covering of chalk, has been exposed. The suitability of these soils for cattle-raising in conjunction with the presence of abundant water, has produced the celebrated pastures of the region. Poplars mark the courses of the streams, and thick hedges divide these meadows, where graze and ruminate those well-contented herds of Charolais, Cotentines and (increasingly) Friesians, whose milk goes to provide the double creams and cheeses of Neufchâtel and Gournay. It was from this geological displacement also that rose the ferruginous springs which have brought kings and statesmen, among others less exalted, to take the waters of Forges-les-Eaux.

Throughout the Pays de Caux and the Pays de Bray the nobility of earlier times have left monuments of their presence in great estates and fine châteaux, many of which have been preserved. That of Eu is certainly not fine but the site is of great historical interest. The original castle was built by Rollo, the first Norman duke; it was at Eu that the future Conqueror married Matilda of Flanders, and rather forcibly entertained the Saxon Harold. Joan of Arc spent the night at Eu on her journey from Compiègne to the stake at Rouen. Long afterwards it came into the possession of Mlle de Montpensier, la Grand Mademoiselle, the lover of Lauzun, and thence to the Orléans branch of the French royal family. The château was a favourite residence of Louis-Philippe, who twice received Queen Victoria at Eu, when she landed from the royal yacht at Le Tréport.

Normans, with understandable patriotic pride, have claimed for their countrymen some outstanding contributions to early French literature, beginning with the celebrated *Chanson de Roland*, which was said to have been on the lips of the minstrel-warrior Taillefer as he died at Hastings. With this innocently biased end in view, much has been read into the last line of the earliest existing copy of the *Chanson*, which is in the Bodleian Library at Oxford. This concludes with the words, '*Ci falt la geste, que Turoldus declinet*', and it is the last two—'Turoldus declinet'—that present the problem. The Scandinavian name Turold seems to favour the pro-Norman partisans—but 'declinet'? Nobody can be sure what it means in this context. All that can be safely said is that it could possibly point to a Norman author. Perhaps we are on somewhat surer ground in deciding in favour of a Norman origin for the 'Thomas of Britain' whose work, written in Anglo-Norman French, played so important a part in the final development of what is universally recognised as a masterpiece of mediaeval romance, the story of *Tristram and Yseult*.

However, among these questions of literary antecedents there is one in which the Abbey of Fécamp plays a most important part—and this one happily leaves little room for the same kinds of doubt. In the abbey church of Ste-Trinité is preserved a sixteenth-century tabernacle, containing the relic of the Holy Blood, the *Saint-Sang*. The legends which have grown up around the miraculous preservation of the Precious Blood are very ancient and have come down to us in many variants. One such is that Joseph of Arimathaea (or Nicodemus), in burying the body of Christ, kept a phial of the blood and some of the instruments of the crucifixion, and bequeathed them to his nephew Isaac in Jerusalem. In possession of the precious blood Isaac prospered; but his wife, discovering the cause of this prosperity, denounced him to the priests. Saved from death by Christ's intercession, Isaac moved to Sidon, where, fearing the coming of Titus and Vespasian, he hid the relics, sealed in leaden containers, in a fig-tree. Again, warned by a voice of the danger from the Romans, he cut down the fig-tree and cast it into the sea, with the prayer that God would cause the trunk to be carried to one of the farthest provinces of France. It was indeed cast up on the shore of the valley which thenceforward has been called *Fici campus*, the field of the fig-tree, or Fécamp.

These miraculous events were held to have taken place in the first century of our era; and on the spot where the relics came ashore (the relics that today are in Ste-Trinité) a spring gushed forth, which supplies the Fountain of the Precious Blood in Fécamp. (It is located in the court, which is entered from No. 12 rue de l'Aumône.) The relics and the therapeutic qualities of the spring draw many pilgrims to Fécamp; and in about 660 a convent of nuns was founded by St Waneng, but this religious house was destroyed in the raids of the Vikings. The Norman Duke Richard I later rebuilt a sanctuary on the spot in honour of the Trinity; and his son Richard II raised there an abbey of Bene-dictine monks, which in 1003 he placed under the celebrated William of Volpiano. The abbey of Fécamp, with the active patronage of the Norman dukes and the Anglo-Norman kings, who early formed the custom of spending the festival of Easter there, became the chief place of pilgrimage in Normandy before the development of Mont-St-Michel. A flourishing guild of minstrels and jongleurs, enjoying the protection and encouragement of the abbots, spread the fame of the relic of the Holy Blood throughout northern Europe. And they did more: it was largely by their means that European literature was en-riched in poetry and prose by the epic cycle of King Arthur and his Knights of the Round Table.

The connection between the great Benedictine houses of Fécamp and Glastonbury was close, both being linked with the legend of Joseph of Arimathaea—or rather, of Arimathaea-Nicodemus, since the monks, like the evangelists themselves, confused the two men. For Glastonbury also had its *Saint-Sang* legend; in the tomb of Joseph of Arimathaea, who was claimed by its monks as the founder of their abbey, was buried with him a phial of the Blood of Our Lord. Further, at Glastonbury were the tombs of King Arthur and his Queen Guine-vere. The myth of the search for the Holy Grail was in its origin British, related as it is to the primitive cult of the regenerative forces in nature. The myth was inseparably bound up with the Arthurian cycle; one of the most sacred tasks of the Knights of the Round Table—of Gawain, Perceval and Galahad in turn—was the quest for the Grail, in all its successive transformations. With time the original nature-cult elements of the legends gave way and were transfigured beneath the weight of the Christian mystical, sacramental accretions. The text of the Grail romance *Perlesvaus* (Perceval) was from an original written at Fécamp. This version, as Jessie L. Weston has maintained, 'alone, of all the Grail romances, connects the hero alike with Nicodemus, and with Joseph of Arimathaea, the respective protagonists of the *Saint-Sang* legends; while its assertion that the original Latin text was found in a holy house situated in the marshes, the burial place of Arthur and Guinevere, unmistakably points to Glastonbury'. Fécamp and Glaston-bury then share between them the glory of having nurtured within their walls and transmitted to posterity this literary cycle, which embodies so much of the feelings and aspirations of northern society in the Middle Ages. And since both these abbeys are no more, in this cycle they have left us their memorials.

The Norman Vexin

South of the Pays de Bray extends the Norman Vexin, a generous countryside of large farms, magnificent beech woods—the Forest of Lyons being considered one of the most beautiful in France—and pleasant valleys. The Vexin constitutes much of the western marches between the lands of the Dukes of Normandy and those of the Kings of France, and both banks of the River Epte, the boundary, once bristled with fortresses, whose imposing ruins can be seen today, especially at Gisors, and at Richard Cœur de Lion's Château-Gaillard on the Seine. Nothing could be more charming than the little town of Lyons-le-Forêt, wrapped round with its mantle of green. The Duke-King Henry I (Henri Beauclerc the Normans call him) died at Lyons in 1135. In the vicinity of Lyons-le-Forêt are the ruins of the Abbey of Mortemer and the château at Vascœuil, recently restored in all the glory of its warm brick, where the historian Michelet lived. Apart from the beautiful churches of Gisors, Le Grand- and Le Petit-Andelys, the Vexin contains a number of parish churches of great interest for the quality of their early fourteenth-century statuary: Pont-St-Pierre, Lisors, Ecos, Mezières-en-Vexin, Saussaye-la-Campagne, Guiseniers, Mainneville—and above all, Ecouis. The collegial church of Notre-Dame d'Ecouis is a museum of exquisite French gothic carving. Its stalls of the same period are prized as some of the finest in Normandy, and the walls of the choir have beautiful carved panelling of the renaissance (sixteenth century). This church, which the Abbé Bretocq considers as the source and inspiration of a Vexin school of sculptors, was founded in 1313 by the munificence of Philippe le Bel's Chamberlain, Enguerrand de Marigny.

The Evrecin and the Pays d'Ouche

South and south-west of the Norman Vexin, across the valley of the Seine, lies the region of the Evrecin, which abuts to the west on the Pays d'Ouche. These regions consist in the main of large fields of 'grandes cultures', and of woods which appear pale in the distance, seeming to hem them in: a wide countryside, at moments showing a rather sad visage, of almost mournful, sparsely inhabited spaces, under the powdered azure or marine greys of the vast concavity of the sky; except in the river valleys—and of these happily there are many, a radiant veining of clear streams: the Eure, Avre, Iton, Rouloir, Risle, Charentonne, and their tributaries. And here again there is no lack of

woodland—in dense, impenetrable forests, scattered woods and intermittent spinneys. How beautiful and how carefully preserved are these
State (and in places private) forests, where the main roads which cross
them are shaded and grassed avenues, and an interlacing of rides has
been cut through (many from ducal times) to allow them to be hunted
—impossible otherwise. In the clearings stand neatly stacked piles of
measured timber, and everywhere one marks the absence of broken
boughs and neglected undergrowth. These are the Forests of Evreux,
Beaumont, Conches, Breteuil and Ivry, or woods like the Bois
d'Acquigny or that of Broglie.

In the north and in the south of the Evrecin we find respectively the
market-towns of Le Neubourg and St-André-de-l'Eure, both of which
have given their names to *pays*. Evreux is a very ancient city, now recovered from the fearful destruction of the last war. In the vicinity have
been unearthed many Gallo-Roman remains, the best known, a statue
of *Jupiter Stator*, being conserved in the museum. But the most renowned
of Evreux's monuments is the cathedral, whose stained-glass windows
brought Marcel Proust here in his armadillo of a motor car driven by
his beloved Agostini. It was at Evreux that he studied the glass, which
(with the windows of St-Ouen at Pont-Audemer) served as a model for
that of St-Hilaire at Combray, and here he noticed how at dusk the
light seemed to come from within the building outwards. The romanesque church of St-Taurin shows some Byzantine influence (come by
way of the Normans in Southern Italy) in the blue and red lozenges on
the external face of the south transept; and in the reliquary (*chasse*) of
its eponymous founder it possesses one of the finest examples of the art
of French gothic goldsmiths, the gift of St Louis.

Verneuil, on the River Avre, was a frontier outpost of the Norman
Duchy from earliest times. A stake was said to have been placed in the
river bed for the purpose of demarcation, thus separating 'French'
from 'Norman' water. The town has two beautiful churches—that of
the Madeleine, with its tower rivalling the famous Butter Tower of
Rouen Cathedral, and its glass and statues; and that of Notre-Dame,
another museum of local carving of the early 1500s. It also boasts some
fine mediaeval half-timbered houses. Breteuil, Rugles, Conches-en-
Ouche (with the beautiful apsidal windows of the Church of Ste-Foy),
Beaumont-le-Roger, Orbec, Broglie, Bernay . . . so many small towns,
so rich in their interest. It was at Orbec, in the garden of the Hôtel
du Croisy in the main street of this charming unspoilt town, that
Claude Debussy—the composer from the neighbouring Ile-de-France

who perhaps best reflects the graduated nuances of the Norman land-scape and seascape—wrote his *Jardins sous la pluie*. And everywhere in the countryside one comes upon charming old manor houses, mostly in warm weathered stone.

In the south of the Pays d'Ouche there exist still some remains of two famous monasteries: that of the Cistercian Breuil-Benoît at Marcilly, and away to the west the early eleventh-century Benedictine founda-tion of St-Evroult-Notre-Dame-du-Bois. At Bernay the abbey church of another foundation of this period is at the moment being restored, after years of neglect: the magnificent romanesque building of Judith, wife of Duke Richard II, begun in 1013. The Duchess Judith has her tomb in the nearby Basilica Notre-Dame-de-la-Couture, a pilgrim Church, where on Whit Monday gather, with their banners, the con-fraternities of the Charities.

The Charities, although not a peculiarly Norman institution, as some have claimed—they appear to have parallels in Italy, for example in the Neapolitan confraternities, and also in those of Taranto (although these may well be Norman in origin)—have always been numerous in Normandy, surviving the French Revolution, when they were banned, as well as the advent of the welfare state. The *Confréries* grew up in the early Middle Ages with the practical aim of ensuring Christian burial for the dead, and perhaps of succouring survivors. These two purposes they have continued to serve, earning a name for devotion, even for heroism, throughout the Middle Ages, especially at the periodical visitations of the plague. They consist of bands of men, thirteen in number, a master and twelve brothers (in imitation of Christ and the Apostles), of all ages and every social rank. On the Bayeux tapestry a man with a handbell appears in the scene depicting the funeral of Edward the Confessor, and the Charities claim him as one of them. In the parish churches of Normandy the visitor will sometimes find dis-played the Charities' *torchères*, the poles often beautifully wrought in bright metal, and their banners of faded silk worked with gold and silver thread, each bearing the local name and the date of the founda-tion. Orbec is thought by some to be the oldest existing Charity (1006), followed by Broglie (1055) (although it was then known as Chambrais, only changing its name in 1742 when it was raised to a duchy in honour of the famous Piedmont family of Broglio, now called Broglie). Some, however, prefer the claim of Menneval (1060); early, too, were those of the villages of Ailly, Giverville, Hauville and St-Victor-d'Epine. In processions the master and brothers advance, preceded by bellmen, sounding their *tintenelles* according to an unvarying, traditional rhythm. They wear their varicoloured *chaperons* (hoods), again worked with gold and silver, crossed over one shoulder; their heads are covered by caps, shaped like an ecclesiastical biretta.

The Perche

To the south of the Pays d'Ouche, and bordering on the Ile-de-France, lies the Perche, a region of folding hills which rise at places to a thousand feet and form a watershed, with rivers running both north and south. It is a moist countryside, besprinkled with ponds, and heavily wooded with dense forests like those of Bellême, Perche, La Trappe, Reno-Valdieu, Longny and Saussay. Centuries ago much of this primeval forest was cleared, and consists now of well-watered pastures, separated by close-clipped hedges. This is a corner of Normandy which has always been celebrated for the raising of horses; here are reared those stalwart, powerful grey Percherons, the war-chargers of the Normans. It was the Norman Roger de Bellesme (Bellême) from the Perche, a follower of William the Conqueror, and afterwards Earl of Shrewsbury, who introduced French horses (with possibly some Spanish stallions) into England, greatly improving the native breed. The only sizeable towns are Mortagne-au-Perche and Bellême; but there are a number of pleasant villages: Nocé, Rémalard, Longny-au-Perche, Tourouvre. Besides the châteaux of Feillet, Rémalard and Les Feugerets, there are many smaller stone manor-houses of the fifteenth and sixteenth centuries, whose pepper-pot towers and turrets, and their machicolations, suggest (it is in appearance rather than fact) warlike resistance in these marches of Normandy and France—L'Argenardière, Ste-Gauberge, Les Chaponnière, Courboyer, Lormarin, de la Vove. At Serigny, just outside Bellême, is La Tertre, the house where the writer Roger Martin du Gard lived and worked. The Perche, in the seventeenth century, sent out many of its sons and daughters as colonists to Canada; from the little village of Parfondeval, for example, emigrated members of the Trudel family, who settled on the banks of the Saint Lawrence, and today their Canadian descendants are numbered in thousands.

Near the northern limits of the Perche, by a small lake or large pool among the trees of the Forest of La Trappe, stands the Abbey of the Grande-Trappe, the mother-house of the Trappist Order, those communities of the strictest observance, regarded as possibly the most penitential régime in Western monasticism. Originally an abbey of the

Cistercians, La Trappe had suffered much during the English wars of the fifteenth century, and also from the feudal practice of appointing commendatory abbots, so that the congregation had fallen to merely seven monks, whose manner of living was cause for great scandal when Armand Jean Le Bouthillier de Rancé became regular abbot in 1664. With the new appointment, all was changed.

Rancé's reforms of the Cistercian observance, as set out in that handbook of asceticism, *Holiness and Duties of the Monastic Life* (1683) and in his regulations for the community, are so elaborately detailed as to appear to some of us as a work of masochistic pedantry, of terrifying, inhuman casuistry, the minutiae of maceration. The monk was to live only for God, to live in this world a living death, with eternal matters alone occupying his mind—to turn his gaze from God was a 'spiritual fornication'. Every act of his day was regulated, every action, every movement or gesture was prescribed or proscribed: he must not use the arm of the chair, he must not rest his elbows on his knees when bending down, he must not yawn; he must always look cheerful, he must not move the furniture of his cell, on retiring to bed he must sit up at first and not lie down. In like manner he was directed in church, refectory, cloisters, in all his menial tasks. He must die on a litter of straw and ashes. Austerity, obedience, perpetual silence. The silence has been resounding; many have heard all over the world the call of the Abbé de Rancé from his austere cell in the Perche, and have obeyed.

The Roumois and the Lieuvin

North of the Plain of Neubourg and of the Pays d'Ouche, and bounded beyond the Seine by the Pays de Caux and the Norman Vexin, and to the west by the River Touques, lies the rich countryside of the Roumois and the Lieuvin. The gently-flowing Risle provides a clearly identified line of demarcation between the two *pays*. However, it soon becomes clear to the visitor to Normandy that this division into *pays* is only very approximate. In the Roumois, the *pays* of Rouen (*pagus rothomagensis*), how dissimilar are the luxuriant rich, flat meadows of the drained fens of the Marais Vernier from the rolling countryside around Bourg-Achard. From the point of view of nomenclature, in the Lieuvin (*lexoviensis pagus*), the *pays* of Lisieux, the city itself is not only on the extreme edge of its 'country', but Lisieux is regarded by many people as the capital of the neighbouring Pays d'Auge. The reason for the extension of this latter *pays* to cover districts with which it was not historically connected is a brashly commercial one: to cash in on the cachet, as it were, of the products of the celebrated Vallée d'Auge. Furthermore, limited parts of one *pays* can be very similar to those of another: the incredible beauty and fertility of the hills and valleys behind Honfleur in the Roumois, a paradise of verdure, are matched by the landscape, say, around Vimoutiers in the Camembert-producing country of the Pays d'Auge. In the matter of names confusion is often doubly confounded.

Everywhere in the countryside of the Roumois and the Lieuvin we come upon scenery singularly intimate in its tranquil charm, in the emerald freshness of orchards, meadows, hedges and woods, in smiling river valleys and sylvan hills—in all this luxuriant harmony of greens. Besides the grandeur of the woods on the left bank of the Seine—the Forests of La Londe, Mauny and Brontonne—the high ground behind Honfleur and the Côte de Grâce is covered with the beech-trees of the Forest of St-Gatien, and here, and in the adjoining hills and valleys, the lanes become tunnels of green gloom, while all around are orchards of apples (and pears), white and pink blossomed in May, when the hedgerows and banks are bright with primroses, bluebells, campions and wild orchids, and the copses are filled with the fresh and tender leafage of elms, limes and flowering chestnuts. Here, if anywhere, we feel impelled, with Marvell, to

> Annihilate everything that's made
> Into a green thought in a green shade.

On the southern bank of the estuary of the Seine from the Marais Vernier to Trouville the road follows the shore, in its later stages rising to form a delightful *corniche*. At Grestain, in an orchard, a memorial tablet on what little ruins remain of ancient stonework informs us that on this spot lie buried Arlette, the mother of William the Conqueror, and her husband Herluin de Conteville, who founded an abbey here about 1050. And then there is Honfleur, this small port gathering together around a dock, the Lieutenance, its ancient houses—a town of the rarest distinction, perhaps the most beautiful in all Normandy. The church of Ste-Catherine d'Honfleur is constructed in timber by those master-builders of the *caravelles* for the Honfleurais corsairs, who sailed the seven seas and were rivalled in the intrepidity of their maritime exploits only by the *armateurs* of Dieppe. The church and its unusual free-standing *clocher*, which seem to have been hewn and shaped solely by the use of a shipwright's adze, are (I am assured by M. Dupont-Danican) common in Scandinavia. They are unique in Normandy. Above the town, on the Côte de Grâce, among a grove of limes and chestnuts, planted here three hundred years ago by Mlle de Montpensier, is the sailors' chapel of Notre-Dame-de-Grâce, with its curious coiffed porch and steeple of pewter-coloured slate. And below at Vasouy, on the Trouville road, stood the Ferme de St-Siméon, where Mère Toutain dispensed, under the shade of the apple-trees, her homely food and her good strong Norman cider to the band of impecunious painters who were to constitute the nucleus of the impressionist school.

Charles Baudelaire had a particular affection for Honfleur, where he had stayed with his mother, and it was perhaps the sight of the ships drawn up in the basin of the Lieutenance that furnished him with the images of *L'Invitation au voyage*, which he wrote there:

> *Vois sur ces canaux*
> *Dormir ces vaisseaux*
> *Dont l'humeur est vagabonde;*
> *C'est pour assouvir*
> *Ton moindre désir*
> *Qu'ils viennent du bout du monde.*
>
> *—Les soleils couchants*
> *Revêtent les champs,*
> *Les canaux, la ville entière,*
> *D'hyacinthe et d'or;*
> *Le monde s'endort*
> *Dans une chaude lumière.*
>
> *Là, tout n'est qu'ordre et beauté,*
> *Luxe, calme et volupté.*

At Criquebeuf (a Norse name, by the way, improperly spelled 'Criquebœuf'), standing above a pond, is the little ivy-covered church which Proust remembered from his youth in a letter to his actress-love Louisa de Morand. It was here, between Criquebeuf and Trouville, in the leafy avenue of Les Allées Marguerite and above the cliffs of Les Creuniers that he had walked with Marie Finaly, whose green eyes set him humming Gabriel Fauré's setting of Baudelaire's poem *Chant d'automne*:

> *J'aime de vos longs veux la lumière verdâtre.*

A cottage near Lisieux

The quay at Honfleur

Recalling that Baudelaire had written the poem while at Honfleur, Proust wondered (or rather the narrator in *A la Recherche* wondered) 'whether Baudelaire's "ray of sunlight on the sea" [*le soleil rayonnant sur la mer*] was not the same that at this very moment was burning the sea like a topaz, fermenting it till it became pale and milky as beer, as frothy as milk. . . .' These heights above Trouville were occupied by sumptuous Victorian villas, set in park-like gardens, and inhabited by so many of Proust's friends. Trouville was, in the middle ages, only a smaller offshoot of the port of Touques, where the troops of Henry V of England landed in 1417; it was 'discovered' by the painter Isabey early in the nineteenth century, and popularised by Alexandre Dumas *père*. Gustave Flaubert remembered with nostalgic regret the little fishing village, where as a child and youth he spent the summer holidays with his family and their relations. In 1853 he wrote to his importunate mistress Louise Colet of the phantoms of the past raised by a revisit to 'this already too popular resort': 'I cannot take a step without running on some youthful memory. Each wave as it breaks re-awakens within me impressions of long ago. I hear a roar of days that are past, and an unending surge, like the surge of the sea, of vanished emotions. I keep remembering my old spasms, fits of melancholy, gusts of desire blowing like a wind in a rigging, and vast vague longings whirling in darkness like a flock of wild gulls in a storm-cloud. . . .'

The two largest towns of these regions are Elbeuf on the Seine, famous for its cloth, whose sombre ugliness is partly relieved by its two churches of St-Etienne and St-Jean, which have some sixteenth-century stained glass; and Lisieux, the centre of popular pilgrimage to the Convent of the Carmel, to the hideous modern Basilica and to the house of Les Buissonnets (the more correct spelling is Bissonnets) in recognition of the young Norman woman, Thérèse de l'Enfant-Jesus (Marie-Thérèse Martin), who was already venerated by many simple and ardent souls before she was canonised by the Church on 17 May 1925. Lisieux suffered devastation in the last war and few of its mediaeval timber-framed houses, with their exotic or grotesque carvings, have survived. Of the smaller towns Pont l'Evêque on the Touques, celebrated for its cheese, also suffered war damage, but Pont-Audemer, on the Risle, got off more lightly. As we have already remarked, the church of St-Ouen possesses beautiful renaissance glass so admired by Proust. At the excellent inn of Le Vieux Puits we are reminded of Flaubert and *Madame Bovary*. Behind the inn lies the garden, which now covers a space formerly open to the waters of one of the branches of the Risle.

B

Until some short time after the First World War this whole area was occupied by a tannery, owned and run by a Monsieur Harlay, who in about 1920–21 erected here the large wooden construction, with its two great ropewheels to haul up water, which we now see. This was the well from the Hôtel du Cygne formerly in the Place Beauvoisine in Rouen. In *Madame Bovary* Charles Bovary takes Emma on a visit to Rouen, where they put up at the Cygne, referred to in the novel as the 'Croix Rouge'—'a good old house, with worm-eaten balconies that creak in the wind on winter nights, always full of people, noise, and feeding, whose black tables are sticky with coffee and brandy, thick windows made yellow by the flies, the damp napkins stained with cheap wine, and that always smells of the village, like ploughboys dressed in Sunday clothes. . . .' This old coaching hostelry was demolished in 1909, part of its contents finding their way into the museum at Rouen, and the well, purchased by M. Harlay, being later erected at Pont Audemer, where it has given its name to this pleasant inn. One of the specialities of the house is *Truite Bovary au champagne*.

In the flowering valley of the Risle, between Montfort and Brionne, near the junction of a little stream or beck, stand the impressive remains of the Abbey of Bec-Hellouin, which was a radiant point of civilised light in the dark ages of the eleventh and twelfth centuries. Bec-Hellouin may with justice claim to be the university of its age, famed far beyond the confines of Normandy, and of France—'the most renowned school of Christendom', in the words of the historian J. R. Green. The quiet beauty of its secluded site among the plane trees and massy chestnuts is still today most moving.

A hermitage was founded near the village of Bonneville in 1034 by the unlettered Norman knight Herluin (Hellouin), son of Ansgot the Dane, a typical member of the Scandinavian ruling class. The spot chosen proving unsuitable, the community which had grown up around Herluin's cell moved twice before becoming established on the banks of the Risle. In 1042, the year after the abbey had been dedicated by Mauger, Archbishop of Rouen and uncle of the young Duke William, the Lombard scholar Lanfranc arrived at Bec-Hellouin, where later he set up a school which became famous throughout Europe. Among the many educated there was the future Pope Alexander II who, it is said, even as Pope always rose to his feet in the presence of his former master. Apart from his teaching, Lanfranc was given the superintendence of the resuscitation of the Abbey of St-Evroult in the Pays d'Ouche, founded in the sixth century, but destroyed by the Vikings. To Lanfranc's gifts as a teacher must be added those of an administrator. Within a few years St-Evroult could almost rival Bec-Hellouin as a school of scholarship. In the same century as its refounding, it sent out five monks, Geoffrey, Gilbert, Odon, Turic and William to teach in England. Among the fens at Cottenham they built their huts and began their humane work; in this way they may make a strong claim to have been the founders of the University of Cambridge. It was here that Duke William, about the year 1047, first met the man who was to be his close adviser, first in Caen, and later as Archbishop of Canterbury. Tooting Bec, on the outskirts of London, derives its name from one of the many manors bestowed on the Abbey of Bec-Hellouin by the Conqueror.

The Pays d'Auge

It has been said of the Pays d'Auge that it is 'the heart and symbol of the traditional Normandy'. Properly so called, it consists of the hilly countryside between the Rivers Touques and Dives, and extending to the south somewhat beyond Vimoutiers. It is not for nothing that the region to the east of the Touques, the beautiful country behind Honfleur and around St-André-d'Hébertot, should frequently (if wrongly) be included in the Pays d'Auge, since the whole of this area, so rich in its carpet of green meadows, its orchards, hedges and copses, is remarkably similar, so very characteristically 'Norman'. This is the moist country of the *'clos normands'*, the orchards, corresponding to the *coursmasures* of the Pays de Caux, in which are found the timbered farmhouses and outbuildings, most often washed over in white between the brown wooden frame, but sometimes in salmon and pink. One of the characteristic features of the buildings of the Pays d'Auge is the narrow brick (*tuileau*), used with most decorative effect in designs between the framework. It is also a countryside of châteaux, old manors and charming thatched or tiled cottages. So dense is this mantle of verdure that the difference in soils is obscured; for here again, as in the Pays de Bray, a displacement of the earth's surface has occurred, which has raised the underlying bed of chalk to form these hills, cut through only by the valley of the lower Touques, and which drop away steeply from a height of some three hundred feet in the west, over the Dives' valley and the Plaine de Caen—the abrupt edge of the Côte d'Auge. The name of 'Auge' is very ancient, and has been variously explained. Perhaps a possible derivation is from *pagus augensis*, the domains, that is, of the Counts of Eu, since the first count, William, the natural son of Duke Richard I, and his wife Lesceline (whose tomb has recently been placed in the apse of the abbey church at St-Pierre-sur-Dives) held the greater part of these regions.

The Pays d'Auge has, perhaps not quite justifiably, the reputation of being the country *par excellence* for the making of cider, the national beverage. Equally good is that made in the Cotentin, Roumois and the Pays de Caux. Who has not seen those orchards, where the trees often are planted in quincunxes, in April and May a symphony of pink, green and white (this from the pears and cherries), or in autumn, with rustic ladders propped against branches, when the farmer's family gather into pyramids the tiny cider-apples? For the small varieties are preferred—'*Petites pommes, gros cidre*', is the Norman expression. Even in England Norman varieties have found favour, as their charming names indicate: Cherry Norman, Cummy Norman, Handsome Norman, Strawberry Norman, White Bache or Norman, Broad-leaved Norman, and others which are common on both sides of the Channel: Argile Grise, Bramtôt, De Boutville, Fréquin Audièvre and Medaille d'Or. The circular grooved stone of the cider-mill with the great stone crushing wheel on its wooden arm and the enormous tuns for storage of the cider are much in evidence, but thousands of bushels of apples are now pressed and the juice extracted and fermented in modern factories; and the itinerant distiller of apple spirit, Calvados, with his contraption of a still on wheels, is passing into memory. Formerly Calvados was made in the *clos* and the farmer would reverently store away the precious spirit in oaken casks under the roof to be matured for years—fifteen to twenty years are necessary to achieve perfection, when the Calvados has turned from a fiery white to a solemn softness of amber. Newcomers to an old Norman farm would wonder what could occupy the farmer so long, when he mounted to the loft on a summer evening. Calvados is one of the most delicate of spirits, and, for those who might require a practical reason for drinking, an excellent *digestif*. It constitutes the celebrated *trou Normand*, the tiny wooden noggin (or rather nipperkin) partaken between courses. Calvados is very widely drunk; a '*café Calva*', the coffee laced with the spirit, is demanded everywhere in Normandy.

Cider was not always the Norman national drink. The apple-tree, cultivated in quantity, only appeared about the fourteenth century, being introduced, it is thought, by the Kings of Navarre, who had large estates in Normandy. (The tradition that it was brought in by the

Crusader Robert Bertrand II of Bricquebec at the end of the eleventh century appears to be without foundation.) Cider is still made and drunk in Navarre, coming from the fertile upland valleys in the Pyrenees and around Pamplona, where the trees will grow from seed, and do not need grafting as is demanded by the harsher climate of the north. Evidence of this origin is that formerly the apple-trees were known in Normandy as bisquaits, that is, coming from the regions of the Bay of Biscay. In the reign of Henry VIII English troops under the Earl of Dorset, engaged in attacking Navarre, complained that the cider made them sick and that the wine was too 'hot'. Until the eleventh century wine was made in the Duchy, and pretty coarse stuff it must have been, since it was called *arrache-boyau*, tear-gut. Presumably beer was also widely drunk. Later wine was imported from localities of superior growths, only altar wine being produced locally, as, for example, that by the monks of Jumièges—although it must be recalled that Rheims and Laon are in the same degree of latitude as much of Normandy. The only vineyard I have seen in Normandy was a small, meagre-looking one near Gaillon. Cider, *le bon bère*, is drunk bottled, *bouché* (when it should be soft—not sharp—and 'quiet', with just a mild, delicate sparkle) or still—but it is wiser to know the provenance of the latter. From the small hard Norman pears a good perry is also made. It is not usually appreciated that perry is the older beverage; it keeps longer than cider, and can become of a most delicate flavour with age.

The excellence of the Norman cuisine owes much to the quality of its cream, and none is finer than that produced in the Pays d'Auge, coming from those gentle, vacuous-faced cows, whose variegated coats, pied, flecked, brindled, freckled, relieve the emerald uniformity of the meadows. (How often in Normandy does one see the elsewhere unfamiliar sight of cows and horses grazing together.) The cream is the colour of ivory, smooth, with a texture of velvet, opulent—*onctueuse* is their word for it. From such material it is small wonder that their cheeses achieve perfection. Of the three most renowned, Pont l'Evêque, Livarot and Camembert, the first two have been made at least since the thirteenth century. Pont l'Evêque is very much the cheese of the farmer's wife, the cheese of the *clos*, which on market days is offered for sale in the squares and streets of Norman towns by these spare women dressed in black, displayed alongside the butter, cream, eggs, poultry (live and dead), domestic rabbits, fresh vegetables, fruit and bunches of herbs and of flowers. The reason for this farmyard economy is that the process of making Pont l'Evêque must be begun when the milk is still warm and creamy. Livarot is a fine cheese and one should not be put off by what to some at first seems to be too pungent an aroma. As a matter of fact, there is a tendency, especially in England, to eat all these cheeses when they are over-ripe; they are best eaten, as they are in Normandy, when they are matured, but firm and fresh. I am told by a Norman that women should not be allowed to buy the cheese for the family; only a man can be a connoisseur of cheese—he alone has a nose for it.

The most famous of all is undoubtedly Camembert—ninety per cent of the cheese produced in the department of Calvados being of this type—and this would suggest that there was not much room for the other twenty varieties of cheese which, it is claimed, are the 'glory' of Normandy; but then the production of Camembert by modern methods is immense. Originally Camembert was a blue cheese, until the advent of Mme Harel, a farmer's wife from the village of Camembert, which is some three miles south-west of Vimoutiers, in Charlotte Corday's country. Mme Harel had the brainwave (or perhaps it was a miraculous intervention from on high—it could hardly have been less) of introducing a mould from the *bondons* of the Pays de Bray into her cheeses. The fame of Camembert was ensured. And Mme Harel's no less. At a road-junction outside her village a fitting memorial has been raised to her genius, which reads:

In
Honour
of
Mme Harel
née
Marie Fontaine
1761–18 [*sic*]
who
INVENTED
THE
CAMEMBERT

And at Vimoutiers, where the greatest production of Camembert is carried on, and where is held annually at Easter one of the largest cheese fairs in France, there are no fewer than two further memorials to the illustrious lady. One, a rather more than life-size stone statue, represents her proffering with one hand to the passer-by her precious flat, round cheese.

A region so rich as this abounds, as we have remarked, in châteaux, manors, and ancient farmhouses and cottages. But there is one small sixteenth-century château, or rather, large manor-house, which is quite perfect both architecturally and chromatically; this is St-Germain-de-Livet, whose walls of chequered stone and brick (the bricks glazed green, turquoise, blue and red) are reflected in the still surface of its moat. Besides a number of parish churches of great charm and interest, two larger edifices are particularly worthy of note: Notre-Dame-de-l'Epinay at St-Pierre-sur-Dives, and another Notre-Dame, that of Dives-sur-Mer, both of which were romanesque structures rebuilt in part in the fourteenth and fifteenth centuries. In the chapter house of Notre-Dame-de-l'Epinay the floor is covered with early thirteenth-century tiles of great rarity and beauty. By a coincidence both these towns still possess their covered markets. But, alas, in Dives-sur-Mer the sixteenth-century hostelry of Guillaume-le-Conquérant, a museum of Norman furniture and mementoes, is no more. This famous old inn, whose name recalls that William the Conqueror gathered his fleet here at Dives in the summer of 1066, and whose cider met with the approval of that connoisseur of all things Norman, Marcel Proust, is up for sale. Let us hope that it may yet be saved.

The coastal strip of the Pays d'Auge from Cabourg to Deauville is occupied by an almost unbroken series of more (or less) fashionable seaside resorts, with stretches of fine sand on either side of the cliffs of the Vaches Noires. These resorts are largely the creation of the Second Empire, of shrewd speculators like Napoleon III's half-brother, that magnificent illegitimate, the Duke of Morny. To the admirers of Proust Cabourg is today something of a sad memory; the pivotal point of the town, the great building of the luxurious Grand Hotel, with its three hundred bedrooms, and its glassed dining-room, from which Proust could watch the *jeune filles en fleur*, is boarded up. And next door, the casino, where he saw the young people gamble away the gold coins he had so liberally bestowed on them, has now a desolate air. Only the gardens behind the hotel are bright with flowers, and a mixed crowd of visitors strolls along the Boulevard des Anglais, overlooking the old bandstand on the beach. But Deauville maintains still its pride of place, holding its own (at least for two weeks in August) in the rich and elegant world, which has, since the First World War, largely forsaken the Norman beaches in favour of the Côte d'Azur. For those who have the means and wish to see and be seen, there are the August races, luncheon at Ciro's on 'the planks', the bar of the Potinière, the golf-course, night-clubs, yachts and the garish splendours of the casino. But, as has been rightly said, Deauville is rather an extension of Paris than part of Normandy.

The Plaine de Caen and the Pays d'Alençon, d'Argentan and de Sées

West of the River Dives, and cut through by the River Orne, stretches the Plaine or Campagne de Caen, which, if we include with it its extension in the Bessin, is bounded in the very west by the River Vire, on which stands the important 'butter town' of Isigny-sur-Mer. Coming from the Pays d'Auge, the visitor is quickly aware of a difference in the farmhouses and their outbuildings; the high walls and great barns, and the houses themselves, are all of a light-coloured stone. In fact, the whole countryside seems to be powdered over at times with a pale, almost white, dust. From quarries to the south of Caen, the capital city of Basse-Normandie, comes the celebrated stone of Caen, a handsome, easily worked but durable limestone. Round Caen much of the flattish land is arable, a countryside of large fields, of herds and crops, softened by the charm of the river valleys—the Orne, Laize, Laizon, Odon, Seulles, Aure, Vire—and many small streams that find their way to the sea, opposite the *plateau de Calvados*, the area on either side of Arromanches made famous by the Normandy landings of June 1944. To the south of all this region the land rises into hills often covered with woods and forests—the Forêts de Cerisy, de Grimbosc, de Cinglais. . . .

The memory of these landings of the Allies on this stretch of the Norman coast recalls that in this region have been fought three earlier battles of great historical consequence. The first was in 1047 at Val-ès-Dunes some miles to the south-east of Caen (the monument is near the village of Vimont on the Lisieux road, but perhaps the site of the battle was somewhat to the south), where the young Duke William, with the aid of the King of France, overcame his rebellious barons. The second battle took place near Varaville to the south-west of Cabourg, when in 1051 Duke William, with the aid this time of his barons, routed the troops of the invading King of France, Henri I, at the crossing of the River Dives. The Anglo-Norman historian Wace reports the king's discomfiture: 'From that day he never again carried sword or lance,' adding slyly, 'I do not know if this was by way of penitence.' In the west of the region at Formigny, between Bayeux and Isigny, a battle was fought which put an end to the Hundred Years' War, a war disastrous for both England and France and utterly ruinous for the fields and towns of Normandy, the scene of much of the fighting. The triumph of Henry V's expeditionary force which took Harfleur and went on to gain Agincourt in 1415 still sounds in the chorus of praise and thanksgiving.

> *Deo gratias, Anglia, redde pro victoria*
> Our king went forth to Normandy
> With grace and might of chivalry
> There God for him wrought marv'lously
> Wherefore England may call and cry
> > *Deo gratias.*

But all this triumph was muted with the appearance of Jeanne d'Arc; Rouen surrendered to the French in October 1449; and the force sent out as a last resort under Sir Thomas Kyriel was annihilated by the French army of the Count of Clermont at Formigny on 15 April 1450. Normandy was thenceforth French.

Caen, the favourite town of William the Bastard, well deserves its reputation, with Rouen, as a cultural capital of Normandy. And the countryside around it, so ancient and well endowed with all material blessings, is filled with memorials of the past—with abbeys and priories, such as Ardenne, Troarn, Ste-Marie, Longues, Cerisy-la-Forêt, Mondaye, St-Gabriel-Brécy, to say nothing of the two ducal foundations at Caen; and it is covered with parish churches of amazing variety and beauty. The cathedral, old churches and houses of Bayeux have been miraculously preserved from war damage—and its famous Tapestry. Furthermore, the châteaux are almost too numerous; but there are some which cannot be overlooked, such as those of Carel, Canon, le Breuil, Outrelaise, Fontaine-Etoupefour (the old pavilion), Lasson, Bénouville, Lion-sur-Mer, Fontaine-Henry, Lantheuil, Creully, Creullet, Vaussieux, the Manoir d'Argouges, and Balleroy.

Balleroy and Beaumesnil in the Pays d'Ouche perhaps share the honours of being the most *seigneurial* of all Norman châteaux; and it would be hard to judge between them in respect of perfection of form, splendour of allure and beauty of setting. But if one has to decide and plump for one or the other, I feel that it is Balleroy which must take pride of place. And architecture apart, this fascinating house, with its gardens and park—and, indeed its town, for this was designed to go with it—has several other important claims on our notice. Something of the history of Normandy, of France, is represented here. The family fortunes of the Choisy were made by Jean I, who was but one of the twenty-four wine merchants who served the itinerant court of Henri Quatre. It was his son Jean II who began in 1626 to raise the present château, employing a young architect who, together with his relative Jules Hardouin, was to exemplify the best of late renaissance architecture in France, one Nicholas-François Mansart, then twenty-eight. Mansart made a daring and ingenious use of the hilly site; the very wide, straight street of the town that he designed leads to the entrance, which precedes a balustraded ramp over a declivity, which in turn fans out in lawns, and brings the visitor to the ironwork gates. In front of him the main drive crosses a court formed on either side by domestic offices, the carriageway being flanked by a most beautiful specimen of the French formal decorative garden, the scrolls, borders and arabesques of low box separating a variegated pattern of coloured groundwork, the reds of crushed brick, copper-green gravel and the gleaming white of pounded seashell. Then follows a deep moat, empty of water and carpeted with an emerald lawn, behind which rises the stone balustrade of the court of honour, reached by means of a bridge and a flight of shallow steps arranged in concentric circles, convex first, then concave. Two free-standing pavilions form the approach to this court, and it is at this point that the visitor can form a just view of the proportions of Mansart's building—the high central section capped by a lantern, supported by two lower wings, the whole in what from a distance appeared as brick, but is now seen as schist, bound together by the light-coloured stonework of quoins, level courses and windows. From afar, and according to the light, the intervening stonework takes on differing colours, at times rust-rose, violet or grey-violet. No statuary, no flamboyant embellishment, the whole is a perfection of harmonised colour and refinement of proportion. And the grandeur is enhanced by the surroundings—the charm of the formal *parterres*, the majesty of the ancient trees.

Balleroy has remained, by female descent at times, in the same family until today—or one should say 'virtually in the same family'. The celebrated transvestite Abbé de Choisy, engrossed by his *affaires* in Paris, sold the property in 1700 to the Princesse d'Harcourt; but the latter was the proprietor only for some months, since, according to the 'custom of Normandy', a member of the family can exercise in such cases of the alienation of property a right of pre-emption (*retrait lignager*). Madeleine de La Cour, acting as the grand-daughter of Madeleine de Choisy, made use of this ancient legal prerogative, and through her husband Jacques de La Cour, a king's counsellor, acquired the estate in 1701. Balleroy henceforth was owned by the La Cour, being raised, by the French practice of attaching titles to land, to a marquisate in 1704. The two sons of the second Marquis de Balleroy had adopted the profession of arms and distinguished themselves in the Seven Years' War; but at the Revolution they retired to Normandy, where on 27 March 1794 both were arrested at Balleroy, to perish later on the scaffold.

South of Caen the River Orne has carved for itself a valley through hilly country of beautiful woods, a countryside of picturesque charm, but nothing vaguely resembling its vulgar description as *La Suisse Normande*. This is in truth the beginning of the Bocage country, 'wooded', much broken in gorges, cliffs and outcrops of rock—Thury-Harcourt, Maizeray, the Pain de Sucre (above the delightful village of Clècy), the Croix de la Faverie, Pont d'Ouilly, the Roche d'Oëtre, the Gorges de St-Aubert, the Barrage de Rabodanges and its artificial lake (north-west of Putanges)—the wildness tempered everywhere by the beauty of the trees, the shaded dells, the silver of splashing streams. Travelling south from Caen, at first somewhat to the east of the Orne (the country rising in folds), the visitor comes to the Pays de Falaise, then the Pays d'Argentan, and right in the south, where the Norman boundary makes a loop to include it, the Pays d'Alençon. In these regions are the Forêt des Monts d'Etraines, the Bois du Roi and de St-André, the Forêt de Gouffern, and the great stretch of woodland which forms the Forêt d'Ecouves. This last forest covers the easternmost buttress of the Armorican massif, reaching in the Signal d'Ecouves the height of 1,368 feet, one of the highest points in Western France. It consists of some 37,000 acres of oaks, beech and pines, and provides a shelter for animals of many kinds—wild boar, deer, foxes and hares principally. Mushrooms are plentiful, and the edible kinds have in French such delectable names as *cèpes, girolles, bolets, pieds de mouton, coulemelles*, although *trompettes de la mort* sound rather fearsome. These hills constitute a watershed, running roughly east–west, and from their crests the distant country to the south has the appearance at times of being one extended, unbroken forest; although, in fact, the many meadows are parcelled out between boundary trees, hedges and copses. To the south-east lies the Perche; to the west and north-west stretches the Bocage proper.

The road from Caen to Falaise passes through the village of Pontigny where the existence of iron-mines does little to mar the delightful landscape. Here the high hedgerows are yellow in spring with the tassels of laburnum. Just to the east rises the plateau of Saumont-St-Quentin on the edge of which, at a spot known as the Brèche-au-Diable, is the tomb of a famous eighteenth-century actress, Marie Joly, whose devoted husband carried out her wish to be buried in this romantic spot, now become popular as a place of pilgrimage for aspiring actors and actresses. From this height, where the plateau falls away in a sheer cliff, there is a fine view over the oak woods immediately below and out over the valley of the Laizon and the rolling country beyond, marked by long lines of poplars. At Bons-Tassilly, another village nearby, Louis XVI's minister, Turgot, had his country-house; and it was he who founded the nurseries at neighbouring Ussey, which have become famous all over the world for their young fruit trees—apples, pears, peaches, apricots, nectarines, quinces and plums. Two statesmen of the *ancien régime* seem to be representative of the Norman character in their practicality and their sound common-sense—Colbert and Turgot; and both of them have left their mark on this part of Normandy.

The Turgots are an ancient Norman family, the tradition being that they are of Scandinavian origin; but they appear to have been in Scotland for several centuries, where one was a minister of King Malcolm III before settling in Normandy. There were several branches of them: one family, that of the Marquis de Naurois-Turgot, still inhabits the château of Lantheuil, some ten miles north-west of Caen. Here there is preserved a precious collection of pictures, papers and mementoes of the family and its relations by marriage: of Michel-Etienne Turgot, the provost of the merchant guilds of Paris (for the Turgots did not disdain business), his youngest son Anne-Robert-Jacques, the minister and economist, and the Countess of Albany, the wife of the last Stuart. The great Turgot, in his honesty and clear-sightedness, might have done something to remedy the abuses that brought down the throne, had he known how to measure his words and conceal his contempt, and had he served someone less indolent and infirm of purpose than Louis XVI. Instead, Turgot retired to cultivate his Norman garden, and to resume his scientific and literary studies and his attendance at the best salons of Paris.

Colbert was born in 1619, the son of a draper, at Rheims; but there is a persistent tradition that his family was from Rouen, which certainly seems more likely than the fantastic claims made, when he had reached a position of power and fortune, that his family derived from the 'barons of Castlehill in Scotland', who had transferred to Normandy in 1281. However, we have it on the authority of Saint-Simon that King James considered that they were of the lowest extraction. The titles came later to his many connections, but they came thick and fast, including the marquisate of Croissy, that of d'Ormoy, and the dukedom of Estouteville. For, if Colbert brought profit to the state, he also, in a true Norman way, brought honours and riches to his own relatives. France, and with it Normandy, owes much to the vigorous policy of protecting and encouraging commerce and industry; in this the master-mind and indefatigable controller was Colbert, who agreed with the king, his master, in one thing—that France was to be the indubitable mistress of nations.

Nine miles due east of Argentan, in lovely rolling country of green pasture and lofty beech woods, is the celebrated Haras-du-Pin, the state stud, which owes its existence to Colbert by an *arrêt du conseil* of 1665. The plans were drawn up by Jules Hardouin-Mansart, with some assistance from Le Nôtre; but the financial crisis at the close of the reign of Louis XIV, brought about by the king's and Louvois's war-policy, which Colbert was powerless to restrain, caused the postponement of building. It was only in 1715 that work got under way. Everything at the Haras-du-Pin is conducted with a military precision, the likeness being extended to the scarlet jackets of the grooms. With the appointment as administrator of Charles-Eugène de Lorraine, Duke of Elbeuf and Prince of Lambesc, in 1764, the stud consolidated its reputation for the excellence of its breeding. At the Revolution the state-run studs were abolished; but the director, the Citizen Théobald Wagner, discreetly saw to it that the stallions were not too widely dispersed, so that when a few years later the ruling was reversed the stud quickly regained its life. War in 1870, and again twice in this century, has threatened its continuity, but it has managed to survive.

From 1823 races have been regularly held at the Haras-du-Pin (on the second Sunday in October), the president being for many years the Comte de la Genevraye, the model for the superb hero of Comte Jean de la Varende's great romantic novel *Nez-de-Cuir*. A painting in the château shows him, with the mask he habitually wore to hide his terrible mutilation, in a crowd of officials welcoming the royal party on a state visit to the stud. La Varende says of him: 'Who has seen, in the ravaged visage, the apprehending glance, the smile full of charm of the Count de la Genevraye, understands that he has always been listened to by men, understood by women.'

Usually about two hundred stallions are kept, thoroughbreds (*pur sang anglais*), Norman hacks and cobs, French trotters and the stalwart grey Percherons. The English thoroughbred stallion Carmathen, a magnificent chestnut, standing some sixteen hands, has earned a sum of money which seems extraordinary to the uninitiated, as does the number of times the name of a single stallion appears in pedigrees, and indeed the fact that any thoroughbred living today will have the blood of three English horses in his veins—the Darley Arabian, the Byerly Turk, and the Godolphin Arabian or Barb. In Normandy the raising of horses has always been, since the days of the first Normans, an aristocratic pursuit, and in the meadows of the many *haras* which are found in all this region the visitor will see in May most beautifully bred mares, running out with their foals. William the Conqueror prided himself on his Spanish horses, and his followers (Roger of Bellesme for one, according to Giraldus Cambrensis) introduced Spanish stallions into England. At the time of the Crusades there was an infusion of eastern blood into English horses; again, the period of the Stuarts brought a fresh importation of Arabian and Barb stallions; and by the eighteenth century the race of English thoroughbred was becoming firmly established, to be brought to perfection after the first compilation of the Stud-Book in 1791. This bloodstock is now world-wide, and the traditional Norman skill in horse-raising is proved by the frequent French successes on the racecourses of Europe.

The Normans owe another debt to Colbert for his establishment of Alençon and Argentan as centres for the making of lace, which previously had been imported into France at great cost from Italy, particularly from Venice and Genoa, or from the many lace-making districts of Flanders. Since prohibition of importing it from abroad had proved ineffective, Colbert resolved to invest state funds in companies designed to produce locally what was thenceforth to be known, in imitation of '*point de Venise*' (he had procured from Venice lace-workers to serve as teachers), as '*points de France*'. An edict of 1665 allowed an advance to be made by the Treasury to a Dame Gilbert for the setting-up of a factory at Alençon, a town already famous for the skill of its women in needlework. Indeed, somewhat earlier a Dame La Perrière had invented a *point*, bearing a resemblance to Venetian work, but original in its design. During the eighteenth century this was developed into the *point d'Alençon*, a light and graceful pattern of bouquets of tiny flowers on a rectangular mesh, which became preferred to most others. The work was done either by the use of bobbins, with the lace held firm on a pillow or cushion ('pillow-lace'), or simply with a needle ('needlepoint'). Pieces of different designs could be made by women at home and assembled at a 'factory', which often served as a school of lace-making. It will be remembered that Mme Martin, the Alençonnaise mother of Ste-Thérèse of Lisieux, although she was not economically dependent on working, considered herself as obeying a divine injunction to go on supervising her work-girls and turning out 'a beautiful lace'—for which, indeed, she was well rewarded. At the same period as Colbert's edict, the industry was established at other centres, such as Caen and Argentan, the latter becoming a friendly rival to neighbouring Alençon. The industry, notwithstanding changed fashions, continues in both towns today; the fortunate discovery in 1874 of the pattern-instructions of the eighteenth century, which had been neglected and forgotten with the changes in taste, allowed the resumption of the manufacture of the famous *point d'Argentan*.

The chief places of the region other than Alençon and Argentan are Falaise, which was terribly battered in the Second World War, and the sleepy, cathedral town of Sées. In Falaise, repaired from wartime damage, stands the castle from whose dominant height the young Robert, then but Viscount of Exmes, watched Arlette, the beautiful daughter of a citizen of Falaise, washing linen with her young companions in the waters of a fountain in the Val d'Ante. From their union sprang William the Bastard, Duke of Normandy and Conqueror of England. The commune, with a taste which can only be deplored, has recently erected a sham 'Norman' memorial at the Fountain of Arlette. The nineteenth-century equestrian statue of the Conqueror has survived the holocaust of war, and so have three churches: the romanesque St-Gervais, the gothic Trinité, and in the suburb of Guibray, once famous for its annual fair, Notre-Dame, which is both romanesque and gothic. Argentan also suffered heavily from the war, and its church of St-Germain remained still unrestored in 1972. Alençon was more fortunate, so the visitor may still enjoy the architecture of this cultivated capital of the Valois Dukes of Alençon. Of particular interest are the church of Notre-Dame, with its flame-like porch, reminiscent of that of St-Maclou in Rouen; the eighteenth-century town hall, the remains of the ducal château (now a prison), the seventeenth-century Hôtel de la Préfecture (once owned by the Guise family), the fifteenth-century Hôtel d'Ozé, and many fine old shops and dwellings. Both Alençon and Argentan possess museums important for the history of French lacework. Sées, too, appears today unruffled by the ravages of war, with its thirteenth-century gothic cathedral, austere in its peculiarly

Norman simplicity, raising its twin spires above the clustered old buildings and winding narrow streets.

Between St-Pierre-sur-Dives and Falaise, outside the village of Courcy, a farm now occupies the space within the solid walls of a very early stronghold, once owned by members of the Norman-Anglo-Irish family of Courcy. It is an impressive ruin. And no visitor to these southernmost parts of the province should overlook the charming little village on the border with Maine, St Céneri-le-Gérei, whose fortress was once in the possession of the powerful family of Giroie (hence its name), whom we have already remarked as the rebuilders of the Abbey of St-Evroult in the Pays d'Ouche.

The Bocage Normand

We have noticed the generic use of '*bocage*' to mean 'a wooded country-side', but this term is also particularised, being employed to refer to a region of western Normandy, vague enough in its limits, which goes by the name of the *Bocage Normand*. And taking advantage of this vagueness of application, we shall, for sake of convenience, extend its use to cover a countryside which has, in spite of local differences, many characteristics that can be regarded in common. The nature of the whole region is hilly, the main direction of these hills running west to east, the southernmost range being from Avranches, through Mortain and Domfront, to Bagnoles-St-l'Orne, and beyond; then to the north runs a series of parallel lines of hills, culminating in the northernmost boundary of the region in the edge of spurs just to the north of Coutance and St-Lô. This pervading east–west direction of the folds is not always apparent on the ground, from the presence of numerous river valleys that cut across them, notably the Vire and the Orne—the latter of which we are taking as our (rather arbitrary) eastern boundary. The rivers that have followed these folds and flow westwards into the sea are the Sienne, the Sée and the Sélune. Forming the frontier of Normandy and Brittany is the River Couesnon, which runs north and meets the sea in the Bay of Mont-St-Michel.

The whole region, then, is well wooded, and this does not merely refer to the forests, to the great Fôrets d'Andaine and de la Motte around Bagnolles, to the Fôret de Halouze, south of Flers, to the Fôrets de Mortain and de Lande-Pourrie, near Mortain, or to the Fôret de St-Sever, west of Vire—these forests of oak, beech and, increasingly, of conifers, spruce and larch. More characteristic of the Bocage are those wide areas of rolling countryside, penetrated by deep, winding lanes, where hedges and trees divide orchards of apples and pears—those lands in which some of the fiercest fighting occurred in 1944, in the 'warfare of the hedges'. From the height of the town of Domfront, built, like Mortain, on a granite outcrop, the visitor can look out over a magnificent landscape seemingly covered with a thick pile of green leafage, not, as farther to the east, of forest so much as of small copses, isolated trees, orchards and their intervening hedgerows. It is these that are typical of the delightful countryside of the *Bocage Normand*, a region of sturdy small proprietors, of charming manor-houses, and of industrious towns.

Vire is looked on as the capital of the Bocage, a town severely tried in the last war, but now risen again, well-built and prosperous, with its granite town-gate and clock-tower, the *Tour de l'Horloge*, which survived the destruction. Below, in the valley of the Vire, cragged, rocky and verdant at the same time, is the passage known as the Vales of Vire, the *Vaux de Vire*, which has given us the word 'vaudeville' from the tradition that here (his house is still shown) lived the fuller, Olivier Basselin, the fifteenth-century writer of drinking-songs and sketches. The tradition also has it that Basselin met a patriot's death in the Hundred Years' War at the hands of the English (the *'Godons'*, 'God-damns' as the Normans called them), when he was caught, with his companions, near St-Gilles in the Cotentin, about the time of the battle of Formigny, 1450. And Olivier Basselin brings to mind another Norman patriot of those dangerous times, also a poet, and a stern critic of contemporary society, yet one who never lost faith in an ultimate French victory—Alain Chartier of not-so-distant Bayeux, reputed to be the ugliest man of his day. Nevertheless, such was his fame that it was said that Margaret of Scotland once imprinted a kiss on the lips of the sleeping poet, on '*la précieuse bouche de laquelle sont issus et sortis tant de bons mots et vertueuses parolles*'. It was Chartier who wrote *La Belle Dame sans Merci* and made popular a form of song known as the *virelai nouveau*, the 'new virelay' as opposed to the older, charming 'bird-song virelays', once so fashionable at the French court. '*Virelai*' is considered by some to have been derived from the verb *virer*, to turn or veer, and is thought on somewhat obscure authority to have originated in Provence. It would be pleasant to be able to think that this etymology was erroneous and that vaudevilles and virelays both had their origin in the little Norman town of Vire.

The town of Flers also suffered severe war-damage, but fortunately its château has escaped. It stands, reflected in the pools formed here by

the River Vire, today the Hôtel de Ville, but successively the possession
of a curious alchemist, Nicolas de Grosparmy, then of the Pellevé
family and of the La Motte-Ango. The industrial town of Tinchebray
will recall to Frenchmen the name of the proud aristocrat Nez-de-Cuir
of La Varende's novel (a disguised form of the family name of La
Genevraye), and to Englishmen that nearby was fought in 1106 the
battle, in which Henry I of England defeated and took prisoner his older
brother Robert Courteheuse, Duke of Normandy. Farther north is
Torigni-sur-Vire, with its great barracks of a château of the famous
Matignon family, one of whose members today is Prince of Monaco
and married to the Irish-American actress Grace Kelly. And then,
again to the north (sometimes considered as already in the Cotentin),
is St-Lô, which was quite overwhelmed by war, 'the most devastated
city in France', as it has been called. The rebuilding of these ruined
Norman cities, both from the point of view of town-planning and of
architecture, must be regarded as a signal success.

Close to the southern boundary of Normandy with Maine, surrounded by woods, once the haunts of Chouans, is the thermal establishment of Bagnolles-de-l'Orne, a town seemingly far removed from
the cares and strains of the modern world (unless the ailments that
bring people are included in these), a spa which caters in every sense
for *confort cossu*, in a setting evocative of—by a somewhat indulgent
imagination—the backcloth for a performance of *Lac des Cygnes*. A mile
or so due south of the town is the sombre château of Couterne, inhabited since 1542 by the old Norman family of Frotté, many of whose
members were Huguenots and one of whom, Louis de Frotté, was at
the time of the Chouannerie, general in chief of the Royalists in
Normandy. He was captured, and met his death before a firing squad
at Verneuil in 1800, on the orders of the First Consul. I understand that
a memorial to him is shortly to be erected on the place of his execution.
Westwards, raised high on a granite pedestal, is picturesque Domfront,
its houses built into the walls of this ancient stronghold of the terrible
Bellême family, inveterate enemies of any form of peace. The countryside around is rich in beautiful manor-houses, particularly of the
periods from the fifteenth century to the age of Louis XIII. A list of
some of them reads like an honour-roll, written by a Villon in praise
of the beauties of ladies dead and gallant knights: la Challerie, la
Saucerie, la Guyardière, la Guerinière, la Bonnelière, la Motte-
Egrenne, Loraille, le Boise-Vezin, la Maigrère, Champsecret, L'Yvon-
nière, Mevzon, le Bois de Maine, la Servière, la Bérardière, and so

many others. And below Domfront, beautifully placed by the bridge over the Varenne, is a priceless jewel of romanesque architecture—the little church of Notre-Dame-sur-l'Eau. Then farther to the west rises the grey granite town of Mortain above its leafy cascades; and on its outskirts the grim iron-bound austerity of the Cistercian (inappropriately named) Abbaye Blanche, with the remains of its twelfth-century cloister, one of the oldest in Normandy.

Motoring westwards towards Avranches, the traveller sees, as he turns north after Ducey, the high silhouette, rarefied by a golden mist, of the 'Marvel of the West', Mont-St-Michel. This distant view of St Michael's Mount affects the viewer's memory as if by an indelible, inexpungeable after-image. On a clear day the visitor can see the Mount again, anchored in its sands, from the belvedere in the public gardens, on the site of the former Capuchin monastery, in Avranches —which Effie Ruskin ill-temperedly called 'a stupid town'. Higher still in this eyrie city of Avranches, on the terrace where once stood the old cathedral, a square of chains surrounds the stone on which Henry II Plantagenet made public penitence for his part in the murder in the cathedral, the martyrdom of St Thomas Becket in 1170. Avranches, too, has a nearer claim to celebrity as having, in the last century, provided for close-cut English lawns the fashionable game of croquet.

To the north-east of Avranches is Villedieu-les-Poëles, a town well-known for the casting of bells and for the manufacture of copper utensils; to the north-west stands weather-beaten Granville, the old town built above the harbour, with its shelter from the fury of western gales, an important port for communication with the Channel Isles. And then there is Coutances, a city again built on high ground, and celebrated for its soaring cathedral, considered so highly by Ruskin. Bishop Geoffrey, failing to raise the enormous funds required for a building such as he envisaged (for he appears to have been a big man in every sense) had the bright idea of appealing to the sons of a local family who had made good in Southern Italy.

North-east from Coutances, about eight miles as the crow flies, is the village of Hauteville-le-Guichard, a small place in the hills amid a countryside which even today does not present the richness found elsewhere in the Bocage. In a poor manor, some two hundred yards from the parish church, lived a descendant of the invading Northmen, one Tancred, whose marriage had been more fertile than his lands, producing him, from more than one wife, twelve sons. These, as their forefathers before them, sought their fortunes abroad, this time in the

South of Italy. About 1016 a party of Normans, visiting that older shrine in honour of St Michael on Monte Gargano in Apulia, were persuaded to intervene as mercenaries in the endemic local warfare between Byzantines, Lombards and the autonomous dukes of Naples. Two of Tancred de Hauteville's oldest sons, William and Drogo, were so successful that by 1042 William was recognised as 'Count of the Normans of all Apulia and Calabria', with his headquarters at Melfi. Other brothers followed, and finally Robert arrived, the sixth son, whose appearance—tall, blonde and powerfully voiced—is vividly described by the Byzantine historian Anna Comnena. Robert's character is summed up in his nickname 'Guiscard' ('resourceful', or, better, 'cunning'). It was said of him that he was 'more eloquent than Cicero and more wily than Ulysses'. Guiscard, who succeeded as leader of the Normans on the death of his eldest brother, had so consolidated his position by 1059 that he was invested by Pope Nicholas II and confirmed in the possession of his actual, and future, gains—'by the Grace of God and St Peter Duke of Apulia and Calabria and, with their help, hereafter of Sicily'.

This was the man that Geoffrey, Bishop of Coutances, journeyed to the shores of the Mediterranean to visit; and his long journey was far from being unrewarding, for he came home laden with gifts that allowed him to build the choir, ambulatory and transept, and to crown his building with three spires. It was Guiscard's youngest brother Roger who finally took Sicily, and it fell to the latter's son Count Roger II, who succeeded to the family possessions on the mainland, to join Sicily with Apulia; but it was only after many years of fighting with the rebellious barons, and by defeating an invasion of his lands by Pope Innocent II, that Roger was invested in 1139 by the Pope as 'King of Sicily, of the Duchy of Apulia and of the Principate of Capua'. King Roger, by an able policy of religious toleration for his Muslim and Greek subjects, of parity between languages, creeds and customs, of vigorous centralised administration and economic expansion, created the strongest state on the Mediterranean. It was also the most civilised —the great cathedral at Monreale and the Capella Palatina at Palermo reflecting the hybrid splendour of his culture and tastes. There, living in an oriental luxury, surrounded by savants of all races, by the women and eunuchs of his seraglio, did this quick-witted Norman make the best of all possible worlds.

In a region where small independent proprietors preponderate it is but natural that châteaux should be fewer than in, say, the Plain of Caen or the Pays d'Auge. Nevertheless, of ecclesiastical foundations it possesses the imposing ruins of the Abbaye de la Lucerne (now being well restored by its owner, the Abbé Le Ligard), the Abbaye de Hambye, and the monastic buildings, restored after war damage, of Lonlay-l'Abbaye—and, of course, that which remains one of the most celebrated abbeys in all Europe, Mont-St-Michel.

The Cotentin

The Presqu'île du Cotentin, the peninsula pushing out prominently into the English Channel on the north-west of Normandy, is usually regarded as extending south to about the latitude of Granville. A more restricted region, better known under its old name of the *Clos du Cotentin*, is bounded on the south by something resembling a moat of marshlands and streams running south-west from Carentan to just north of Coutances. This is the Cotentin proper, a remote and beautiful part of Normandy, breathing the air of a still-living, mysterious past of legend and sorcery, and having a strange life of its own, best understood, perhaps, not in its smiling landscape of woods, orchards and meadows, but in other more sombre parts—in the *landes* of Lessay, those often desolate heaths, or in those wild hilly stretches above the sharp cliffs of the Nez de Jobourg, in the haunted *enceinte* of the Hague-Dick. Travelling northwards from Carentan the English visitor may think of the words used by the historian Freeman in referring to the Bessin, and feel that he has not left his native land. The appearance of many of the inhabitants is also familiar; for this was the *litus saxonicum*, the shores open to the raids of Saxon pirates, even before the coming, and settling here, of the Vikings. The men of the Cotentin were more Northmen than the Normans; their barons and fighting men were the cream of the warlike caste, veritable *berserkers*. At the battle of Val-ès-Dunes the warriors of Cotentin, fighting under their chief Nigel against Duke William, threw to the ground the King of France, his ally. Guillesen paid for his temerity with his life, but his deed became legendary:

> *De cela parfois parlent les paysans*
> *Et disent encore en gabant:*
> *'De Cotentin issit la lance*
> *Qui abattit le roi de France!'*

(Of this sometimes talk the peasantry
And they speak still in pleasantry:
'From Cotentin issued the lance
That struck low the King of France.')

On fine warm days no landscape could be more placid and genial than this *clos*, this garden, of Cotentin, with its hedgerows of thorn and hazel, the high trees (not pollarded, as elsewhere) forming also its meadow boundaries—oak, ash, poplar, beech, lime, and the occasional chestnut, walnut and sycamore—with its coppices and woods in an undulating pelt of varied greens, turned violet in a distance subdued and softened by the prevalent haze. It is difficult to imagine a country-side more beautiful than that around the château of Chiffrevast, a few miles north of Valognes, where the bright green meadows run up like fjords to be closed in by the towering cliffs of the beech woods. A land of lanes, leading, when one comes out of the valleys, to high points from which the view enchants by the sweep of far horizon, by the diversity of landscape and by its quiet serenity. Marcel Proust knew it so well: 'It is possible that the eyes of M. de Cambremer retained behind their eyelids a trace of the sky of the Cotentin, so soft upon sunny days, when the wayfarer amuses himself in watching, drawn up by the roadside, and counting in their hundreds the shadows of the poplars. . . .' A little north of the road from St-Sauveur-le-Vicomte to Portbail rises the Mont de Besneville, above the village of that name. There, from where once stood three windmills, a magnificent panorama extends all round, over woods and hills, with the sea lying away to the west, where in clear weather may be seen the island of Jersey, floating diaphanous amid the deeper blue. From this spot, a circular sweep will pick out, with the naked eye, the steeples or towers of thirty-six village churches.

But if this is the fair side of the picture of the Cotentin, there is another—harsher, grimmer, more turbulent—derived from the coast-line that the peninsula presents to the sea. This darker aspect is not so marked on the east, in the long stretches of sand which are now known as Utah Beach, commemorating the successful American landings there in June 1944. The huge Atlantic waves, thrown forward in angry succession by western gales, are hurled at the Cotentin, to buffet and break on the cliffs of Jobourg, as against a natural breakwater. Then low clouds come scudding in to shroud the land, and men seem dwarfed to insignificance before the force and roaring of the wind. The very architecture of this northern region, the thick granite walls, the low eaves, the shuttered windows, speaks of the human need of pro-tection against the elements. And even in calmer weather these seas can be treacherous, with submerged reefs and dangerous currents, like those of the Raz Blanchard and the Raz de Barfleur, the races of swirling waters round the Cap de La Hague and the Pointe de Barfleur. In November 1120 many of the court of King Henry I (Beauclerc, as the Normans called him), with his only lawful son William, embarked at Barfleur for England in the White Ship—the *Blanche-Nef*. It seems strange that the captain should have so miscalculated as to have been off this hazardous coast on a winter's night, but so it was, and the White Ship struck a reef and went down with all hands, save for the butcher Berold. Again, between 29 and 31 May 1692, these waters were the scene of a naval action disastrous to the French fleet, known to the English as the battle of La Hougue. Louis XIV had assembled an army to replace the exiled James II on his throne, and the Norman Admiral Anne-Hilarion de Cotentin (or Costentin), Count of Tourville, was given orders to attack and pursue vigorously the combined Anglo-Dutch fleet gathered in the Channel, under the command of Admiral Russell. In spite of the discrepancy in numbers (he was opposed by ninety ships to his forty-four) Tourville launched his attack on the allied centre and did some damage, before he was forced to withdraw with his own damaged flagship, the *Soleil Royal*. The decision which followed was fatal: he ordered his fleet to round the Cap de La Hague and seek safety at Brest, while he came on with the stricken vessels. Some ships escaped, but others were wrecked on reefs between the cape and Jersey, others still were driven by a change of wind towards Cherbourg, where they were engaged and destroyed. To complete his ruin, he, with the *Soleil Royal* and fourteen ships, was compelled to redouble Cap Barfleur and take refuge in the bay of St-Vaast-la-Hougue. Here, besieged by the allies, he beached his vessels; whereupon fireships were dispatched against them, and their destruction was completed. King James was in the Cotentin, ready to cross to England; like Xerxes he was a witness of his Salamis. He is said to have wept at the cross-roads of the village of Quinéville.

At the time of the battle of La Hougue Cherbourg was a small port exposed to Atlantic storms. It was the seventeenth-century engineer Vauban who conceived the construction of an artificial harbour behind breakwaters. Progress was slow, the waves defying the work of men. Napoleon, seeing the value of such a naval and military base for his proposed attack on England, took up the work, boasting that 'he was resolved to renew at Cherbourg the marvels of Egypt'; yet the moles and docks were only completed in 1858 under Napoleon III. Today Cherbourg is a transatlantic port and chief town of the region. Of greater interest to the visitor is the little town of Valognes, whose provincial aristocracy, visiting each other in their elegant eighteenth-century hôtels, appeared both pretentious and not a little comic to Lesage, the author of *Gil Blas*, who mocked them in his stage-comedy *Turcaret*. This was the society cherished in retrospect by Barbey d'Aurevilly, who lived in Valognes for a time, but was born in St-Sauveur-le-Vicomte. In the latter town the house of his birth has survived from the last war, which caused such severe damage to the towns of the Cotentin. Barbey's bust by Rodin stands outside the castle, in which has been assembled a museum in his memory; and in the charming orchard-cemetery beneath its walls are the graves of the Aurevilly brothers, the writer and the priest.

Architecturally, the Cotentin is not so rich as some other regions, but it does possess buildings of a high quality and unique interest. At the village of Querqueville, high on a hill to the west of Cherbourg, in the cemetery beside the parish church stands the chapel of St-Germain, which is considered by some to be one of the oldest churches in western France, contemporaneous perhaps with the chapel of St-Saturnin in the grounds of the Abbey of St-Wandrille at Caudebec-en-Caux. At Lessay the abbey church, founded about 1060 by a local lord whose name betrays his origin, Turstein Haldup and his son Eudes au Chapel, was badly shattered by the fighting of the last war, but the stones have been replaced with the care of a mosaicist by M. Yves Froidevaux, and it now rises after the centuries close by the locality famous also from the past for its fair. The fair of Lessay is the most celebrated in Normandy, once for its horses and cattle; still today farmers, hucksters and others come in large numbers in September for the sales, and eat in the open the *gigots* of lamb and drink the *bon bère* of fresh Cotentin cider. Not far distant, to the north of Lessay near la Haye-du-Puits, are the ruins of the Abbey of Blanchelande, with so beautiful a name, which will be remembered by readers of Barbey d'Aurevilly and La Varende.

In 1557 Marie d'Estouteville, widow of the Duke of Nevers, presented the château of Tourlaville to Jean de Ravalet, the Abbot of Hambye, who, with his brother Jacques, pulled down much of the old house and built the present château. The gardens today show, by the juxtaposition of sub-tropical flora with plants of northern latitudes— a feature common in the Cotentin, from the presence of the Gulf Stream—something of the languorous South, something almost discordant, unquiet, even restless among these fragile, deciduous trees. Tourlaville was left by the Abbot of Hambye to his nephew, who became the father of eight children, among whom were Julien and

Marguerite. These two—Julien was the elder by four years—formed early a more than fraternal attachment, which ended by so worrying their parents that Julien was sent away to study in Paris, and Marguerite, then only thirteen, was married to Jehan Lefèbre, Sieur de Hautpitois, her senior by thirty-three years. He appears to have been both brutal and vulgar. Early in 1602 Marguerite fled from her husband's house in Valognes, but was caught and strictly confined at home, being further punished by her husband's refusal to allow her to wear her hair *en arceaux*—the style, high in front, then in fashion. Once again she fled and was retaken; and this time she was sent back to Tourlaville, her husband filing an accusation against her of an incestuous relation with Julien. From Tourlaville on the night of 27 December 1602 Marguerite escaped to Fougères in Brittany, the original home of the Ravalet, and there, cutting off the tresses of her beautiful hair, she sent them to Julien, with a letter telling him that she would meet him in Paris. For some months they lived together undetected, but at length on 3 September 1603 they were arrested. Condemned to death for incest, and refused clemency on account of their youth by Henri IV, they were decapitated by the common executioner on the Place de Grève (opposite the Hôtel de Ville) in Paris on 2 December 1603. They met their death with great fortitude. Whatever their crimes, their lives were pitiful, and their end excited indignation and regret. 'Those young people were so beautiful,' wrote a contemporary, Pierre de l'Estoile, 'that it might have been said that Nature had taken pleasure in forming them to show us one of its miracles.'

Such, then, in broad brush-strokes is Normandy, the Norman landscape, the background against which the Norman people have lived, and live. And, outside the larger cities—Rouen, Caen, Le Havre, Cherbourg—it is essentially the countryside, the landscape, that determines the kind and quality of Norman life. It is a country not largely provided with mineral resources or with natural products other than those that derive directly from the soil; but it is here, in these last, that its richness lies—a moist temperate countryside of hills, plains, rivers and streams, of woods, orchards, and fields, and of lush meadows, which have no need of plough to bring forth their verdant grasses, pasturage for the magnificent breeds of horses and dairy herds. Everywhere in Normandy we feel that if nature has proposed, it is man who has disposed. Behind all the natural luxuriance of woodland and meadow we are immediately aware of the controlling hand of man.

Between the natural and the human there is in Normandy a contiguity, a commingling—almost a consanguinity. André Gide has expressed this point in *L'Immoraliste*: 'From this ordered abundance, this joyous acceptance of service imposed, this smiling cultivation, has arisen a harmony that is the result not of chance but of intention, a rhythm, a beauty at once human and natural, in which the teeming fecundity of nature and the wise effort of man to regulate it are combined in such perfect agreement that one no longer knows which is more admirable.' And perhaps it is somewhere here, in this conjunction, that the traveller must look to uncover the source of much of what is undeniable—the fascination and unfailing charm of Normandy.

CHAPTER II

The Norman Conquerors

THE EXPRESSION IS frequently heard that Normandy is a creation of history. This may serve to remind us—what a map will quickly show—that, with the exception of the sea to the north and west, there are no prominent geographical reasons why this particular region of France rather than any other should have become autonomous, homogeneous; why it should have remained thus for so long and have maintained its 'Normanity' to this day. There are no reasons, that is, save the actions and the will of men—history being above all a record of such actions, of such human will to survive. When the Romans came to Gaul they found these northern parts occupied by the Celtic peoples, who had absorbed the earlier 'Ligurians', and were grouped territorially in 'nations': the Veliocassi (around Rouen), Caletes (in the Pays de Caux), Lexovii (Lisieux), Viducassi (Caen), Baiocassi (Bayeux), Abrincatui (Avranches), Unelli (Carentan) and the Aulerci-Eburovices (Evreux)—these formed the chief divisions. After the unsuccessful revolt of 56 B.C. the region was quietly and effectively Romanised, with its towns and their surrounding countryside (*civitates* and *pagi*), and with the more rural areas worked in large estates grouped around 'villas' (*villae*). This Gallo-Roman civilisation has left an indelible mark on Normandy. From the end of the second century of our era, the Roman peace was disturbed by raids of Saxon pirates, who pillaged not only the coastal areas but farther inland, and actually achieved at a date unknown a foothold for their colonists in the Bessin and Cotentin. Under the Emperor Diocletian (A.D. 245–313) the future Normandy constituted a part of the province of the Second Lyonnaise (*Lugdunensis secunda*), with its capital at *Rothamagus* (Rouen). During these last centuries Christianity, following often the tracks of merchants, had effected its silent revolution, with increased rapidity after its official recognition by Constantine in 313.

About 383, to meet the disintegration which was threatening the province from without and within, a revision was made of the boundaries of the Second Lyonnaise, possibly by the Emperor Valentinian II, which, with quite uncanny administrative perspicacity, laid down the

limits of the historical Normandy—in fact, it has been said that
Normandy was born of this imperial decree. It was the Romans who,
while fixing its eastern and western frontiers at the Rivers Epte and
Couesnon, and also to an extent its southern limits, gave the province
its administrative divisions; and it was on these that the nascent church
built its dioceses: Rouen, Bayeux, Evreux, Lisieux, Sées, Avranches and
Coutances. Rouen, which from the beginning had a primacy both
secular and ecclesiastic, is claimed by some to have had as early as 260
a bishop, St Mellon, who was invested by Pope Stephen about this
time. The collapse of the Roman Empire from pressure of the barbarians on its northern frontiers, and from their intrusion within the
state itself, culminated in the victory of Clovis, king of the Salian
Franks, at Soissons (486), and the inauguration of the western kingdom
of Neustria in Gaul, north of the Loire. The succeeding centuries, when
the Merovingian dynasty was replaced by the Carolingian, were
marked by a flowering of monasticism and the spread of sanctuaries,
hermitages and oratories, which later were to grow into the cathedrals
and parish churches. The Church had begun its great civilising role in
the province. The first monastery this side of the Alps of which we
have evidence, had been built by Bishop Victrix in Rouen at the close
of the fourth century. But from the foundation of the abbey at Les
Andelys by Queen Clotilde in 526, the building of other monasteries
followed rapidly, so that soon the land became 'filled' with abbeys
and their beneficent hard-working communities: St-Samson (Pental,
c. 540), St-Evroult, St-Marcouf, St-Valéry, St-Wandrille (or Fontenelle,
649), Jumièges (c. 654), Pavilly, Fécamp (c. 658), Montivilliers, Ham
(679), and, for its future the greatest of all, the most celebrated abbey
of the West, Mont-St-Michel, founded by St Aubert, bishop of Avranches, in 709. At first these monasteries followed the Irish pattern introduced by St Columban. Then the Benedictine rule was adopted from
England, and became by the eighth century almost universal.

The military aristocracy formed a landed caste, their properties extending beyond the confines of the province, with the result that there
developed a genuinely Frankish civilisation on the Gallo-Roman basis.
The trouble that came with the close of the Merovingian age brought
a weakening of social ties and a ruthless exploitation of monastic
property by the aristocracy. In general, however, this western province
of the Empire of Charlemagne, benefiting from the prosperity which
came with external peace (despite intermittent warfare and acts of
violence, chiefly among the higher ranks of society), showed by the

ninth century a fair face to the world—alas, too fair to go unnoticed. Only too soon would terrified priests and congregations intone an added invocation in the litany: *A furore Normannorum libera nos, Domine.*

The Vikings struck there where the richest booty was most easily got. Since the cessation of the Saxon incursions centuries earlier the inhabitants of Neustria had ceased to heed the possibility of hostile attacks from the sea. When, in the last years of the reign of Charlemagne, the longships drew up on the strand, the natives crowded round to inquire whence these seafarers came and what was their business. We may presume that they were not long in learning. Like the unfortunate shire-reeve of Dorset, when the 'three ships from Heretheland' beached at his port, they 'would fain have known what manner of men they might be'; like him, they paid for their inquisitiveness with their lives. The first raid on these coasts of which we have documentary knowledge was in 820, when thirteen ships of the 'Northmen', after an unsuccessful foray in Flanders, appeared in the Seine—the 'Way of the Swans', as they called it—but they were driven off, with the loss of five men. At first the Vikings' object was booty, particularly the gold and silver of the unprotected monasteries, as well as captives, whom they sold as slaves. They massacred indiscriminately, ravaging and setting fire to the dwellings. In 841, led by Osker the Northman, they stayed for three weeks, burnt Rouen and the abbey of Jumièges; the captured monks of St-Wandrille were ransomed by appealing to the abbot of St-Denis, outside Paris. Then in 845, under that 'king of the sea' famous from the *Sagas*, Ragnar Ladbrok, they ascended the Seine, brushing aside any opposition, and took Paris. In the autumn of each year, returning to their homes in Norway and Denmark, the Vikings spread the news of the ease of their enrichment; next spring fresh fleets of their longships (*snekkja*) would be launched on these exceedingly profitable ventures. Their raids continued with the rhythm of the seasons; but before long the rich valley of the Seine and those regions most easily accessible to their ships were exhausted and destitute of portable booty. In 851 the Vikings for the first time wintered in the lower Seine, employing the coldest months, when the Frankish forces were immobilised, in pushing farther inland. Before retiring in June 852, they burnt the abbey of St-Wandrille. Thenceforth bodies of the Northmen, each captained by a 'king of the sea', not only continued their forays (for example in the Cotentin and the Bessin), but set up permannet bases, like that on the island of Jeufosse in the Seine, between Vernon and Bonnières. The successors of Charlemagne were

powerless to protect their subjects. In 864 Charles the Bald had built
fortifications across the Seine at Pont-de-l'Arche, and strengthened
them in the following years; but to no avail. The Neustrians were left
to their own devices; the towns had been dismantled of walls, and the
strong-points could hold out only for a matter of weeks. Their only
safety lay in flight; but the Normans (we shall adopt the name which
was now but too well known) pillaged far and wide, riding on captured
horses. A contemporary wrote: 'There does not exist a road which
was not littered with the dead. . . . Despair spread throughout the land
and it seemed that all Christian people would perish.' The young
Viking warriors viewed these exploits differently, although the end was
the same. In the *Corpus Poeticum Borealis* a youthful Norseman sings:
'I have walked with bloody brand and the whistling spear, with the
wound-bird following me. We Vikings attacked fiercely, raising a
furious storm, and the flames ran over the dwellings of men. We laid
the gory bodies to rest at the gates of the city.' Evidence of the widespread destructiveness of the Vikings is seen today in the fact that there
has survived in Normandy practically no monument anterior to the
tenth century.

The kings had experienced the inefficacy of bribing the leaders of
Viking bands to depart and forage elsewhere—for example, in England;
this expedient had been used too often; they merely pocketed the ransom or bribe, moved off, and left the market open to the next-comer.
Danegeld being no remedy, what other means were at the disposal of
the Carolingians? In 863 Charles the Bald had granted the Breton
chief Salomon the quasi-royal rights over western Anjou; four years
later the king yielded to him 'the County of Cotentin with all the taxes,
the royal *villae* and the abbeys situated in the county, and all those
things appertaining to him, except the bishopric', in return for swearing
fidelity and aid against the king's enemies. It seems clear that the
Avranchin was included in this grant, if not legally then by fact of
possession. Elsewhere, on the island of Walcheren, in Germany and
Flanders, the Frankish kings had made similar grants, but with little
success, since the Scandinavians merely used the lands as bases for
further attacks. However, in England the Danes had learnt the ad-
vantages of territorial possession; and now, with the exhaustion of the
Seine Valley and adjacent territories as a field for extortion and
robbery, the Vikings there might look on a grant of lands as a more
secure, permanent source of wealth. This was the background to the
'treaty' ('agreement' is better, since there was no written document) of

St-Clair-sur-Epte made in 911 between Charles the Simple and the Viking chieftain Rolf (or Rollo), whereby the Frankish king granted to the Norman leader lands about the lower Seine, which he had already occupied for a number of years, on conditions similar to those made by Charles the Bald to the Breton Count—namely, that he would defend the territory against other Viking marauders, accept Christian baptism and remain faithful to the King of the Franks.

The *Sagas* are full of lively descriptions of these Viking raids; in vigorous vivid language, fresh as the salt wind that twanged in their taut cordage and whipped the spray from the oar-blades to flail the long line of shields on the gunwale, the Norse literature is a paean of warlike exultation in remembrance or anticipation of victorious pillage. Although only committed to writing long after the events related, the collections in verse and prose of the Icelandic *Eddas*, legends transmitted verbally over the generations, reveal, with an intimacy only more poignant and real from the sparseness, the very terseness of their diction and imagery, the world as seen and felt by these northern Vikings, the makers of Normandy. One of the earliest glimpses we get of the Normans and of their relations with their countrymen in Norway is from the *Heimskringla* in the *Saga of King Olaf Haraldson the Saint*(!). Olaf, as a boy of twelve, went on his first Viking cruise in 1007; he afterwards visited England, and in 1012-13 he was in Western France (*Valland*), plundering on the Garonne and the Loire, where he, 'the young king, blythe and gay', burnt Poitou, Tours and 'rich Parthenay', and laid waste the countryside. Snorre Sturlason continues: 'King Olaf had been two summers and a winter in the west in Valland on this cruise; and thirteen years had now passed since the fall of King Olaf Trygveson. . . . During this time there were two earls in Valland, William and Robert; their father was Richard Earl of Rouen. They ruled over Normandy. [Snorre is wrong here, Richard II would be reigning; but he goes on correctly, giving an interesting sidelight on the Normans' continued connections with their Norse kinsfolk.] Richard the Earl of Rouen was a son of Richard son of William Long Spear, who was the son of Rolf Ganger, the earl who first conquered Normandy; and he again was son of Ragnavald the Mighty, Earl of More, as before related. From Rolf Ganger are descended the Earls of Rouen, who have long reckoned themselves of kin to the chiefs in Norway, and hold them in such respect that they were always the greatest friends of the Northmen; and every Northman found a friendly country in Normandy, if he required it. To Normandy King Olaf

came in autumn [1013] and remained all winter [1014] in the River
Seine in good peace and quiet.'

The epic figure of Rolf (*Hrôlfr*) or Rollo—let us plump for the latter
name, if for no better reason than that it approximates closely to the
Norman-French *Rollon*—is made of the heroic stuff of these Norse
legends. He is said to have been immense in stature, of a height such
that he was unable to find a horse in his native land that could raise
his feet off the ground, so that once on land he always marched to
battle—hence Rollo *Ganger*—'the Marcher'. It seems that as a 'king of
the sea' his pirate-band was for the most part of Danish origin, although
he himself was Norse, son of this Earl Rögnwald of More, one of the
right-hand men of King Harold of Norway. The story is that the young
Rollo, about the year 875, raided the coast of Vik (where Oslo now
stands) and carried off cattle (*strandhug*) right, as it were, from the
king's doorstep; for this he was banished. This tendency to rob and
fight among themselves, if no better prey were offering, is characteristic of the Vikings, as was seen later in Normandy. Rollo put himself
at the head of similarly minded young men, and joined in the forays
from the Vikings' base on the Seine. Under the leadership of Sigfrid,
he appears to have been one of the chiefs in the attack on Paris in 890,
from which the Vikings, worsted by Odo, Count of Paris, marched
across country to the Cotentin, sacking and burning St-Lô (and perhaps
Bayeux). Two years later we find him besieging Evreux, which he took;
and it must have been about this time that he was rewarded, as part of
his share of the booty at the taking of Senlis, with Popa, daughter of
the slain Count Berenger. We know nothing of the steps which brought
him to the command of the Vikings settled in the lower Seine, although
he does appear in the persistent struggles with the defenders of Paris;
indeed, just a few months before the treaty of St-Clair-sur-Epte, he was
defeated in a battle near Chartres. He would have been a seasoned man
in his fifties when he was recognised by Charles the Simple as the ruler
of the territories around Rouen and Evreux. (Further cessions soon
afterwards completed for the Normans the possession of much of the
historical Normandy: the dioceses of Bayeux and Sées in 924 and the
Cotentin and Avranchin, taken from the Bretons, in 933.) It is important to note, for an understanding of the future, that the whole of
Normandy had not been conquered by Rollo, but that much had been
achieved also by other Norman bands, who doubtless were not pleased
to find themselves under the chiefs of Rouen. A firm hand above all was
to be needed.

The coast at Etretat

Traditional Charities procession at Giverville

Detail from the Bayeux tapestry

The character of the Norman conquerors has been strikingly portrayed by a contemporary, Geoffrey Malaterra: 'They are to be sure a cunning race, vengeful of injuries, despising their own patrimony in the hope of gaining more elsewhere, eager after gain and domination, given to imitation of every kind, holding a certain mean between ostentatious luxury and avarice—their leaders are very lavish in their desire to make a good impression. A race skilful in flattery, much attracted by the studies of eloquence, so much so that their very boys are something of orators; a race entirely unbridled unless restrained by the yoke of justice. They are enduring of toil, hunger and cold, when need be; devoted to hunting and falconry, delighting in extravagance of dress, horses and warlike accoutrements.' Such were the men who were about to rule Normandy. Their submission to Christian conversion was often something of a farce, a matter largely for profit. A Norman chief would ribaldly admit that he was indeed a Christian, 'well-stocked with white shirts', referring by this to the practice of penitents wearing a white shift at baptism, which, with the Normans, was invariably accompanied by valuable gifts—and the sacrament could be endlessly repeated. At the beginning of the tenth century the Archbishop of Rheims wrote to Pope John X: 'They have been baptised and re-baptised, and after their baptism have lived as pagans, killing Christians, massacring priests and sacrificing to idols.' Many remained pagans; even when converted they could conveniently slip Christ and the saints in alongside Odin, Thor and Balder. Further, they were polygamous; very few of their country-women emigrated with them, and they co-habited, at first almost entirely, with women of the conquered people, or later with those who took their fancy, if they were powerful enough to impose their will. 'Danish marriage' (*more danico*), a union unsanctified by the Church, was most common in Normandy. Of the first six dukes after Rollo (although they were not styled thus before Richard I) all were illegitimate save the two brothers Richard III and Robert the Magnificent; illegitimacy bearing no social stigma until Christian influence began to bear fruit at the time of the birth of Duke William.

Although documentation is lacking, subsequent events show that the new province of Normandy was built on firm foundations by Rollo, who based and exercised his rule partly on traditional Carolingian rights and practices, but more especially on Scandinavian custom. As a Viking chief he could command a disciplined body of men faithful to himself personally; furthermore, both he and his succcsesors could call

c

on aid from other 'kings of the sea'; the 'jarls of Rouen' (*Rhudu jarlar*) still profited by *danegelds* extracted from Flanders in 923–4 and in 926; and Rollo had at his own disposal the lands and revenues (however nugatory at first) of the destroyed monasteries and escheated estates. To become prosperous, Normandy required a strong hand, and peace; and this Rollo and his descendants gave it. It is not for nothing that an ancient Danish legend should have been resuscitated to find a local habitation in the Forest of Roumare, west of Rouen, where on an oak tree, *Le Chêne à Leu*, Rollo is said to have suspended his chain of gold, and returning three years later to have found it still there, untouched. Of Scandinavian customs Rollo is reported to have introduced the personal appeal direct to the duke for redress of injustice (the *haro*), and the system of banishment (which he had suffered in his own person) for offenders against the state, i.e. himself (*ullac*—outlaw). Save for the vague recognition of Frankish overlordship, the Norman dukes enjoyed in their duchy as full a sovereignty as that of an emperor like Charlemagne. Rollo died in 933, and was succeeded by the son of the Christian concubine Popa, William Long Sword (*Longue Epée*).

To William (who reigned 933–42) must be attributed the success of what has been called 'the Scandinavian graft on the Franco-Roman stock'. His marriage to the Carolingian princess, Liégarde of Vermandois, displeased the Viking element among his subjects, and a rising under Riouf in the first years of his reign shut him in Rouen; but after the collapse of this revolt William played an active part in French politics, supporting King Louis IV d'Outremer in securing his throne. His forward policy on the frontier of his duchy, in Brittany and Flanders, brought him in the latter case into collision with Count Arnoul of Flanders. On a pretext of negotiation Arnoul sought an interview with William at Picquigny on the Somme, where he was treacherously set on and murdered by the count's orders on 17 December 942.

His only son Richard I, born of a (perhaps Breton) concubine named Sprota, was only ten at his father's murder, and was in the custody of King Louis IV at Laon, who now, together with Hugues the Great, Duke of France, laid hold on Normandy. The Vikings called on the help of a 'king of the sea', Sytrygg, and it was with Scandinavian aid that Richard, escaping from Laon, assisted in this by Yvon de Bellême (who later was to be well repaid for his services), drove out the French and re-established the Duchy. Richard married Emma, a daughter of Hugues of France, but when she died childless he regularised his union with a Danish concubine Gonnor. From the Duchess Gonnor and her numerous relations sprang many of the Norman noble families of the eleventh century. Their children were: Richard II, successor to the Duchy; Robert, Archbishop of Rouen and Count of Evreux; Mauger, Count of Corbeil, and father of William, Count of Mortain; Emma, who married the English king, Ethelred the Unready, whence came Duke William's claim to the throne of England; Havoise, married to the Count of Brittany; Mahaut, married to the Count of Chartres. Of other concubines Richard had Godfrey, Count of Brionne, William, Count of Hiesmes, and two more daughters. From these, and the equally numerous progeny of Richard II, were filled the highest posts in the land, including the most important bishoprics, those of Rouen and Bayeux, and five counties. Their descendants were the so-called *Rollonides*, who gave so much trouble to Duke William. All honours were held directly of the duke, and could be revoked at will. The counts acted in the duke's name, but withheld for themselves certain of the revenues, as well as those from the estates granted them. Of lower rank were the viscounts, who, while also acting for the duke in the ancient *pagi*, remitted him the revenues from taxation; for loyal services these viscounties could be made hereditary. No foreign prince held lands in Normandy. Thus, with the army at their disposal alone, the dukes held their duchy on a tight rein, increasingly assisted as time went on in detailed administration by the hierarchy of the clergy, whose appointments they also controlled.

Under the first devastating attacks of the Northmen, the cathedrals and abbeys, since richer than parish churches, suffered most heavily. Baltfridus of Bayeux in 858 and Lista of Coutances in 890 were murdered, and Adalhelmus of Sées carried overseas as a slave. Only the see of Rouen remained when Rollo took over his province and was baptised in 911, and of the abbeys Mont-St-Michel alone retained a handful of monks. It has been a matter of admiration and surprise that Rollo and his successors, from being savage pirates, polygamous and heathen, could have within so short a time created the most strongly centralised and administered state in the west. The Normans (like the Arabs before them) were not originators so much as great assimilators and users of the talents of others. They adopted as much as was left to them of old organisations, and adapted them to their own clearly envisaged purposes. Nowhere was this more clearly seen than in their handling of the Church, which became, with the army, one of the twin pillars of ducal rule. This began under Rollo, gathered momentum under William

Long Sword, and reached a high level under the Richards. Towards 990 all the episcopal sees had incumbents (although Herbert Bishop of Coutances did not move from his refuge in Rouen until 1024), and already we find the rebuilding of the mutilated or destroyed abbeys: St-Ouen (*c.* 930), St-Wandrille (960), Mont-St-Michel (re-animated *c.* 966), Fécamp (1001), the last-named under the Italian Guillaume de Volpiano, who was also responsible for the construction of St-Taurin at Evreux; and at Montivilliers and Bernay. Cerisy was founded by Robert the Magnificent in 1032. Later, the nobles joined in the foundation or restoration of abbeys, such as Bec-Hellouin, St-Evroult, Troarn, Lonlay and Lessay. The Norman Church was ready for the cultural developments of Duke William and his advisers Lanfranc and Anselm.

Richard II reigned thirty years (996–1026) and with him the duchy of Normandy reached a summit of power in Europe only to be excelled under the rule of his grandson. A revolt of the peasants, a *Jacquerie*, most likely in protest at aristocratic and military outrages, was brutally put down by the cutting off of feet and hands and blinding, so that Richard's surname 'the Good' seems at first out of place. But it was under his administration that the Cluniac reforms of monasticism began to have an effect, and prepared the way for the Norman renaissance of Herluin, Lanfranc and St Anselm. Richard's legitimate marriage to the Breton Judith produced two sons who followed him. The eldest, Richard III, on succeeding to the duchy, asked for and received the hand of Adèle of France, but he died within a year, in 1027, most likely poisoned by his younger brother Robert.

Robert the Magnificent or Robert the Devil?—which of these names that he is known by is the appropriate one? The answer is most certainly both. It is seldom taken into account, when judging him, how young he was. He was born, in all probability, in 1010, and died in 1035—that is, at his death he was twenty-five. On his brother's poisoning and his accession he was only seventeen, the luxurious Count of Hiémois, leader of a high-spirited (unprincipled, rather), ambitious band of young nobles of whom Robert de Montgommery was typical. To gain their loyalty, Robert made over to them large estates taken from the Church, until his uncle the Archbishop of Rouen's quick excommunication caused him to pause, then to withdraw, in order to save his throne. This action is typical of him; he is said to have lived in a tension between the ardours of a morbid mysticism and the drives of ungovernable desires, fluctuating between spectacular magnificence

and debilitating repentance. Once duke, he had to meet the rebellion
of his barons; successful in these battles and against the Bretons, he
intervened in Flanders and in a revolt against the King of France.
From his highest successes he fell suddenly into despair at the heinous-
ness of his own crimes. He was clearly unbalanced in mind. He founded
the abbey of Cerisy, the first re-establishment in the west of Normandy,
by way of expiation. But nothing less than a pilgrimage to the Holy
Land, to beg forgiveness at the Holy Sepulchre, would satisfy the intensity of his despairing remorse. His subjects heard from time to time
of his flamboyant eccentricities *en route*, at Rome and at Constantinople;
it seemed that his mind was failing. A pilgrim from Pirou in the Cotentin
met the duke's litter borne by negroes near Jerusalem, and, greeting
his sovereign, asked if there were any message he could take home to
his people. The duke, already foreseeing his end, joked of it in verse.
Pointing to his black porters, he rhymed:

> *Dictes à mes amis*
> *E à la gent de mon païs*
> *Ke as diables trestus vifs*
> *Me faz porter en paraïs.*

> (Say to my friends
> And to the people of my country
> That by living devils
> I have myself carried to paradise.)

The unfortunate man died at Nicaea in Anatolia in the summer of
1035; his final resting place is unknown. His heir he had already named;
at a convocation before his departure the barons had sworn to acknowledge his successor. It was the boy William, aged only seven years.

When the modern Englishman thinks of William the Conqueror, the
figure he conjures up is only vaguely Norman; by his very conquest of
England William has become an Englishman—not a native, it is true,
not a naturalised, but a *natural* Englishman. To a Norman, however,
William is nothing but a Norman, the greatest of all Normans, the
representative of the qualities of the race. On confirmation of the death
of Duke Robert, Arlette had married Herluin de Conteville, whose
estates were on the River Risle, near its junction with the estuary of the
Seine. The duchy soon was aflame from end to end, at the mercy of
baronial faction and anarchy. The boy-duke had been brought to

Normandy from Paris; but both his tutor, Gilbert of Brionne, and his seneschal Osborn were murdered, the latter in bed at the boy's side—he could never for a moment leave him. It was his mother and her new relations who at this juncture saved William's life; he was hidden away in isolated parts of the country, where he lived with peasants, sharing their lives and their poverty. It was as a sturdy, silent boy of fourteen that William the Bastard (as he was known, and as he signed himself —'*Guglielmus Nothus*') first appeared in public. Very soon he showed his subjects the mettle of their prince. A revolt of the governor of the Hiémois, Toustain Goz, aided by Henry I of France, was effectively put down by the speedy capture of Falaise. Then in 1047, when William was nineteen, conspiracy broke out in the open in the Great Revolt of the Barons. The duke was in Valognes when, warned by a jester, he managed to elude the rebels and, making his way to his suzerain, Henry of France, sought his feudal aid. The result was his great victory at Val-ès-Dunes. At the siege of Brionne, which followed, William first met Lanfranc, who was to become his most trusted counsellor, and who persuaded the Pope to lift the ecclesiastical ban on his marriage with Matilda of Flanders. As a sign of their penitence for ignoring the ban, William and Matilda built four hospitals in the largest Norman towns (Rouen, Caen, Bayeux and Cherbourg) and the two magnificent abbeys we see today in Caen.

In the course of a concerted action with Henry of France against Geoffrey of Anjou, the latter, giving William the slip, occupied Alençon. Here, on the one occasion in his life, William tarnished his reputation for clemency, stung by the allusions of the besieged to the illegitimacy of his birth. Stretched over those places in their walls vulnerable to fire were skins, on which the citizens beat, as if on drums, shouting, 'Skins, skins for the tanner!' The thirty-three prisoners taken had their hands and feet hacked off and flung back over the walls. Alençon capitulated. The barons remained restless; risings led by his own relations, the so-called Rollonides, were frequent; but the energy of the duke and his military skill gave him the upper hand. On one occasion, the news of the revolt of his uncle, Count of Talou, brought him the 160 miles separating Coutances from Arques in thirty hours. The attempt was quickly crushed. Two invasions by the French king resulted in William's overwhelming victories at Mortemer (1054) and Varaville (1057). Finally, the conquest of Maine by 1062 consolidated the borders of his duchy; and the subjugation of the barons completed thirty years of warfare to secure his possession of Normandy. By 1066, at the experienced age of thirty-eight, Duke William was ready for his greatest feat of diplomacy and arms, the conquest of England.

There seems little doubt that, whatever the legality of the matter, William thought justified his claims on the English throne, left vacant at the death of Edward the Confessor on 5 January 1066: by inheritance (Edward and Robert the Magnificent were first cousins), by Edward's promise given, and by Harold's oath to support his claim. He had very considerable difficulty in persuading the barons of Normandy to accompany him; and he had to exert all his powers of cajolery, flattery and implied threats at a council held at Lillebonne. Finally he succeeded. The Pope, advised by Hildebrand, proclaimed the invasion a crusade; the King of France declared his neutrality; the Emperor Henry V guaranteed the safety of his state in his absence; a second front was opened from Scandinavia; and by late August the great armada was centred on Dives-sur-Mer. All this required planning and diplomacy—considering the state of communications at the time—of the highest order. Contrary winds and storms delayed the sailing. On 14 October 1066, at Hastings, William of Normandy won the throne of England. Henceforth, Normandy had only a part-share in her duke, but Normans had the lion's share of conquered England.

CHAPTER III

Rouen

ROUEN WAS ALMOST certainly a Celtic strongpoint long before the
Romans conquered Gaul in the middle of the first century B.C.; its
name Rothomagus is a Latinised form of earlier Celtic words which
perhaps referred to the existence of a 'market at the cròssing'—that is
of the Seine. Possibly as a consequence of the great Germanic invasion
of the year 275, the Romans fortified this their chief administrative
centre for the province; they built walls on three sides (the fourth
being protected by the river), and laid it out on the customary plan
of a *civitas quadrata*, with the typical *cardines* and *decumani* criss-crossing
at right angles, a form to which the present old quarter approximates,
since, despite modern efforts at 'Haussmanisation', the Rue du Gros-
Horloge still traces part of the ancient *decumanus maximus*. The figure of
St Mellon hardly emerges from the obscurity of the third century; it
is with St Victrice, the friend of St Martin of Tours, that first light
dawns. In the church of St Gervais, which he began in 386 outside the
walls, to the north-west, there still exists beneath the modern building
a Gallo-Roman crypt, which has a right to be considered part of one
of the earliest Christian churches in France. The crypt appears to have
been the *martyrium* of the ancient *ecclesia civitatis*, that is, the original
episcopal basilica of the province of the Second Lyonnaise. On one
of its Gallo-Roman capitals can be seen the imprint of the legionary
eagle of the Roman Imperial armies. Then the barbarian darkness
descended, lit only by occasional flickers of light. In the sixth century
it appears that the bishops transferred their seat to the church which
arose on the site of the present St-Godard, for it was here that the
saintly Bishop Praetextas was murdered in his own church by orders of
the terrible Queen Fredegonde.

There followed the Scandinavian incursions. Even before the treaty
of St-Clair-sur-Epte in 912, when Charles the Simple relinquished his
feeble hold on the province which was to become Normandy, Rollo had
already chosen Rouen as his *point d'appui*. It was he, the first of the
Norman dukes, who refounded Rouen, filling in the creeks and con-
solidating the islands on which it is built, and constructing the quays,

Lessay Abbey

Abbey tower, Le Bec-Hellouin

which served also to withhold the river. Under the Norman dukes, then, Rouen resumed its pre-eminence, as capital and chief ducal residence. It was Archbishop Robert, uncle of Duke Robert the Magnificent, who decided to move his cathedral from St-Godard's to within the walls; and in 1034 he began, over the ancient forum, the building of a church grander in conception than anything attempted hitherto. The original plan included a double choir, one above the other, as is found in romanesque Italy. The restoration after the fires and bombardments of 1940 and 1944 has allowed us to see again the lower choir, although it is noticeably less high than first designed. This early cathedral was overwhelmed by fire on 9 April 1200, and little of it now remains.

The young Ruskin, on his honeymoon, was delighted with the city of Rouen—'this is *the* place of North Europe as Venice is of the South'; and he was equally emphatic in his approval of its cathedral of Notre-Dame—'my idea, as it always has been, of Gothic proper'. If the visitor comes out into the Place de la Cathédrale from the Rue du Gros-Horloge, the western façade rises before him like a cliff of chiselled stone, imposing in its intricate grandeur, and without any of its sharp angularity softened, as it is in Monet's celebrated paintings in the Beaux-Arts, where the cathedral appears refracted in coloured luminosity, following the dictates of his impressionism. (But, seen enveloped in the Rouen mist or in the suffused glow of sunrise or sunset, the artist's vision of this façade is strikingly vindicated, quite astonishing in its veracity.) Flanked with dissimilar towers, the middle section is sharply accented by light on structure and ornament against shadow in time-blackened recesses, in a masterly composition of pointed doorways, central high openwork gable (partly masking the rose-window), buttresses, bays and tapering spires. The eye is drawn upwards, travelling over fretted arches and pinnacles, spiked with crockets and finials, over all this expanse of stonework encrusted with carving, from the tree of Jesse in the tympanum of the main doorway, up, beyond the crowded archivolts, through band after horizontal band of seemingly free-standing statuary.

A more detailed study of the west front reveals the remarkable harmony achieved in the blending of successive gothic styles on the base of the original romanesque edifice. In the tower of St-Romain (that on the left) the bottom-most storey is romanesque from the early twelfth century; then follow four storeys built later in the same century in the early gothic style; the topmost storey, still hidden by scaffolding, is in flamboyant gothic. From the early gothic period are the two lateral doorways, that of St John the Baptist on the left and of St Stephen on the right. Rebuilding after the fire of 1200 was begun almost at once under the architect Jean d'Andely, who was followed in 1214 by one Ingleram (or Enguerrand), and work was pushed on with extraordinary rapidity, so that by 1250 the main construction was complete, but not the external decoration or the tower on the right, the Tour de Beurre. The name of Butter Tower is said to derive from the means by which the expense of its erection was defrayed. No Norman would cook without a plentiful use of cream and butter, but these were forbidden during Lent. The Church, ever flexible in these matters, was willing to relax—if the faithful paid for the dispensation. An incredible consumption of butter must have gone to the raising of this beautiful tower, a fitting monument to the Norman cuisine. The architect for this and for the top storey of the Tour St-Romain, both in the flamboyant style of the late fifteenth century, was Guillaume Pontifz, who was also responsible for the sculptured gallery in the Cour des Libraires on the north side of the cathedral and for the staircase to the canons' library in the north transept. The tympana and archivolts of the two lateral doors, as well as the little arcade above them, are from the thirteenth century. Above this arcading the seven narrow bays, with openwork arches (reputed to be English in inspiration), are filled with sculptured figures—not the finest of gothic statuary, but vigorously treated, and of high decorative value. The three bays to the right of the central rose-window and the one flanking it on the left are in the *rayonnant* style of the fourteenth century; the three bays to the left (those nearest to the Tour St-Romain) are of a century later, in flamboyant gothic. These bays mask the four square towers with their elaborate pinnacles, which are all fourteenth-century work. At the beginning of the sixteenth century the whole central section immediately above and including the main doorway threatened to collapse; the architects who conceived this splendid lacework of stone are known to have been Jacques and Rouland le Roux. In 1514 the slender spire of wood and lead was consumed by fire, its replacement, also wooden, suffering a similar fate in 1822, when it was struck by lightning. The present *flèche*, 495 feet in height, was begun in 1827, but not completed until fifty years later. Built of cast-iron and bronze, and dirtied and darkened by time, it has its detractors; for my own part, whatever my aesthetic feelings, I should be infinitely sad to see it removed—and replacement is hardly likely.

The thirteenth-century sculptor of the tympanum of the St-Etienne door has represented the stoning of St Stephen and Christ in Majesty; the little scenes adjoining repeat the former event, and possibly further incidents on St Paul's journey to Damascus. The St-Jean door, showing episodes from the life of John the Baptist, may have been before Flaubert's mind when he conceived the Herodias story in *Trois Contes*. The amusing figure of the acrobat walking on her hands is that of Salome, and it is interesting to compare it with the similar motif in a contemporary stained-glass window in Bourges Cathedral. The carving in both archivolts and jambs, of the same period, is bizarre in conception and worked with a bold plasticity. The tympanum of the cental doorway, the tree of Jesse, was carved in 1512 by Pierre des Aubeaux, one of the band of sculptors brought together by Rouland le Roux, who carved the host of curious figures, both religious and profane, which fill the archivolts, as well as the prophets, patriarchs and sibyls of the jambs. Above the rose-window, but difficult to pick out in the fretted canopy, is the Virgin between two angels.

Flaubert has left us in *Madame Bovary* a picture of the cathedral square, as it appeared in the last century, filled with a matutinal freshness of sunlight, and gay with the coloured awnings of the market stalls. (To the south of the open space, and extending to the *quais* of the Seine, stood a picturesque warren of streets and mediaeval half-timbered and gabled houses, annihilated by bombs and fire in the last war, and replaced today by wide streets, squares and modern shop-buildings.)

It was a beautiful summer morning. Silver plate sparkled in the jewellers' windows, and the light falling obliquely on the cathedral made mirrors of the corners of the grey stones; a flock of birds fluttered in the blue sky round the trefoil bell-turrets; the square, resounding with cries, was fragrant with the flowers that bordered its pavements, roses, jasmines, pinks, narcissi, and tuberoses, irregularly dispersed among moist pot-herbs, cat-mint and chickweed for the birds; the fountains gurgled in the centre, and under large umbrellas, amid melons piled up in heaps, flower-women, bareheaded, were twisting paper round bunches of violets. . . .

Sitting in this square on a summer evening, perhaps in front of the rebuilt Brasserie Paul, Rouen's oldest *brasserie*, the visitor may be charmed by the sound of bells floating out from the Tour de Beurre. In 1920 a carillon of 29 bells was installed here, and after being augmented in 1954 to the number of 55, giving a range of more than four chromatic scales, it became one of the most celebrated carillons in Europe. Operated by means of a manual keyboard (which is struck by the fist clothed in leather) and by pedals, not only the simpler religious music can be played, but classical composers like Bach. One evening I was fascinated to hear, clear and limpid over the noise of traffic, the sonorous, gay notes of M. Maurice Lenfant's rendering of Wolf-Ferrari's *serenade-entracte* from *The School for Fathers*.

Rounding the Butter Tower, we come to the southern flank of the cathedral, badly damaged in its counter-supports and flying buttresses by the aerial bombardment of the last war, but now felicitously restored. In the transept is the beautiful *rayonnant* gothic doorway of La Calende, built between 1280 and 1325 to the design of Jean Davy, and acclaimed as a masterpiece of the period. By standing well back in the square, we may enjoy a view of the magnificent composition of the Calende façade, with its two flanking towers pierced by high lancet openings, and its splendid rose-window, set against the richly decorated central tower, its elegant corner pinnacles and the soaring verticality of the spire. The sculpture of the doorway repays a closer inspection. Below the statues of the apostles are panels in low-relief, depicting the story of Jacob and Joseph, scenes from the lives of St-Romain and St-Ouen and representations of the wicked rich man of the New Testament and Aristotle's magnanimous man. Above the apostles are medallions enclosed in quatrefoil and heart-shaped frames, the carving of which seems to have been influenced by contemporary French ivories. In another quatrefoil medallion in the principal openwork gable is a group representing the coronation of the Virgin. Below is a majestic tympanum, divided into three horizontal strips, which are decorated (again in strong relief) with episodes from the life of Our Lord, and, in the apex, the scene of His Passion. The sculpture of the archivolt, extremely fine in its execution, is of figures of prophets, martyrs and angels.

Behind the cathedral apse (or rather, chevet), and forming with it a remarkable complex of buildings, is the archbishop's palace, built in the fifteenth century by the princely cardinals d'Estouteville and Georges I d'Amboise. The great main entrance is ascribed to Mansart. (Visits are allowed by application to the concierge.) Particularly impressive are the gothic rooms on the ground floor. The quarters of the guard and the kitchens vaulted over the twelfth-century cellars convey some idea of the opulent lives led by these courtly prelates. The fifteenth-century great hall (known as that of the Estates of Normandy), with its beautiful woodwork, was extensively remodelled under Louis XVI.

It is hung with specially commissioned paintings by Hubert Robert, representing the towns of Rouen, Le Havre, Dieppe and Gaillon.

Retracing our steps to the front of the cathedral, we see opposite, on the corner of the Rue du Petit-Salut, the old Bureau des Finances today occupied by the Syndicat d'Initiative. This building was erected between 1505 and 1510 by the same Rouland le Roux who rebuilt the central section of the cathedral façade and the beautiful late gothic Palais de Justice. Here in the Bureau des Finances we see how rapidly the renaissance style had caught on, this innovation introduced into Normandy from Italy by Cardinal Georges d'Amboise, who on his return from Louis XII's expedition to Italy in 1500 continued the transformation of his château at Gaillon in the new taste. The little of gothic decoration that remains, as on the corner angle, only serves to point the architectural transition to the flat pilasters, the deep window recesses, and the horizontal cornices, as well as the decorative carving in low-relief arabesque and deeper relieved leaf-fronds, and the medallions supported by cupidons—all these outward signs of the supplanting of gothic in Normandy by the too successful styles of the Italian renaissance.

The north side of the cathedral is approached by the narrow Rue St-Romain, which is flanked on the left by mediaeval houses in wood and plaster, with their projecting upper storeys sheltering an arcade of shops, and with their characteristic gables. So little of these old streets and the ancient buildings à pans du bois, which were 'quite Paradise' to the young Ruskin, has survived undamaged the ravages of the last war. (In assigning a date to these half-timbered houses, it is useful to remember that those whose fronts are stepped outwards at successive storeys must have been built before 1525, since in that year a civic ordinance forbade this form of encroachment on the limited space and light of the narrow streets.) Corresponding to the Portail de la Calende in the southern transept is Guillaume Pontifz's Cour and Portail des Libraires in the north, which are equally beautiful. This was once the spot where booksellers had their shops in stalls built into the stonework of the court—hence the name to both the approach and doorway. Unfortunately much of the most fascinating sculpture is still not visible, being hidden by scaffolding and wooden supports, restoration not yet having been completed after the damage of war. In the doorway of the Libraires is a particular little figure about whom both Ruskin and Proust have written. In 1900, the same year as Ruskin died, Proust, who was at the time deep in the study and translation of his architectural works, paid a special visit to Rouen with some friends. He had read in *The Bible of Amiens* Ruskin's description of a strange carved manikin on the cathedral, 'vexed and puzzled in his malice; his hand is pressed hard against his cheek-bone, and the flesh of the cheek is wrinkled under the eye by pressure'. How in the multitude of figures on façade and flanks were they to find him? It was the young architect Madeleine Yeatman who pointed him out, just as Ruskin had described him, in the kind of canopy above the sculptured figure of a bishop in the central jamb of the Libraires' doorway, below the Last Judgement.

To appreciate most fully the magnificent simplicity of the interior of the cathedral it is best to enter by the main west doors. The effect of the great height is enhanced by the clusters of slender columns, flowing unimpeded from floor level up through the three storeys of the bays and between the top clerestory windows, to continue beyond, fanning out in the groins of the vaulting. The aisles also are remarkable for their height; their bays were transformed in the fourteenth century into lateral chapels. Most impressive is the disposition of light, especially from the well of the great lantern and from the apsidal windows.

A considerable portion of the stained glass has survived the calamities of war. This glass is of many periods, from the beginning of the thirteenth century to the realistic renaissance work of the late fifteenth and the sixteenth centuries—to say nothing of the modern glass, such as that of the chapel of St Joan of Arc by Max Ingrand (in the right transept). The rose-window of the west front is of the sixteenth century; those of the transepts have not yet been replaced. The glass in the choir, the ambulatory and the Lady Chapel includes some most interesting work, particularly the five thirteenth-century windows in the ambulatory, depicting the legend of St Julian the Hospitaller, the life of Joseph, the Passion, and the parable of the good Samaritan. The Joseph windows are the only ones of the period to be signed: '*Clemens vitrearius Carnotensis me fecit*', 'Clement the glazier of Chartres made me.' The window, presented by the guild of fishmongers, which shows scenes from the life of St Julian the Hospitaller has become famous for a literary reason: it is said to have given Flaubert the idea for one of his *Trois Contes*, that of *La Légende de St-Julien l'Hospitalier*. This may indeed be so; but it is not the only source. Flaubert concludes his tale, written in 1875, with the words: 'And that is the story of St Julian the Hospitaller, such almost as one finds it in a church window in my part of the world'; but Flaubert had for some thirty years carried in his mind the prospect of writing the story. Maxime du Camp in his

Souvenirs littéraires tells of a visit that he made with Flaubert to the beautiful church of Notre-Dame in Caudebec-en-Caux in 1845–6, and states explicitly that Flaubert conceived the idea of writing *St-Julien* there and then. Possibly Flaubert had mistaken the stained-glass representation of the story of St-Hubert (or is it St-Eustache?) in the church for that of St Julian; and these two windows of Rouen and Caudebec had become fused in his memory with a small statue in the latter church which is inscribed 'Saint-Julien', although in fact it depicts a bishop. He often recurred to the theme in the intervening years, but it was only in 1875, as a relief from physical disabilities and acute financial distress, that he took up the tale—and completed it.

The choir, in the elegance of its proportions, shows the perfection achieved by the gothic architects of the thirteenth century. Above the modern altar is the figure of Christ by the eighteenth-century sculptor Clodion, formerly part of the choir-screen; and on each side is an angel in gilded lead, the rococo work of one of the Caffieri family (Jacques or Philippe?), coming from the church of St-Vincent, which was completely destroyed in 1944. In the ambulatory or in chapels are the tombs or memorials of Duke Rollo, William Long Sword, Richard Cœur-de-Lion (once containing his heart, which is now in the Museum of Antiquities), the Empress Matilda (daughter of Henry I and mother of Henry II Plantagenet) and the Duke of Bedford. But pride of place must go to two of the tombs in the Lady Chapel; the renaissance monument (by Rouland le Roux) of the two Cardinals Georges d'Amboise, both Archbishops of Rouen; and the memorial tomb raised by Diane de Poitiers between 1536 and 1544 in honour of her husband Louis de Brézé, Grand Seneschal of Normandy. In a tomb nearby lies another Brézé, also Grand Seneschal, who fell fighting against the Duke of Burgundy at Montlhéry in 1465—this Louis' grandfather. Philippe de Commynes tells how he deliberately flouted the king's orders and brought on the battle. Commynes adds laconically: 'So he did; the first man to die was himself and his men with him.' The tomb erected by Diane de Poitiers was designed by the celebrated Jean Goujon, who carved part of the lower ornamental sculpture. At the foot of the recumbent effigy of the dead man stands the Blessed Virgin; at his head his wife Diane weeps. The caryatids represent Virtue, Prudence, Faith and Glory, a pretty mixed bag of cardinal and natural virtues, which, if characteristic of the deceased, are hardly of the donor. Diane de Poitier's inscription requires a tolerant interpretation: '*Fidelissima coniunx ut fuit in thalamo sic erit in tumulo*'—'The most faithful spouse as she was in the marriage bed so will she be in the tomb.' But between the one and the other she was fully occupied elsewhere.

In 1536, when she began this tomb, she was already mistress to Henry, second son of François I, who on his elder brother's death in that year became Dauphin. Born of an old family of Dauphiné, Diane de Poitiers had been married at fifteen to the aged and misshapen Seneschal, by whom she had two daughters. She was twenty years Henry's senior, but her hold over his feelings and mind was such that, on his succession to the throne in 1547, she remained his confidante, and it was wearing her colours that the king fell to the lance of Gabriel de Montgommery in 1559. The slighted Queen Catherine de' Medici thereupon drove her from court and forced her to relinquish her beautiful château of Chenonceaux; but she still possessed Anet on the River Eure, which here forms the border of Normandy, and it was there that she retired to live out her days. This magnificent residence, regal in its prodigality of riches, was designed by Philibert de l'Orme, and decorated by such consummate artists as Benvenuto Cellini, Jean Goujon, Germain Pilon and Primaticcio. Diane de Poitiers was a patron of the arts, and artists repaid her by somewhat exaggerating her beauty. Her good taste, however, seems to have failed her in her flaunting inscriptions. Over the main gateway of Anet the visitor may read the distich:

> *Phoebo sacrata est almae domus ampla Dianae*
> *Verum accepta cui cuncta Diana refert.*

(This splendid house of life-giving Diana is consecrated to Phoebus, but in truth Diana owes to him all that she has received.)

The cathedral treasury has suffered from the pillages of Huguenots and of Revolutionists, but it still retains its famous reliquary of the city's patron, the Fierte de St-Romain. About the beginning of the twelfth century the chapter of Rouen Cathedral claimed as an ancient right, in honour of St Romain, the privilege of freeing a criminal who had been condemned by the civic authorities. In the part of the city most devastated by the bombardments of the last war, between the cathedral and the Seine, on the ancient Place de la Haute-Vieille-Tour, still stands the Fierte St-Romain, the only building in the area to escape destruction. This is a kind of classical loggia of the renaissance (1542), approached by two ramps of steps, standing against the rebuilt Halle-aux-Toiles, the old Cloth Market. Each year on Ascension Day, until 1792, the Archbishop and Chapter led here in solemn procession a condemned criminal, bound with chains; then, kneeling, he made confession and received absolution. Having lifted the heavy reliquary three times before the assembled crowd, he was pardoned and set free.

Leaving the cathedral by the north transept and the Portail des Libraires, we may turn right in the Rue St-Romain, passing under the fifteenth-century walls of the archbishop's palace. The remains of a gothic window is all that is left of the chapel in which the trial of Joan of Arc took place in 1431, and it was here that her rehabilitation was proclaimed in 1456. At the end of the narrow street we glimpse the central doorway, the sharp-pointed openwork gable and richly en-crusted spire of the church of St-Maclou. This church, dedicated to the Welsh St MacLaw or St Malo, was built by rich merchants and ship-owners, the saint's relics having been brought here from St Malo in Brittany to escape the Normans. St Maclou is today the patron of the French Lifeboat Society. Without a doubt, St-Maclou, which was begun in 1437 on the plans of the master-mason of Charles VII, Pierre Robin, and also owes much to the munificence of the two Cardinals d'Amboise, is one of the most beautiful examples of flamboyant gothic in existence. It is as if the architect, inspired by the art of the goldsmith, had translated a reliquary into stone, or—if we may in our admiration use a well-known metaphor from another art—it is pure frozen music. The spire, originally in wood and lead, was destroyed in 1794, and re-placed in 1868 by the architect Barthélemy *père*, with a taste in perfect keeping with the stonework it crowns. The fretwork of the façade is topped by a single gable, broken by two pinnacled columns on either side of the central window, the sloping lines and lacework of crockets and quatrefoil apertures supported on delicate openwork arcading. The intricacy of the decoration as the eye follows upwards to the tower and steeple defeats description. The three doorways are preceded by an unusual fan-shaped porch, formed by a wide central bay flanked on each side by two narrower bays, all capped by high sharp-pointed openwork gables, a miracle of lambent lightness and grace. The excel-lence of the renaissance wood-carving on the left and central doors (the inner sides are also carved) has led to their attribution, at least in part, to Jean Goujon, who is mentioned in the accounts of St-Maclou as working there in 1540. This sculptor, who may have been by birth a Norman, certainly carved the capitals of the organ loft, and perhaps also had a hand in the beautiful door on the north side of the church. The tympanum of the central door depicts the Last Judgement; the licking flames pursuing the lost souls reminded Ruskin of Orcagna and, of all people, Hogarth. The interior has not been entirely restored after wartime damage, but, beside the organ loft, the renaissance stairway is remarkable for its lacework decoration.

The little *place* which surrounds St-Maclou and the adjoining streets have retained much of their mediaeval charm. From the rear of the church the Rue Martainville leads to the curious cloister (*Aître*) of St-Maclou, the entrance being on the left of the street at Nos. 184–6. Aître is derived from the Latin *atrium*, an enclosed court. This, and the cemetery of Brisegaret at Montivilliers, are among the few remaining charnel-houses in France for the burial of victims of the plague. It has not, however, been used as a burial-place since the Revolution, and today it houses the Ecole des Beaux Arts. In appearance it resembles nothing so much as the mediaeval court of a Cambridge college. The greater part of the building was carried out between 1526 and 1533, except the right-hand side as one enters, which dates from 1640. Stone columns support at intervals the wood and plaster upper storeys; the bays of the ground floor, now closed in, were once used as shopkeepers' stalls. Above them run wooden friezes carved in low-relief with skulls, tibias and fibulas, gravediggers' picks and spades, the whole grisly apparatus of death in the macabre taste of the time, a minatory *momento mori*. A gayer note is struck by the planting of trees in the centre of the court, where the sunlight filters through the green freshness of leaves.

From the Place Barthélemy in front of the entrance to the church of St-Maclou, to the right, runs the narrow alley of the Rue Damiette, through a quarter which has escaped the worst of the bombing and retains much of the tenebrous picturesqueness of mediaeval Rouen. Past the dark Impasse des Hauts-Mariages, at the end of another passage (No. 30) is the Hôtel de Senneville (d'Aligre), where in the 1670s was to be seen 'a fair, ruddy, fat, middle-statured, handsome man', whom 'gusts of envy' had blown to France in 1667. This was Edward Hyde, 1st Earl of Clarendon, one time Lord Chancellor of England, historian and the statesman to whom, more than to anyone, Charles II owed his restoration; but now, driven by his own rigid temperament and the king's ingratitude, into exile. He retired to Rouen, and it was there in the Rue Damiette that he died on 9 December 1674.

Many of these seventeenth- and eighteenth-century frame houses have their original carved doorways—for example, No. 19, and several others in the Place Lieut-Auber. Just beyond the *place*, to the left in Rue d'Amiens, is the fine Hôtel d'Etancourt, its seventeenth-century façade decorated by bold baroque statues. Continuing north from the Rue Damiette by the Rue des Boucheries-St-Ouen, we come out facing the

magnificent southern flank of the Abbatiale de St-Ouen. Before entering the church, it is pleasant to walk round the gardens behind it and
the adjoining Hôtel de Ville. It was here, in what was then the cemetery
of the abbey, that on 24 May 1431 Joan of Arc was forced publicly to
declare her 'heresy'. Through the leafy framework of the trees can be
seen the *chevet* of St-Ouen, the flying buttresses, the high steep-slanting
roof of the choir, and the flamboyant gothic tower—this last, the pride
of the Rouennais, who refer to its hexagonal top, with its little pinnacled
coronet, as the 'crown of Normandy'. Ruskin, whose taste was for
earlier and 'purer' styles, disagreed most heartily: 'one of the basest
pieces of gothic in Europe . . . resembling, and deserving little more
credit than, the burnt sugar ornaments of elaborate confectionery'.
Even if we may regret the coronet, yet Ruskin's remark does appear
perhaps a little bad-tempered and over-hasty. This crown is usually
compared with that of the Madeleine at Verneuil—I must confess that
I deplore the latter. The south transept has a curious fourteenth-century
doorway, known from its grotesque figures as the Portail des Marmousets,
which is preceded by a porch (fifteenth-century) remarkable for the
somewhat disconcerting key-pendants of its vaulting. The tympanum
shows the Burial, Assumption and Glorification of the Virgin Mary.

From the extensive square, re-named the Place Général de Gaulle,
with its equestrian statue of Napoleon, cast in bronze from cannon
captured at the battle of Austerlitz, we can see both the church and
the adjoining Hôtel de Ville, the whole of which before the Revolution
formed the ancient Abbey of St-Ouen. (By the way, at the southern end
of the *place* are two beautiful examples of eighteenth-century town
houses.) The monastery is traditionally held to have been founded
during Roman times, and to have been reconstituted by Archbishop
St-Ouen in the seventh century. The initiator of the present church,
which replaced a romanesque building (the sole remnant of which is
the little apse to the east of the north transept), was Jean Roussel
—known for some strange reason as Marc d'Argent—who was the
twenty-third abbot. Work began on the choir in 1381, and was carried
on in the following century by the Bernevals, father and son. The nave
was completed in 1519, the original plans having been followed
throughout, with the result that—excepting the rebuilt west front and
towers, a work of nineteenth-century vandalism—St-Ouen is one of the
finest examples of *rayonnant* gothic in France. Although the earlier
planned façade was known from drawings and engravings, the architects of the age of the Citizen-King Louis Philippe declared roundly

that they were not 'dupes of the corruption of taste of the time of François Ier', and built the present front, which, as the well-known Norman historian, M. Herval, has recently remarked with bitterness, 'reveals on the part of its author, the architect Grégoire, neither soul nor genius'. At first sight, especially if seen on a dull day, the interior is austere to a degree almost forbidding. Only with some attention do the purity of line and harmony of composition stir the visitor to admiration for the grandeur of its conception. In certain lights the reflections in the stoup at the western entrance of the church give a fascinating impression of the intricate construction of the building. Not all the earlier glass has been replaced—what glass there is comes mostly from the fourteenth to the sixteenth centuries, with some rather disturbing modern windows. There is a tradition that the glass of the rose-window in the north transept, the work of a pupil, so surpassed in beauty that of Alexandre Berneval, the master, that in a fit of jealousy he killed him. Berneval was executed, but the monks, in recognition of their architect's work, allowed him burial within the church in the chapel of Ste Cécile, where his son also has his tomb. The grille which encloses the choir is of gilded ironwork, from the eighteenth century.

The Hôtel de Ville, occupying since 1800 the seventeenth-century monastic buildings, reflects in its statues, busts and murals the civic pride of the Rouennais. A short way up the broad Rue Louis-Ricard is the Lycée Corneille, a continuation of a former Jesuit college, whose famous pupils have included Pierre Corneille, the poet and dramatist, and his brother Thomas, the Sieur de la Salle (the discoverer of the Ohio), Fontenelle (Corneille's nephew, that *'ésprit infiniment distingué'*), Flaubert, Maupassant and André Maurois. In the seventeenth-century court of honour is a statue of the great Corneille (1606–84) by Duparc. At the unveiling of this statue in the 1830s, at the height of the warfare between classicists and romantics, a perfervid academician was inveighing against these corrupting innovators with all the very considerable force at his disposal, while beside him on the platform, smiling broadly, sat one of the worst of the culprits, Alexandre Dumas *père*. The Lycée's chapel, which is entered from the Rue Bourg-l'Abbé, is worth a visit for those curious to see how gothic style can be adapted to the floridities of the Jesuit manner.

We may leave the Place Général de Gaulle at its southern end by the Rue de l'Hôpital, and continue west to arrive at the Carrefour de la Crosse, with its fountain and mediaeval houses, at the intersection of the busy commercial Rue des Carmes. Turning left in the Rue des

Carmes and crossing over, we come to the Rue St-Lô, which we take, noticing the doorway of a church once belonging to an ancient priory, and ahead, the north façade of the Palais de Justice. Again on our left, the short Rue Eugène-Boudin, named after the celebrated Norman painter, brings us to the Rue aux Juifs, on which opens the court of honour and principal façade of a masterpiece of late gothic secular building, Rouland le Roux's Palais de Justice. The extreme damage suffered in the last war has been to a great extent repaired, with a care and skill that are beyond all praise.

Three sides of the rectangular courtyard are occupied by buildings, the wing on the left, the oldest part, being begun in 1493 as a meeting place for the guild of merchants, those rich Rouen entrepreneurs, whose corporate arms carried the proud device: 'O sun, we shall follow you over the whole earth.' The stairway in the angle, which was replaced at the beginning of this century, leads up to the magnificently panelled Salle des Pas-Perdus, once used as a courtroom, where Pierre Corneille (the father of the dramatist) pleaded in the seventeenth century as advocate of the king at the so-called Cour de la Table de Marbre, the marble table which is seen at the end of the room. The modern parts of this wing, entered from the Place du Maréchal-Foch in the Rue Jeanne d'Arc, were erected in 1880, and serve today as the offices and courts of the Tribunal Civil. The central block (facing the Rue aux Juifs), the Palais Royal, was built at the command of Louis XII in 1508–9 for the meetings of the Exchequer of Normandy, a body transformed by Francois Ier into the Norman Parlement. The façade, like that of the Bureaux des Finances, shows the transition from the gothic to the renaissance style, only here you might say the trend had been reversed. The ground floor is of an almost severe renaissance simplicity of form and decoration, which becomes more elaborate in the first floor, in the gothic columns and windows with their carving and cross-bars, and finally, above the elaborately decorated balustrade, the dormer windows are almost hidden by a forest of pinnacles, buttressed and fretted open-arches, and statues, in a glorious riot of flamboyant gothic. To the right of the main doorway the hexagonal *tourelle* with the high pointed roof was once the chapel. Within, the ancient Great Chamber of the Parlement of Normandy, today a courtroom, has a fine renaissance ceiling of gilded caissons. In this hall were held several '*lits de justice*' by the kings of France, and it was here in 1563, before his mother Catherine de' Medici and the court, that Charles IX heard his majority publicly proclaimed. The wing to the right of the courtyard,

now housing the courts of appeal, was built in 1842, to replace an
earlier edifice, by the same architect Grégoire of the west front of St-
Ouen. Here his talents were better employed.

The town of Rouen was caught up in the ultimate events of that
heroic tragedy which is the earthly life of Joan of Arc. Today the city
is something of a pilgrimage-place—the scene of her final agony. Her
story is well-known. The Hundred Years' War, which lasted from 1337
until 1453, was a prolonged struggle to maintain the territories of the
kings of England in France against their feudal superiors, the French
kings, in the course of which some of the fairest lands of France were
laid waste and much of Normandy devastated. Henry V, after his
victory at Agincourt, entered Normandy, and in 1418 laid siege to
Rouen, which capitulated after an ordeal which lasted for six months.
Henry's successes reached their highest point when he obtained the
hand of Charles VI's daughter Catherine, with the titles of regent and
heir to the throne of France. On his death in 1422, he left the throne to
his son Henry VI and appointed the Duke of Bedford as his regent in
Rouen. The Dauphin, as he was usually styled until his coronation in
Rheims in 1429, suffered such a series of defeats that Orléans appeared
the last bulwark of royalty in France, and this was closely besieged by
the English under the Earl of Salisbury.

Joan of Arc was traditionally held to have been born of farming stock
in fairly easy circumstances at the village of Domrémy on the borders
of Lorraine, although those are not wanting who see a much grander
origin for her. Although she never learned to read or write, she showed
at an early age a serious disposition and a devotion to religion, coupled
with great physical energy and endurance. She became convinced that
the voices of St Michael, St Catherine and St Margaret urged her to
accept her mission, which was nothing less than to deliver France from
the hated English. Overcoming all difficulties, she obtained an audience
with the Dauphin, and managed to persuade this indolent and untrust-
worthy prince to put her at the head of some four thousand troops for
the relief of Orléans. This she accomplished on 29 April 1429; and it
was her personal leadership and unerring military strategy that brought
about a string of English setbacks, which culminated in the signal victory of Patay, when Talbot was taken prisoner, in June. Standing with
her banner by his side, Joan saw the Dauphin crowned as Charles VII
in Rheims Cathedral on 20 July. On her recovery from a slight wound
received in September, while attempting to capture Paris, she returned
to the army defending Compiègne against the Duke of Burgundy, who

was in alliance with the English. Here, on 24 May 1430, in a sortie against the besiegers, Joan was surrounded and captured. Charles made no move to effect her ransom, callously leaving her to her fate.

Joan, the Maid of Orléans, was now enmeshed in a play of politics and theology, which in its devious entanglements she was intellectually quite unequipped to understand. Through the machinations of Cauchon, Bishop of Beauvais, who had been chased from his see and who coveted the more splendid archbishopric of Rouen, she was sold by John of Luxembourg and Burgundy to the English for 10,000 golden crowns. (Cauchon was to be rewarded for his share in the whole sorry affair by appointment to Lisieux in 1432.) Accompanied by a strong guard of English soldiers, Joan reached Rouen about Christmas Day 1430, and was imprisoned by Warwick in a tower of the donjon of the castle, where she was kept manacled and under the surveillance of soldiers night and day. Remains of this castle, built about 1204 by Philippe Auguste, after John Lackland's loss of Normandy, may be seen today not far from the railway station. The tower where she was first lodged, known today as the Tour Jeanne d'Arc, is in the Rue du Donjon, a short way south-east of the intersection of the Boulevard de l'Yser and the Rue Jeanne d'Arc. When her examination began on 21 February 1431, set in motion by Bishop Cauchon, she was removed from the donjon and incarcerated in what became known as the Tour de la Pucelle, of which some vestiges are still visible in the court of a private dwelling at No. 102 Rue Jeanne d'Arc. Nothing remains of the Salle de Parlement, where the trial of heresy opened, with many Norman bishops, as well as theologians from Paris and Caen, as assessors. On 2 May her fortitude and clarity of conscience ('obduracy' it was called) in face of the legal and theological ruses employed to trick her into an admission of guilt, which was what Cauchon and the English wanted, brought about a threat to extort a confession by force. She was taken back to the donjon and shown the instruments of torture, but she was not actually put to the question. Ultimately she was pronounced guilty of heresy and witchcraft; and on 24 May she was taken from prison to the cemetery of the Abbey of St-Ouen, where a scaffold had been erected; there, before the high dignitaries of the Church, she made a formal abjuration, a declaration which she did not understand. Sentenced to life imprisonment, Joan was escorted back to the castle. But the English and their tool Cauchon were still not satisfied. On Trinity Sunday the soldiers who guarded her removed her women's clothes, replacing them by male garments. She refused to get up until midday, when 'for bodily necessities she was constrained to rise and put on the said clothes', the wearing of which she had been compelled solemnly to renounce. This act was construed as a relapse into heresy and schism. On 29 May in the archbishop's chapel in Rue-St-Romain she was condemned to death. The following day, 30 May 1431, Joan was brought under a heavy guard of English men-at-arms to the market-place, the Vieux-Marché, crowded with soldiers and simple citizens, where the pyre was already prepared. The sentence of death was read out; then, maintaining the self-possession and perfect calm of demean-our that had never left her, she was committed to the flames. On the order of the Cardinal-Bishop of Winchester, her heart (which was not consumed) and her ashes were cast into the Seine.

In 1449 Charles VII entered Rouen; and in the following year the decisive defeat at the battle of Formigny signalled the ultimate loss of Normandy by the English. Under the presidency of Archbishop Guillaume d'Estouteville a second trial was held in 1456 in the same chapel in Rue St-Romain, and concluded with the rehabilitation of the martyred Maid of Orléans. In the last century the clerical party in France, accused of lack of patriotism by the more rabid of the anti-clericals, was able to point to the undeniable motives of Joan of Arc's actions—her religious devotion and her unshaken patriotism. She was canonised in 1920 (only five years before Ste-Thérèse of Lisieux) and has been accepted as the patron saint of France. Joan was the first to raise high the cross of Lorraine.

A simple railing in the square of the Vieux-Marché marks today the spot where Joan was burnt, and under the arcading of the hall nearby is a somewhat sentimental modern statue of the saint by Maxime Réal del Sarte, which is popular with visitors as a suitable background to be photographed against. The Vieux-Marché is well placed as a starting-point for some easy walks of discovery of the old Rouen. At the south-western angle of the *place*, in the short Rue de la Pie, is the much restored house, No. 4, where Pierre Corneille was born in 1606, and lived for many years. The house, reconstituted to represent a well-to-do dwelling of the period, has been converted into a commemorative museum of the poet-dramatist, one of Rouen's most famous sons. (It is not always recognised how remarkable were the Corneille family: the father—named like his more celebrated son Pierre—was a distinguished lawyer in the king's service, and ennobled in 1637; Thomas, the second son, was also an excellent dramatist, over-shadowed by the fame of his brother; Fontenelle was their nephew; and among their

Rouen cathedral

Above:
Abbaye aux
Hommes (St-
Etienne), Caen

Left:
Eu: La Collégiale,
interior

numerous descendants was Charlotte Corday.) When Corneille's
father had made his way in the world, he bought the charming country-
house at Petit-Couronne, today seen in its orchard among the spreading
oil-refineries of the industrial suburbs to the south of Rouen. This too
has been turned into a Corneille museum. On the first floor of the
house in Rue de la Pie is the study, and on the floor above the library,
which contain books important for Corneille scholars, as well as the
rich collection left by the Rouennais bibliophile Pelay. In the same
street, at No. 9, is one of the rare surviving examples of an early
sixteenth-century shop.

Retracing our steps to the Vieux-Marché and continuing along its
southern side, we come, on the right, to a street which almost immediately opens out into the Place de la Pucelle d'Orléans. Here stands
the Hôtel de Bourgtheroulde (pronounced 'Boutroude'). This house
was begun about 1500, or perhaps a little earlier, by Guillaume Le
Roux, Lord of Bourgtheroulde, a village some miles to the south-west
of Rouen, in the Roumois countryside. Guillaume was responsible for
the part of the building which faces the arched and escutcheoned *porte
cochère*; this shows, as so much elsewhere in Rouen, the transition from
gothic to the recently imported style of the renaissance. The two lower
storeys are surmounted by richly ornamented dormer windows with
high pinnacles. Among the bas-reliefs, carved somewhat later in the
century, can be picked out the salamander, the emblem of François
Ier. In the angle is a finely proportioned triple-fronted *tourelle*, which
encloses the stairway. The left-hand wing, with its shallow-arched
window arcades, was built for Guillaume Le Roux's son, the Abbé
d'Aumale, a little after 1520. The architecture here is pure renaissance.
Friezes run above and below the window recesses; in that above is
represented the Triumph of Petrarch (the first two panels are destroyed); the lower frieze depicts the Field of the Cloth of Gold, where
Aumale was in attendance on François Ier at his meeting with Henry
VIII in June 1520. The arms of Eleonore of Austria suggest that the
carvings at least were executed after François's marriage to the princess
in 1530.

From the Vieux-Marché it is some ten minutes' walk to the Hôtel-
Dieu, the hospital where Dr Flaubert was for many years in charge,
and where in the house at the end of the left wing, abutting on the Rue
de Lecat, his famous son Gustave was born in 1821. (From the western
side of the market-place the Rue de Crosne, which is continued by the
Avenue G. Flaubert, brings you to the Rue de Lecat.) A door in the

wall gives entry to the little garden of gravelled walks, nondescript shrubs and a few sad trees in front of the Flauberts' house. Within, there is a small museum, with some objects connected with the writer and his family—as well as old medical instruments, books and *miscellanea*. The house must have been a relentlessly dreary habitation—far different from the beautiful Seine-side villa at nearby Croisset.

The Rue du Gros-Horloge, which runs its narrow way from the Vieux-Marché to the Place de la Cathédrale, has been for two thousand years the commercial artery of Rouen; and by a beneficent fortune it has escaped destruction. Its half-timbered houses (*maisons à pans de bois*), beneath at times their rather too prinked-up refurbishing, date from the end of the fifteenth century—Nos. 148, 150, 80 and 87 are from this period. Opposite No. 87 is the ancient Hôtel de Ville, designed in the Florentine style by Jacques Gabriel in the seventeenth century. The Gros-Horloge itself has escaped serious war-damage—an *ensemble* fascinating in the disparity of its styles, but achieving a homogeneity perhaps more from the passage of time than from any conscious adaptation of design. The oldest part is the communal belfry on the right (south), which was rebuilt in 1389, when the first two visible storeys were raised in *rayonnant* gothic. Nine years later the topmost storey was added in the early flamboyant style; and finally the tower was crowned with a cupola of lead, covering a wooden frame, in the eighteenth century, during the reign of Louis XV. Within is housed what the Rouennais fondly know as the '*auloge*', a clock of forged iron, which is claimed to be the most ancient in existence still capable of functioning. Of its two bells, the older, called the 'Cache-Ribaud', has sounded the hours and the curfew at nine o'clock since the year 1260. From the platform there is a fine view over Rouen (during the summer; but closed on Tuesdays).

The pavilion, with the two clock-faces, which bridges the street, was built in 1525 (or 1527) in the style of the French renaissance. The underside of the shallow arch is sculptured with a scene depicting the Good Shepherd amid his flock, and, in the key of the vault, an escutcheon with the arms of Rouen—the paschal lamb *passant*. The cornice above the richly gilded clock-face (which incidentally has but a single hand, pointing the hours) is surmounted by a ball which shows the phases of the moon; and below is an aperture, forming a segment of the outer circle of the clock-face, where the passage of a triumphal car indicates the day of the week: Apollo (the sun, Sunday), Phoebe (his sister the moon, Monday), Mars (Tuesday), Mercury (Wednesday),

Jupiter (Thursday), Venus (Friday), Saturn (Saturday). At the foot of the belfry a loggia, whose ground floor was built in 1527 and the two wooden upper storeys in the seventeenth century, links the older portions of the complex to the more recent, a fountain of the period of Louis XV (1733), illustrating the myth of the river-god Alpheus and the beautiful nymph Arethusa. By the Gros-Horloge is the fine old carved-wood shop front of the Maison Perier, the celebrated *patisserie* and bakery, where sixteen kinds of delicious bread are baked each day.

As can be well imagined from the vicissitudes that Rouen has undergone, the history of its parish churches is equally chequered. In the priory attached to St-Gervais, whose fourth-century crypt we have already noticed, William the Conqueror died in 1087, abandoned by all. Another early church, that of St-Paul, which stands by the Seine on the Paris road, has retained parts of its romanesque eleventh-century fabric, used today as the sacristy. The church of St-Vincent, which dated from the beginning of the fifteenth century, and was famous for its stained-glass windows, was completely destroyed in the last war; some of the glass (sixteenth-century), however, was saved and is today in the Musée Le Secq-des-Tournelles. Most of the windows of Rouen's parish churches are of one period, that of the renaissance of the late fifteenth and early sixteenth centuries: St-Patrice, which possesses a good series of sixteenth-century glass; St-Godard's, too, are of the same epoch—a *Life of St-Romain*, Rouen's patron saint, and a *Tree of Jesse*, signed by Arnould de la Pointe, a native of Nijmegen; and St-Romain, where glass, again mostly sixteenth-century, coming from destroyed churches, has been brought together. In the Place de la Pucelle d'Orléans stands the still unrepaired fabric of the sixteenth-century Protestant church of St-Eloi, which was used for Protestant worship since the Concordat of 1801. Before the revocation of the Edict of Nantes in 1685 the Huguenot population of Rouen was very considerable, both in numbers and wealth, and the emigration of many of them was unfortunate for the prosperity of the city and of Normandy. In St-Eloi's was a tomb with a curious epitaph: 'Here lies a body without a soul; pray God that He may have it.'

The Rouennais pride themselves on their city's museums. In the Musée des Beaux Arts they have one of the most representative collections in the French provinces, with examples of the work of Perugino, Veronese, Guercino, Caravaggio, Carraccio, Velasquez, Guardi, Clouet, Delacroix, Ingres and Corot. There is a magnificent *Virgin and Saints* by Gérard David of Bruges; and noteworthy are the examples of the famous local painters: Poussin, born near Les Andelys in 1594, and the two Rouennais, Jouvenet (born 1647) and Géricault (born 1791). The works of the last-named include his spirited sketch of slaves restraining a horse. Rooms have been devoted to Norman painters of the last century (particularly the Havrais Boudin and his followers, containing excellent painters little known outside their country), the impressionists and the modern schools. But remarkable for their painterly as well as their literary interest are the portraits by Jacques-Emile Blanche, who was born in Paris in 1861, in the former hôtel of the Princesse de Lamballe (where his father had a famous hospital) and lived for much of his life in Normandy. For the student of European (particularly of French) ideas and letters in the twentieth century Blanche's portraits alone merit a journey to Rouen. His distinguished sitters were all men he knew personally—he was a writer as much as a painter—and it may be that it is from this knowledge of their work and character that something of his flair as a portraitist derives. Everyone knows his portrait of Marcel Proust as the young dandy of the Faubourg St-Germain. That, alas, is not here; but what a gallery of distinction is represented: Bergson, Claudel, Cocteau, Gide, Giraudoux, Max Jacob, Jaloux, Jammes, Maeterlinck, Mallarmé, Mauriac, Maurois, Montherlant, George Moore, Radiguet, Stravinsky, Valéry, les Six. . . . Furthermore, the museum contains a representative and beautiful collection of the famous faïence of Rouen.

In the same building (but with a different entrance) is the Municipal Library, which possesses some 250,000 books and 7,000 manuscripts, some of great value. These include two Saxon MSS., the tenth-century *Benedictionary*, once the property of Archbishop Robert, and used in the coronation of the Anglo-Norman kings, and the eleventh-century *Missal* of St Guthlac. Another priceless possession is the *Historia Normannorum* of Guillaume de Jumièges, copied in the hand of the English monk-historian of St-Evroult, Odericus Vitalis. Opposite the entrance to the library, housed in the fifteenth-century flamboyant church of St-Laurent, is the fascinating collection of ironwork from the third to the nineteenth centuries, named after the donor the Musée Le Secq-des-Tournelles. Among other museums which have earned for Rouen, in the jargon of tourism, the name of the *Ville Musée*, is one that cannot be overlooked—the splendid Musée des Antiquités, which occupies the old seventeenth-century convent of the Visitandines. It is enough to say that this is one of the most interesting museums of its kind in France. Especially noteworthy are the Gallo-Roman antiquities

which have been found in Normandy, the French ivories, the remains
of historical Rouen, and the tapestries. Of these last there is the celebrated Winged Stag tapestry (fifteenth century) and one of a century
later from Anet, which represents Diane de Poitiers as the goddess of
the chase, beseeching Jupiter to grant her the gift of chastity!

CHAPTER IV

Flaubert and Maupassant

ON A LATE afternoon in the early 1830s some friends of the Flaubert
family were seated in the theatre, converted for this purpose from the
upstairs billiard-room of Dr Flaubert's house in the wing of Rouen's
Hôtel-Dieu, and were studying their programmes, which were written
in a childish, though carefully formed, hand. The performance, they
were told, was to consist of four short pieces—two scenes by Scribe and
Corneille and, after the interval, two original works, *L'Amant avare* and
Poursognac, by the eight-year-old impresario, dramatist, actor and pro-
gramme-writer Gustave Flaubert. The actors were Gustave and his
sister Caroline, three years his junior; Ernest Chevalier, who was ten;
and Laure Le Poittevin, who was almost exactly Gustave's age. Dr
Flaubert was not in the audience, as he had been called out on an
urgent case, but Mme Flaubert was present, looking somewhat dis-
approving and anxious, and her eldest son Achille, eighteen and soon
to be off to study medicine in Paris; also among the spectators were
Papa Mignot, from opposite in the Rue de Lecat, who encouraged
Gustave in his love for fantastic stories; and M. and Mme Le Poittevin,
Laure's parents and close friends of the Flauberts, with their son Alfred,
who, four years older than Gustave, was then at school at the Collège
Royal of Rouen. The families were linked, for M. Le Poittevin was
godfather to Gustave, and Dr Flaubert stood in the same relation to
Alfred Poittevin. These theatricals must have been something of a
success, since they were frequently repeated, until in February 1832
Gustave, who had just turned ten, was sent as a boarder to the Rouen
Collège, now the Lycée Corneille. It is permissible to speculate how
much the young Flaubert's interest in the theatre was roused or stimu-
lated by the puppet show of the Foire St-Romain, held each year at
Rouen in the end of October and beginning of November. He was an
assiduous attender at Père Legrain's booth, where this extraordinary
man put his marionettes through a spirited performance of *The Temptation of St Anthony*, complete with the saint, his pig, Satan, God the Father,
supported by angels and devils; the whole hotch-potch of the traditional
lines, spiced with Legrain's topical improvisations, and his calls for the

chorus of approval or disapproval from his audience, appealing immensely to Flaubert, to the boy as subsequently to the man. For some forty years later he escorted George Sand, by then an old lady with white silken hair and a bonnet of an earlier age, to see (and hear) the perennial Legrain at the Foire in Rouen.

The Flauberts were highly respected in Rouen as members of the rich professional upper level of the bourgeoisie. Dr Flaubert was not in fact Norman by birth, his family coming from the Champagne; but his wife was, having been born Caroline Fleuriot in 1794, the daughter of a doctor of Pont-l'Evêque. At eighteen Caroline Fleuriot, whose father was dead, leaving her considerable property in land, was married to Dr Flaubert. Gustave, born in 1821, was the middle one of the three surviving Flaubert children, and inherited his strongly pronounced Norman characteristics from his mother. As a boy he was thought to be singularly good-looking, 'a young Apollo', well-built, with a mass of fair hair and a Viking's blue eyes, which were at once both assessing and affectionate. One day the Duchess of Berry, passing through Rouen and seeing the boy lifted up on his father's shoulders, stopped the carriage and bent down and kissed him. An annexe to a large hospital was scarcely congenial to the upbringing of children. It was to remove the children to serener, more healthy surroundings that Dr Flaubert bought first the property at Yonville on the outskirts of Rouen, and finally the beautiful villa at Croisset, two miles down the Seine from the city.

Gustave hated school from the outset and, as he grew into adolescence, this hatred extended in its objects and increased, until it became pathological in its intensity; early turned inward on himself, he became morbidly introspective and filled with a contempt for the city of Rouen, its smug bourgeoisie, and finally for religion, indeed for life itself—for everything, that is, except Art. The school holidays were spent in Trouville, at that time a simple fishing village, quite unspoilt. And at Trouville one day in the summer of 1836 (at the time Gustave was fourteen and a half) he was walking on the beach when he noticed a woman's red bathing-cloak, which the wavelets of the incoming tide were about to reach and wash away. He rescued it; and he was to retain all his life the vision of the young woman who thanked him. If Mme Elise Schlésinger awakened in him those adolescent passions, which, when he returned to Rouen and school, were to disturb his imagination with constant reveries and to burst at times into spasms of frustrated sexual desire, she remained for him—far different from his more usual relationships with women—an object to be worshipped with the purest of loves. This period in France after the fall of the Empire was a disturbed and disturbing one: the young particularly, who suffered badly from the *malaise de siècle*, were filled with a cynicism, a boredom with life, a neurotic hypersensitivity, which led often to suicide—and many showed, as if by some reciprocal action, a tendency to violence, which found outlets in extremes of imagination or of revolutionary action. France was in a ferment, as the new rulers, the bourgeoisie, settled themselves somewhat awkwardly in the saddle. Rouen, an important industrial centre and a busy port, had its bourgeoisie and its unsettled, neurasthenic youth.

From being somewhat backward on his entry to the Collège Flaubert matured rapidly, helped on by such sympathetic masters as Michelet's pupil Chéruel in history, and Pouchet in biology, and in 1840 he passed his *baccalauréat*; but he spent more than a year in Rouen and Trouville, reading and writing, as well as going on a voyage to Corsica, before departing in 1842 for Paris, where he had entered himself at the Faculty of Law.

Flaubert was no happier in Paris; he despised the law, and although he attended lectures, his mind was elsewhere; he was, and felt, a provincial; and loneliness, a nostalgia for Normandy, depressed him. Then in 1843, in the rooms of a schoolfellow, he met Maxime du Camp, and the two young men immediately became friends. They had much in common: they were the same age, of the same social background (du Camp's father, a surgeon, was dead, leaving him well-off), shared a distaste for the study of law, were similar too in their attitudes to life —and, above all, both saw their future in literature. With Alfred Le Poittevin also in Paris, and some other congenial spirits, they formed a company delightfully limited to the expression and pursuit of their common aims. About this time Flaubert met Victor Hugo in the drawing-room of Mme Pradier, the attractive (too attractive) wife of the well-known sculptor, and resumed his acquaintance with the ever-charming Mme Schlésinger, dining every Wednesday *en famille*, where he could study at close quarters her unscrupulous, flamboyant husband, the Jewish music-publisher Maurice Schlésinger. Not unnaturally he failed his law examinations.

Then in January 1844 Flaubert was struck down with an illness, traumatic in its severity and its consequences for the course of his life. (It is a curious fact how illness at the threshold of manhood has played its part in the careers of three of the great French prose-writers of the

The eleventh-century church of Secqueville-en-Bessin.
The spire is thirteenth century

The cathedral. Evreux

last hundred years—and all of them closely connected with Normandy—Flaubert, Gide and Proust.) He was returning to Rouen from Trouville, where he had been the witness of distressing scenes at the house of an acquaintance, and was met in Pont-l'Evêque by his brother Achille with the gig. The night was of an almost impenetrable blackness, so that the horse was barely visible. As they approached Bourg-Achard, and saw the glow from the village inn on their right, a carrier's waggon suddenly appeared out of the darkness. Gustave, who was driving, drew abreast of the carrier, and was aware of the jingling of bells and the crunching of wheels, when suddenly he slumped to the floor, apparently unconscious. Achille carried him to a nearby house, bled him three times and then hurried him home to their father at the Hôtel-Dieu. Afterwards he remained in an exhausted, highly nervous condition, until gradually, after a period maybe of weeks, he regained his strength. Maxime du Camp declared Flaubert's attacks to be epileptic, but he is an unreliable witness; medical opinion today is inclined to see them as hysterico-neurasthenic. Henceforth normal life was debarred him; he was to be a recluse. One cannot help thinking that he had found the regimen best suited to his tastes—and to his genius. From this time on his habits were sedentary; he over-ate, over-smoked, over-drank both coffee and alcohol, over-indulged in over-hot baths; often the only exercise he took was the walk from his study to the dining room and back, or a stroll on the terrace.

By a curious conjunction of circumstances a legend has been perpetuated about the writing and the characters of *Madame Bovary*. Today the inhabitants of Ry, a village in the Roumois on the banks of the little River Crevon, some twelve miles almost due east of Rouen, point out to tourists the grave of a certain Mme Delphine Delamare, the wife of the village doctor, whom they claim Flaubert used as a real-life model for the Emma Bovary of his novel. They go very much further: Ry is Flaubert's Yonville-l'Abbaye; the *mairie*, the *halles*, the church, Dr Bovary's house, the site of Homais' pharmacy—they are all there, as so minutely and accurately described by the novelist. They will also inform you of the real names of all Flaubert's characters. It is fascinating to discover how such a myth was born and grew, despite Flaubert's own emphatic denials that he was depicting actual characters and actual events in an actual Norman village, and despite all the evidence as to the genesis of his work. Rumours that he had consciously drawn from life were abroad as early as March 1857, the year after the novel's appearance, when he wrote to a correspondent, Mlle Le Royer de

D

Chantepie: 'With a reader such as you, and one so sympathetic, frankness is a duty. I am going, therefore, to reply to your questions. There is nothing of truth about *Madame Bovary*. The story is totally invented.' Three months later he repeated this denial to the same correspondent: 'No model has posed before me. Madame Bovary is a pure invention. All the characters of this book are completely imagined and Yonville-l'Abbaye itself is a part of the world that does not exist no more than the Rieule, etc. . . . That does not prevent one here in Normandy discovering in my novel a host of allusions. If I had done so, my portraits would have been less lifelike, because I would have had in sight certain persons, and on the contrary I have wanted to reproduce types. . . .' Again, he once made the remark, 'My Bovary, without a doubt, suffers and weeps in several villages of France at this moment.' As further evidence that all of his characters came from the crucible of his own imagination and experience there is his remark, lapidary in its incisiveness, '*Madame Bovary, c'est moi!*'

The source of this legend was the unreliable Maxime du Camp in his *Souvenirs littéraires*, which he brought out after the deaths both of Flaubert and Bouilhet, who, living, would not have allowed it to stand. Writing of the day following the fateful reading of the *Temptation* at Croisset, he says:

> . . . we were seated in the garden. We were silent; we were sad, thinking of Flaubert's disappointment and the truths that we had not spared him. Suddenly Bouilhet said, 'Why would you not write the story of Delaunay?' Flaubert raised his head, and cried joyfully, 'What an idea!' Delaunay was a poor devil of a doctor, who had been a pupil of Flaubert's father and whom we had known. He had set up as doctor near Rouen, at Bonsecours. Married for the first time to a woman older than himself and whom he had believed rich, he lost his wife and married again a penniless girl, who had received some education at a private boarding-school in Rouen. She was a small woman, without beauty, whose hair of a lack-lustre yellow framed a face marked with freckles . . . Delaunay adored this wife, who cared nothing for him, who sought *affaires*, and whom nothing satisfied. She was the prey to one of the forms of neurosis which affect anaemic women. Suffering from nymphomania, and excessively lavish, she was scarcely responsible, and, as the only care she was shown was in the form of good advice, she did not get better. Over-whelmed with debts, sued by creditors, repulsed by her lovers, for

whom she fleeced her husband, she was seized by an access of despair, and poisoned herself. She left behind a small daughter, whom Delaunay decided to bring up to the best of his ability, but the poor man was ruined; his resources used up without meeting his wife's debts, and himself openly mocked at, he too became disgusted with life, mixed himself a dose of potassium cyanide, and went to rejoin her whose loss had left him inconsolable.

That was the intimate drama, played by four or five persons in an obscure village, which Bouilhet proposed to Flaubert, which he accepted eagerly, and which has become *Madame Bovary*.

Tongues had already been wagging in Ry, and some vague rumours of these seem to have reached du Camp, when he wrote this highly inaccurate report. First, Delaunay did not exist; one Delamare certainly did. There is no published record of Delphine Couturier, this Delamare's wife, having poisoned herself; nor of his doing so. Furthermore Delamare was still alive at the date that this alleged conversation between Bouilhet and Flaubert took place. Journalists like Georges Dubosc of the *Journal de Rouen*, who wrote an article for that paper on the eve of the unveiling of Flaubert's statue in Rouen's Jardin Solferino on 23 September 1890, were quick to seize on the stories circulated by the villagers of Ry (where the Delamares had lived), whose memories of Delphine Delamare improved each year after reading and re-reading *Madame Bovary*. And how could they be wrong as to the facts, since Flaubert was so scrupulous in ascertaining and presenting the 'truth'? This curiously circular argument has persisted and persists today in, for example, Michelin's *Guide Vert de Normandie*, and in Ry itself, where charabancs unload the tourists to study the church ('described by Flaubert'!) and purchase the *cartes postales* of places 'mentioned in the book'. But the publication of the *Œuvres de Jeunesse* in 1910 put some perspicacious critics on their guard, when they read those *juvenilia* and noticed the germs of *Madame Bovary* in such pieces as *Smahr, Novembre, Mémoires d'un Fou, Agonies* and others—but especially in *Passion et Vertu*, which indeed derived from a news-item in the *Journal de Rouen* of 5 October 1837. When the sixteen-year-old Flaubert read this article and wrote his own *Passion et Vertu* in 1837, Delphine Couturier, aged fifteen, was still a boarder at the Ursulines' convent in Rouen. There is no mention of her, or of Ry, in any of Flaubert's papers or correspondence. With the Norman scholar M. Réne Herval, whose *Les Veritables Origines de Madame Bovary* sets out the argument in convincing detail, we may accept Flaubert's express words, 'There is nothing of truth about Madame Bovary. The story is totally invented.' Flaubert picked and chose what and where he wanted, with his worldly experience behind him and his unfailing taste of a great artist to guide him. It is more likely that Forges-les-Eaux and possibly the nearby village of Buchy furnished him with some ideas for his Yonville-l'Abbaye; but if he were asked where this Norman village existed, he could truthfully answer that it existed first in his imagination and subsequently in his novel. In his deeply moving short story *Un Coeur Simple*, which was also set in Normandy, he used his youthful memories of an old servant at Trouville and of the small town of Pont-l'Evêque, where his mother was born and had property, and which he re-visited to check on topographical details. The old servant of the Flauberts, Julie, who still lived, and with whom he liked to talk over old times, also served him as a type similar to the Félicité of his tale. However, with the exception that in this case Pont-l'Evêque was named, and faithfully portrayed, there is no more reason to assume this story to be literary *reportage* than *Madame Bovary*.

In 1846, the same year as Alfred Le Poittevin married Louise de Maupassant, the latter's brother Gustave de Maupassant married Alfred's adoring sister, the romantic, highly wrought, intellectual Laure. No more than Dr Flaubert were the Maupassants of indigenous Norman stock, although Gustave's father Jules, born in Paris, had settled in Normandy, being the possessor of a tobacco warehouse in Rouen and a pleasant farm and manor-house at La Neuville-Champ-d'Oisel, about eight miles south-east of Rouen. An ancestor had been ennobled in the eighteenth century while in the service of Austria; the use of the particle gave the de Maupassants in the eyes of the bourgeois something of the cachet of *ci-devants*; in the eyes of those who knew better more of the appearance of *parvenus*. These social ambiguities of heredity—of origin and class—as well as others deriving from his environment, were to contribute significantly to the character of Guy, the elder son of Gustave and Laure de Maupassant—later the novelist and story-teller. Gustave, possessing at first an indolent, superficial charm, was absorbed by his own pleasures, especially those he found with women; his wife, as might have been expected in a disciple of Alfred Le Poittevin, was highly imaginative, well-read (particularly in the Romantic poets and in Shakespeare), intense and sensitive to the point of neurosis. She was perhaps rather too intense, in fact, both aesthetically and socially; it was said, no doubt maliciously, that the only quality that husband and wife had in common was their snobbishness. On 5 August 1850 Laure de Maupassant gave birth to her first child Guy. Like the setting and characters of *Madame Bovary*, Guy de Maupassant's birthplace has caused much ink to flow. It seemed that the intention of Laure de Maupassant had been fulfilled, and that the birth of her son and heir took place in a context befitting both her wishes and her assumed status, at the seventeenth-century château of Miromesnil, outside Tourville-sur-Arques, in the delightful countryside to the south of Dieppe. It seemed—but there were some discrepancies in the story too pertinent to be overlooked. It is a strange coincidence that Flaubert's niece, Caroline Commanville, whose extravagances and those of her Norman husband ruined the writer, suffered also from what is often called *folie de grandeur* and tried some years later to rent this imposing house and its magnificent gardens and park among the centuries-old beech woods. It appears that the Maupassants only remained as tenants at Miromesnil for a short period, but while there Guy was registered at nearby Tourville-sur-Arques. To deepen the mystery, his death certificate gives his birthplace as Sotteville, near Yvetot. In reality, it seems, Laure de Maupassant was brought to bed prematurely, before her husband and she had taken up residence at Miromesnil, and that Guy was born in Fécamp at 98 Rue Sous-les-Bois (today renamed Quai Guy de Maupassant), near the birthplace of another nineteenth-century writer, the somewhat unsavoury novelist and gossip Jean Lorrain, with whom Proust fought a duel for a malicious innuendo, and who once escorted the young Colette to a Marseillais brothel. Laure de Maupassant moved from Miromesnil back to Fécamp, where at her family's house she had been so happy with Alfred and Gustave Flaubert; and then on to Etretat, the Norman fishing village made popular by the writer Alphonse Karr and the composer Offenbach. Here, in the comfortable old house Les Verguies, with a large garden, which is still to be seen near the church, Guy was brought up, almost entirely by his mother, who had in a 'friendly fashion' legally separated from her philandering husband after the birth of a second son Hervé in 1856.

The heterogeneous population of Etretat must have delighted the young Maupassant; there he could rub shoulders with the local residents and visitors, with fishermen, country-folk (squireens and peasants), shop people, innkeepers, artists, tramps, rich Parisians and their mistresses. He loved the sea, to swim out, breasting the waves in its chilly invigorating waters; and on a warm moonlit night to launch the boats from the gravelly beach and to sail past the Falaise d'Aval, far out into the Channel, with the little fleet of fishermen, returning at dawn; and he loved equally the rolling countryside, which came right to the cliffs' edge and then spread inland in heaths of gorse, in meadows where dairy herds grazed, in woods and copses where game was plentiful. He grew up thick-set, strong, healthy, able to hold his own, even something of a bully—but not a snob. When he was thirteen, his doting mother, who looked forward to his future as a poet but feared for his education at her hands and the local *abbé*'s, sent him off as a boarder to the Institution Ecclésiastique in Yvetot, a school for the sons of well-to-do local families. This was not at all to his liking; perhaps his scorn for priests developed here into something stronger, his lifelong contempt for religion. A midnight raid for brandy on the reverend father's cellar, and a letter to his cousin, containing a poem in which he declared that 'buried in the cloister' he aspired to something more 'than the cassock and surplice' and languished for the comfort of feminine charms, persuaded the priests to send him back to Etretat and his mother. Laure, however, saw this escapade and his writing poetry as evidence that her Guy was a worthy replica of her worshipped brother Alfred. It was only in his sexual precocity that he differed profoundly from that misogynist, and she turned a complacently blind eye on this. In March 1866 she wrote to Flaubert: 'I have two children whom I love from the bottom of my heart . . . the elder is already a serious young man; the poor boy has seen and experienced much and is almost too mature for his fifteen years. He will remind you of his Uncle Alfred, whom he resembles in many ways and I am sure you will love him.' In the meantime, however, he could not cool his heels in Etretat, making love to peasant and fisher girls, so his mother entered him at the Rouen Collège, and wrote to Flaubert's intimate friend Louis Bouilhet, asking him to keep an eye on him and to help him with his verses. Bouilhet died in July 1869, the very month that Guy passed his *baccalauréat*. Later Laure wrote, 'Had Bouilhet lived longer he would have made a poet of my son. It was Flaubert who wanted to make him a novelist.' Flaubert had willingly taken his friend's place in Guy's education.

In literary terms the relationship of Flaubert to Maupassant was that of revered master and pupil, the practised hand and the beginner; but by 1872, when Maupassant was employed in Paris as a lowly paid clerk in the Admiralty, it had grown into something warmer. 'You cannot believe how charming, intelligent, what a good boy, how sensible and witty . . . I find him,' he wrote to Mme de Maupassant. It was memories of the dead Alfred Le Poittevin which drew the three together. 'Your son reminds me so much of Alfred,' he wrote. 'Now and then I am startled by the resemblance, particularly when he bends his head as he recites his verses.' 'He is my disciple and I love him like a son,' he wrote to the wife of his publisher. Flaubert each week painstakingly went through Maupassant's verses and short prose pieces, correcting, improving, advising; in return 'Gustave's disciple', as he became known to literary Paris, helped his '*cher maître*' in his researches for *Bouvard et Pécuchet*, sending him on one occasion a detailed description, which the older man required, of a landscape around Etretat. Above all, Flaubert taught him to see with his own eyes, and to convey his sight to paper with a meticulous exactness of language. When *Boule de Suif* was published in *Les Soirées de Médan* in 1880, Flaubert was delighted: 'The story by my disciple,' he wrote to his niece, 'which I read in proof this morning, is a masterpiece: I insist on the word, a masterpiece of composition, of comedy, and of observation, and I wonder why Mme Branine is shocked? It makes me dizzy. Is she a fool?' It was a masterpiece, he repeated in a letter to Maupassant. 'Yes, young man, neither more nor less, this came from a master. . . . That little story will live, rest assured.' 'The little blighter has surpassed us,' Flaubert confessed with creative pride to his literary friends. Then within three months he was dead. On 10 May 1880 Maupassant arrived at Croisset and spent the night keeping vigil beside his master's body; the following day in the presence of Zola, Daudet, Heredia, Edmond de Goncourt and many others Flaubert was buried in the Monumental Cemetery of Rouen.

Much of Guy de Maupassant's writings, both his stories and his novels, is located in Normandy, but it would be most unwise to draw from his characters and plots general observations on indisputably 'Norman' characteristics—if any such characteristics exist. For if Maupassant saw life (some aspects of it) clearly, he most certainly did not see it whole. He was too pessimistic, too cynical, too wry, not to have a predisposition towards choosing subjects from the seamy side of life, chiefly of cruder peasant, petit-bourgeois or *putain* life. In spite of the claims made about him, Maupassant is no more *typically* Norman than are his stories. He loved Normandy and he revelled in 'his Normans', but he saw them always as an '*horzain*', the Norman word for 'foreigner', 'one from outside these parts'. Yet historically other Frenchmen have looked on Normans and found in them, like Maupassant, some most unprepossessing qualities. La Fontaine echoed the popular belief, '*Certain renard gascon, d'autres disent normand*'. Earlier still, Robert d'Hauteville, the Norman freebooter in Southern Italy, was always known as Robert Guiscard ('Cunning', 'Wily', 'Astute'). One of the commonest Norman family names is Goupil, which signified in the Middle Ages 'fox'—the sobriquet has become the surname.

The Norman is said to be legalistic, litigious, given to chicanery, sly, covetous, grasping. . . . The epithets, all suggesting an inordinate love of money and a not too scrupulous regard for how it is acquired, can be endlessly extended. Michelet wrote of peasants who every evening set down their sons, weary from the fields, before a copy of the *Code Civil*. Frenchmen have attributed to the Norman this prayer: 'Lord, I do not ask of you riches, only to put me beside those that have them . . . and I will take care of the rest.' And all these rather unsavoury character-istics are summed up by ascribing to the Normans the possession of hands '*aux doigts crochus*'. The expression is a most suggestive one, having a whole range of possible meanings from 'light-fingered', through 'tight-fisted', to 'rapacious'. But what it really adds up to is the peasant's regard for property and for the rewards appropriate to his unrelenting labour. And that is hardly a unique, specifically Norman characteristic, being found wherever there are peasants. Furthermore, not all Nor-mans *are* peasants. Nevertheless, Maupassant did seize on examples of these qualities in his characters, but in isolating them he hypertrophied them out of all human recognition.

Be this as it may, when Maupassant describes the landscapes and seascapes of Normandy all his love of the province comes shining forth, fresh, tender, untrammelled by preconceptions, accurate—this faultless accuracy of perception, sprung from the observation and feelings of the boy who ran wild on its shores and by its streams, and then become sharpened into the engraver's eye from Flaubert's relentless pursuit of literary perfection—it is here that the artist in Maupassant is revealed. What matters, in *Une Vie*, whether he has based the early events of the novel on the relationship of his mother and father, compared with the moving delicacy of his description of the house and garden of *Les Peuples*—the actual château of Grainville-Ymauville, inland from Fécamp, rented by his family? In these, and a hundred other passages, few writers have captured so well the particular 'feel', the evocative and pervasive essence, of Normandy. In this he excels his master, and is perhaps only surpassed by Barbey d'Aurevilly.

Jeanne gazed at the broad surface of the sea, which appeared like watered silk, sleeping peacefully under the stars. In the quietness of the sunless sky all the scents of the earth rose up into the air. A jasmine climbing round the downstairs window gave out its heady scent, which mingled with the fainter smell of the young leaves. The wind came in gentle puffs, laden with the sharp tang of salt and the heavy viscous aroma of seaweed. . . . All the creatures that wake up every evening and conceal their secret lives in the peacefulness of the night were filling the semi-darkness with their faintly heard movement. Large birds were flitting about noiselessly like black blotches or ghosts, and the hum of unseen insects caressed the ear; there were silent scurryings through the dewy grass and the dust of the deserted roads. The only sound was the melancholy, monotonous note of the frogs croaking at the moon.

Une Vie was the book so much admired by Tolstoy, who considered it the best French novel after *Les Misérables.*

Today at Croisset the pavilion alone of Flaubert's house remains; here, where on Sundays he watched through binoculars the vapid faces of the bourgeois who stared from the river-steamers at this local eccentric, who bellowed like a bull in his '*gueuloir*' and kept his light on all night, so that the river-pilots used to steer by it. At Etretat Maupassant's '*bijou*' house still stands in its well-kept orchard-garden, the scene of riotous parties in the days when he was rich and courted, before—although the signs were already manifest—the syphilitic bacillus deprived him of reason and made necessary his confinement in Dr Blanche's luxurious asylum at Auteuil, where he died in 1893. (It is curious how many different ways can meet, leading from this coast of Normandy. While poor Maupassant was suffering at Auteuil, Jacques-Emile Blanche, Dr Blanche's son, was painting his celebrated portrait of Marcel Proust in the studio of this very house.) But it is Rouen where the shades of Flaubert and Maupassant still wander, in this city so damaged by war but now so happily restored. The Maison Tellier, the brothel of the Rue des Cordeliers, which used to run down to the quays by the present Rue Jeanne d'Arc (and not in Fécamp as related in the story), has been bombed into oblivion. And where is today, one wonders, that Rouen hotel, and its room 'with sunlight and a good chimney' kept for Maupassant and his mistresses? But the Rue des Charrettes is still there, just over the Rue Jeanne d'Arc from the former Rue des Cordeliers; here Flaubert, in search of precise local colour, haunted the cafés, taverns and wineshops of what was then the sailors' quarter and was nearly overcome by 'the smell of absinthe, cigars and oysters'. 'At sunset yesterday,' he wrote, 'the walls were oozing such *ennui* that I was almost asphyxiated as I passed.' And sometimes on a still night as you come out of the Rue du Gros-Horloge into the *place* before the cathedral you may catch the echo, the zany chuckle of *Le Garçon*, Flaubert's schoolboy *bête-noire*: 'Yes, that gothic's fine. War's fine too. They're both so inspiring!'

CHAPTER V

Caen

IN THE EARLY 1850s the Reverend George Musgrove, a West Country parson who appears to have spoken French extremely well, made a sketching excursion through Calvados. He must have been something of a rare bird even in that century of English eccentrics abroad; Protestant, patriotic, insular, but open-eyed, well informed, and well disposed, he left us his impressions of the country and its people in his pleasantly discursive book, *A Ramble through Normandy*. He was singularly appreciative of Caen, quoting with hearty agreement Mme de Sévigné's judgement in a letter to her daughter the Comtesse de Grignan, dated 5 May 1689: 'This is a very beautiful part of France, the most prepossessing, gayest and most happily situated of towns. Its streets are the handsomest, its churches, public buildings and walks the finest of their kind; and from this town have come the brightest wits and intelligences of their country.' Vouching for the truth of these remarks, Musgrove, as an experienced traveller, ventures his opinion that:

an enquiring mind will find more than enough to study, admire and relish in the Capital of which I am speaking. With the exception of Paris, there is hardly another city in France involving, even so far as we, as Englishmen, are concerned, so many awakening associations. . . . Architecture, science and war have severally raised those monuments on which the delighted eye still rests with wonder and veneration. And where has early art achieved more signal triumphs!

Alas, in 1944 Caen became the pivot of German resistance to the allied invasion of Normandy; and by 9 July, when the Canadians first entered the stricken city, whole quarters, like those of St-Pierre and St-Jean, were reduced to ashes and rubble, and thousands of Caen's inhabitants lay buried beneath the ruins of their houses. On 6 June aerial bombs had rained down on the city and by the evening the central area, with its charming mediaeval houses of carved woodwork and its elegant renaissance hôtels, was ablaze. It burned for eleven days. Fifteen hundred people sought refuge in the church of St-Etienne,

founded by William the Conqueror, and in the adjoining abbey buildings, the Abbaye aux Hommes, where the refectory was turned into an
operating theatre and the dead were buried in the courtyards. The
nearby mental hospital of the Bon Sauveur was occupied by some four
thousand refugees; and another wholesale massacre was only averted
by members of the French resistance movement, who got messages
through to the Allies, warning them of the existence of this oasis of
survivors. Most of the inhabitants of Caen, however, found safety in
the caves of Fleury, just south of the city, in the vast underground
quarries, whence the famous Caen stone has been excavated—much
of it to be shipped to England by the Normans for the building, among
other edifices, of Westminster Abbey and the Tower of London. By
the time that Caen was in Allied hands little remained of the beautiful
city known to Malherbe, Mme de Sévigné, Charlotte Corday, Beau
Brummell, Barbey d'Aurevilly, Rémy de Gourmont and the Reverend
Mr Musgrove.

But here I should quickly get in a word, lest it be thought that
nothing at all remains, that Caen has nothing to offer the visitor:
happily this is far from the truth. Caen is still today one of the most
beautiful and fascinating cities of Normandy, and perhaps one of the
most successful examples of intelligent civic planning and reconstruction in Europe, and would be worthy of a visit for that reason alone.
Of its churches still standing and repaired from war-time damage are
Duke William's St-Etienne and its early eighteenth-century abbey
buildings, his wife Matilda's contemporary church of the Trinity (or
Abbaye aux Dames), the romanesque gem of St-Nicolas and the part-
romanesque St-Michel de Vaucelles, the seventeenth-century Jesuit
Notre-Dame-de-la Gloriette, the gothic and renaissance Notre-Dame-
de-la-Rue-Froide (erroneously called St-Sauveur—the true, old St-
Sauveur standing disaffected and ruinous on the *place* of that name,
near the former site of the university), the remains of St-Jean seen above
the lawns and flower-beds, and—a Gothic masterpiece—the jewel-like
church of St-Pierre. Augustus Pugin, foremost among the architects of
the English Gothic revival in the last century, and responsible for much
of the decoration of Sir Charles Barry's Houses of Parliament, used to
bring his pupils to Caen simply to study the perfection of St-Pierre.

And of secular building there remain William the Conqueror's
castle, cleared today so that we can see the contemporary chapel of
St George and the Room of the Exchequer (part of the Norman palace),
and the later residence of the governor; the mediaeval houses *à pans*

de bois at Nos. 52 and 54 Rue St-Pierre and the fourteenth-century Quatran's House in Rue de Geôle; the renaissance Hôtels of Escoville and Thaon, and the Hôtel de Colomby of the time of Louis Treize; the old house where Malherbe lived in Place Malherbe; the typically eighteenth-century Place Fontette and off it the Place St-Sauver, with its eighteenth-century houses; and in the Rue Basse the early sixteenth-century Manoir de Nollent (or Manoir des Gens d'Armes). One feels inclined to use the word *miraculous* when one considers that any building has survived such devastation, but wandering in parts of Caen we light on old courts and dwellings, with carved fronts and intricate ironwork, and over high walls catch glimpses of secluded gardens, bright with lilacs, wistaria and laburnum, in front of houses that have the tranquillity of age.

Yet in the centre of the city one is very aware of, but not offended by, its gleaming modernity, the facing of buildings in white *pierre de Caen*. No praise can be too high for the authorities who planned the city's reconstruction. Taking into account what of architectural value was spared—this refers particularly to the churches and the citadel—those responsible for the planning have been zealous in ensuring that these be seen to their best advantage. Streets and open spaces have been designed with this aim in mind, the heights of buildings have been varied and, where necessary, restricted, so that such views are unimpeded. The result is quite magnificent, St-Pierre especially standing out in all the beauty of its slender spire, its candelabra-like pinnacles and its flowing flamboyant tracery. One must add one's tribute to such foresight, practicality and good taste.

A very old tradition has it that in the seventh century St Régnobert, Bishop of Bayeux, created four new parishes on the banks of the Orne: St-Sauveur, Notre-Dame-de-la-Rue-Froide, St-Jean and St-Pierre, which suggests the existence of a considerable population at that period. In a legal document of 1026 (or 1027) Duke Richard III mentions the '*villa* called *Cathim*' as already a place of some importance. But historical Caen owes everything to Duke William. One of his first public appearances was at the Council of Caen in 1042, when as a boy of fourteen he was present at the promulgation of the Truce of God. There exists today a reminder of this curb on the barons' restlessness in the remains of the apse of the little church of Ste-Paix-de-Tousaints, hidden away among the gas-works, between the Rue d'Auge and the Rue du Marais in the suburb of Vaucelles. Its name was derived from the number of precious relics brought here from all over Normandy to herald in God's holy Truce—*Sainte Paix de Tous Saints*—although the chapel was originally dedicated to St Mark. It was to the south-east of the town that in 1047 Duke William crushed the rising of the barons of the Cotentin and the Bessin at the battle of Val-ès-Dunes. But it was his marriage, despite papal prohibition, with his kinswoman Matilda of Flanders that focused William's attention on Caen. One of the conditions for the removal of the ban of excommunication, negotiated by Lanfranc with the Pope, was that William and Matilda, by way of atonement, should found two abbeys and a hospital in Caen. At the same time the duke fortified the rock with a citadel and enclosed the whole area around it and the two abbeys with walls and fortified towers. Even after the conquest of England Caen was William's city of choice, his favourite Norman residence.

An indication of the town's growing prosperity was the purchase by the burghers from King John Lackland of a municipal charter in 1203, the year before that luckless monarch lost Normandy to Philippe Auguste of France. The Hundred Years' War brought destruction to Caen; in 1346 the troops of Edward III entered the town, ignoring the presence of the garrison, but the women made every house a fortress, hurling down stones and even furniture on the heads of the reviled English. The town was thereupon given over to plunder, and some idea of its wealth may be gauged by the necessity of bringing a hundred ships from Ouistreham to carry off to England the booty, which included, among the gold, silver and jewels, 40,000 pieces of cloth. Again in 1417 Henry V, after the defeat of the French chivalry at Agincourt, took Caen with great slaughter, and repeated the pillage of 1346. However, he liked the place and embellished the castle. Henry V's presence in Caen had a profound effect on the building of town houses; hitherto much had been constructed in stone, but after the sack he sequestrated the quarries of the whole region from Beaulieu to Allemagne (now called Fleury), reserving the Caen stone for use in royal edifices in England and Normandy. Consequently the citizens rebuilt their houses with *pans de bois*, and it is since the destruction of these picturesque dwellings in 1944 that there constructed buildings have been faced with the beautiful local stone. Nor were the English come only as destroyers; in 1432 the regent for Henry VI, his uncle the Duke of Bedford, founded the university of Caen. The English were ultimately forced to leave Caen after the decisive defeat at Formigny in 1450. During the Wars of Religion Caen, which like other prosperous towns of Normandy had a large and for the most part well-to-do Huguenot population, suffered much, particularly at the hands of extreme Calvinists in 1562 and 1563. In the latter year the Protestant Admiral Coligny placed some men in the tower of St-Pierre, to fire at the Catholics in the citadel, who replied with cannon, seriously damaging the spire—and is says much for the strength of its structure that it could go unrepaired for more than a century. The damage caused by the Calvinists' sacking of St-Etienne brought about the collapse of the lantern-tower in 1566. The Revolution was first hailed by the Caennais, but gradually the excesses in Paris caused a revulsion of feeling, and a sporadic movement began in support of the provinces and in opposition to the power of the Paris mob grouped in their Sections. The city opened its gates in 1793 to the expelled Girondins, and it was from the house of her aunt Mme de Bretteville at No. 148 Rue St-Jean (destroyed during the last war) that Charlotte Corday set out on 9 July of that year for the capital, to rid France of the ailing Marat.

Duke William began work on St-Etienne, the church of his Benedictine Abbaye aux Hommes, in 1062 or 1063, having summoned Lanfranc of Pavia from Bec-Hellouin to become its first abbot. It would appear that the architects of St-Etienne owed to Lanfranc the form that the building took, inspired by the austere beauty of the romanesque churches of Lombardy and Ravenna. On 13 September 1077 the church was solemnly dedicated in the presence of William and Matilda, now King and Queen of England, Lanfranc (since 1070 Archbishop of Canterbury), and the Archbishops of Rouen and York. Today, in order to appreciate fully the great west front, it is wise to stand as far back as possible in the short street which faces it. The first sight may be forbidding; the whole eleventh-century façade seems functional to the point of austerity, bare of all ornament, until the eye picks out the light, geometrical decoration on the arches of the triple doors, and higher up an ornamental band at the level from which the towers rise, and again on the edge of the gable over the nave. The area occupied by the first three storeys forms an almost perfect square, relieved only by the four powerful Lombard buttresses, the low door-openings and the plain circular-headed windows. The effect is uncompromisingly stern, down-to-earth, blunt, forthright and implacable as the character of the Conqueror himself. But as we lift our eyes upward to the beautiful twin towers, we feel as if this rigour lightens—from the blind Lombard arcading of the lowest storey, through the elegant twin columns supporting the five arches (two with apertures) of the storey above, to the splendid deep-recessed arches divided each by a slender column of the topmost storey. The width of each tower and the interval between them is seen to be equal, and this whole area again has the illusion of forming another almost perfect square. Up to this height all is of the eleventh century; the magnificent tapering octagonal spires, which surmount the towers and turrets and continue from ground level the sheer vertical thrust upward like a lance aimed at the sky, were raised in the thirteenth century. These are the prototypes for so many Norman gothic spires, such as in Caen that of St-Pierre, or those of Secqueville-en-Bessin or Coutances Cathedral—the original model being doubtless the south spire of Chartres. Beneath the (modern) tympanum of the low central door—low, since this was primarily the entrance to an abbey church —is a curious device: the words *Rex*, *Lex*, *Lux*, *Pax* (King, Law, Light, Peace) in the shape of a cross, with the *x* common to the four words forming the link. The most striking difference externally of the earlier church from the present is in its central lantern-tower, which, until its collapse in 1566, was (with its spire) of a soaring height, similar perhaps in its relation to the spires of the west front as the tall *flèche* of Rouen Cathedral is to the Butter Tower and the Tour St-Romain. With its wooden spire it may have risen as high as 380 feet (nearly the height of Salisbury), overtopping by far those of the west façade—which incidentally are not equal, that of the north measuring 269 feet, with its southern neighbour some seven feet lower.

Within St-Etienne we are overwhelmed by its lofty grandeur, by the majesty and purity of its lines, the harmony of the disposition of stone-work and spaces. There is one feature of the construction which contributes greatly to its effectiveness, but is not immediately noticeable. Originally the nave was covered by a flat wooden ceiling; then in about 1130 this was replaced by the earliest type of gothic vaulting, known from its divisions as sexpartite, formed by the transverse and diagonal ribbing—here without carved bosses. To achieve this the bays of the nave are grouped in pairs. Between every second bay an elegant half-column rises from floor-level to the clerestory; alternating with these are similar half-columns, but set in shallow piers, which, just below the clerestory, support embedded columnettes. From the ornamented capitals of the simple half-columns spring simple transverse ribs; from the triple set of capitals formed of half-columns and columnettes spring both transverse and diagonal ribs. No answer perhaps can be given to the question which arises from this happy conjunction of the architectural prerequisites for such vaulting: Did the romanesque Norman builder foresee this eventuality or was it just a singularly fortunate coincidence? Possibly the alteration was primarily aesthetic? In the aisles the change-over from barrel-vaulting to ogival in all likelihood occurred in the fifteenth century; above, in the extraordinarily broad gallery of the triform, the ribs of rounded vaults serve as buttresses to the lofty nave—a step in the direction of developed gothic, with its characteristic flying-buttresses. The triforium's balustrade of quatre-foils, so decoratively effective in the general scarcity and stylised simplicity of ornament, was placed there in the seventeenth century. And here I must confess what seems to be the one failure in the design of this magnificent church. From the west end of the nave, looking through the beautiful lancet arches (so crisp in their cutting) of the apsidal end of the choir, one finds something like confusion in the dis-position of light coming from the truncated rose-window at the height of the triforium and the clerestory windows. At the beginning of the thirteenth century, to meet the demands of liturgical changes, the romanesque choir was rebuilt and the *chevet*, with its ambulatory and lateral and radial chapels, constructed. From the exterior this is very fine, but inside the church (I feel) the problem of light seen through the choir's end has not been satisfactorily solved—not so effectively as it has been, for example, at St-Pierre-sur-Dives. This work was super-vised by a certain 'Guillaume who excelled in the art of stones', as we may read in his epitaph on the memorial stone which the sacristan will point out in the external wall of the Lady Chapel. Another builder whose name must be honoured among those who have preserved for nine hundred years, with such loyalty to the founder's intentions, this abbey church of St-Etienne, is Dom Jean de Baillehache, the prior re-sponsible for restoration after Calvinist depredations of 1566. So much care was given by him to the work of the early Norman masons that it is said to require an expert's eye to distinguish seventeenth-century stonework from that of the thirteenth. This abbey was conceived before the Norman conquest of England, but Englishmen have been laid under contribution for its immense cost; English estates were lavishly be-stowed on the monks of Caen by William, who did not scruple to divert for this purpose the revenues from the dead Harold's favoured abbey at Waltham in Essex.

In the minds and perhaps the hearts of English and Normans alike the Abbaye aux Hommes holds a special appeal as the last resting place of the Conqueror. The present commemorative stone before the high altar was only set there in 1801 by General Dugua, the provincial prefect under the Consulate, to replace the earlier tomb which had

twice been profaned, once by Calvinists in the religious troubles of the
sixteenth century and again by the revolutionaries in 1790. On the
latter occasion what remained of William's bones, carefully collected
and reburied by the Prior de Baillehache in the early seventeenth
century, were finally scattered to the four winds. The wording is in
the indifferent Latin of the general or his scribes:

HIC SEPULTUS EST

INVICTISSIMUS

GULIELMUS

CONQUESTOR

NORMANNIAE DUX

ET ANGLIAE REX

HUISCE DOMUS

CONDITOR

QUI OBIIT ANNO

MLXXXVII

'Here is buried the invincible William the Conqueror, Duke of
Normandy and King of England, of this house the founder, who died
in the year 1087.'

The lurid events at the burial of William the Conqueror in St-
Etienne in November 1087 left a deep impression on his contemporaries.
His wife had pre-deceased him by some four years, and had been
buried in the sister church of the Holy Trinity at the Abbaye aux
Dames. In September 1087 the king, provoked by injuries at the hands
of the French, invaded the French Vexin and in retaliation gave the
town of Mantes over to the flames. As he was watching the conflagration, his horse, treading on live cinders, suddenly reared and fell,
causing him, corpulent as he had become, an internal injury from
which, after lingering for some weeks in great pain, he died at the
Abbey of St-Gervais in Rouen. His strong hand removed, Normandy
was in the greatest confusion, each man looking only to secure his own
possessions in fear of general anarchy. William Rufus returned in haste
to London to secure his throne, and it was William's youngest son,
Henry (later King Henry I of England), who accompanied the Archbishop of Rouen and the clergy on the boat which carried the late
king's body down the reaches of the Seine, to convey it for interment,
in accordance with his wishes, at Caen. With Henry, gathered around
the mound of earth from the open grave in the transept of St-Etienne,

were a great number of high dignitaries of church and state, among them the self-effacing Nicholas, Abbot of St-Ouen, the late king's cousin and wrongfully denied heir to the duchy, and the gentle Anselm, Lanfranc's successor as Abbot of Bec-Hellouin, later to be Archbishop of Canterbury and saint. The requiem mass having been sung, the Bishop of Evereux was finishing his funeral oration when a loud voice filled the church and sent a shiver of fear through the congregation: '*Haro! Haro! Haro! à l'aide, mon prince, on m'a fait tort!*' This traditional cry of *haro*, for the redress of wrongs (long to continue in the Channel Islands), came from one Ascelin, differently called a knight or a rich burgher, who claimed that the land where William was to be buried was legally his, seized by the dead king from his father without payment, when he raised the church. Ascelin had brought with him witnesses; and it was found expedient to pay him the small sum of thirty sous (about thirty English new pence) on the spot, to prevent further scandal and to allow the burial service to proceed. But William the Conqueror was not yet safely in the grave. As the body was being lowered into the ground the opening was found to be too narrow for the coffin, and when force was applied to it the coffin broke away, crashed against some stone and burst asunder. The stench that issued from it spread to the bystanders, and was so noisome that the congregation quickly dispersed, leaving the clergy to race through the committal and the grave-diggers hurriedly to fill in the dreadful cavity.

Of William's romanesque cloister adjoining his church nothing remains, and only very little of (much restored) gothic building, such as the fourteenth-century so-called *Salle* of Duke William's guards. The actual monastery, a beautiful edifice in the style of Louis Treize, which was from 1804 the Lycée Malherbe and today serves as the Hôtel de Ville, was erected between 1704 and 1724 by Guillaume de la Tremblaye, the monk from Bec-Hellouin, the principal builder for the Benedictine Order in Normandy after the reforms of St-Maur and one of the finest French architects of his period. Within may be visited rooms magnificently panelled with light oak—the parlour, refectory, sacristy and the former meeting-room of the congregation (now the chapel) are particularly beautiful—carved by local craftsmen in low-relief cartouches and garlands of flowers, forming ornamental frames for paintings by Jean Restout, Mignard, Lépicié and others. In the sacristy is an interesting *trompe-l'œil*, painted in fresco in the manner of the seventeenth-century Italians. Curious in some rooms is the result of the circular windows' cutting the elliptical curve of the ceilings, which from certain angles produces the geometrical effect of lighted parabolas. The staircases are designed with a bold inventiveness of curve, and have for their railings the most exquisite eighteenth-century iron-work, which is also seen in the grilles of the upstairs passages.

The monks of the Abbaye aux Hommes, right from its inception, found it necessary to provide for their tenants a parish church in the Bourg-Abbé, which was already populous and had two parish churches, St-Martin and St-Etienne-le-Vieux—the latter behind the Abbaye, where its damaged successor stands today. To this need we owe the foundation of the church dedicated to St-Nicholas, a saint very popular at that time, since the removal of his bones from Myra in Asia Minor to Bari by the Normans of Apulia. In 1083 a charter of King William referred to 'the Church of St-Nicholas, recently constructed by the monks for the needs of their parish'. By happy chance St-Nicholas has not suffered the transformations undergone by so many other roman-esque churches; but it has had vicissitudes enough. Suppressed at the Revolution, it has been used subsequently as a shot factory, cavalry stable and a store for fodder, before its restoration began in 1931. And this is still far from complete, but what we can now see of its formal beauties merits our calling it a little masterpiece of romanesque. Until early in this century the fields came right up to its walls, so that it was known as St-Nicholas-des-Champs; and in the charming overgrown cemetery which encompasses it we can still feel around us the peaceful suggestion of the countryside. Behind the apse, with its strange high seven-sided roof, we may stroll on gravelled paths beneath trees clung close by ivy, among lilac-bushes, box, cypress, laburnum and old roses, and between forgotten graves covered with moss, lichen and peri-winkle, while in the tree-tops the birds sing, songs which in this leafy retreat sound cheerful, but only mutedly so, as if restrained by an underlying sadness.

At the other extremity of old Caen, on the hill, stands the Duchess Matilda's foundation of the Holy Trinity, or the Abbaye aux Dames, begun in 1062. Work could not have progressed far when the church was dedicated on 10 June 1066, in the presence of the duke and duchess and a great concourse of ecclesiastics and barons, who were brought together also for a political purpose—on Christmas Day of the same year William would be crowned King of England in Westminster Abbey. On the occasion of its consecration Duke William presented his daughter Cecilia at the altar as a postulant to the convent, and she later became the second abbess. The Abbaye aux Dames was always an aristocratic institution; for the three days of the Fair of the Holy Trinity the standard of the abbess flew above Caen, and during this period she enjoyed complete municipal jurisdiction. In 1083 Queen Matilda was buried in the choir, leaving her crown and jewels to the abbey. Like the remains of her husband, the queen's tomb has suffered two profanations; after the first in the sixteenth century her bones were piously re-interred by the Abbess Anne de Montmorency, and in 1708 a new monument was erected, only to be destroyed in its turn at the Revolution, although then the coffin was spared. The original black marble stone remains today, with its leonine epitaph praising her illustrious lineage—grand-daughter and niece of Kings of France and daughter of the Count of Flanders. Aesthetically the Abbaye aux Dames bears no comparison with its brother abbey, but in parts it is highly interesting. The main façade, which has been badly restored, particularly in the last century, is, to say little, uninspiring; the central doorway is an absurd anachronism, the work of the architect Geoffrey Dechaume.

Inside the church we are immediately aware of the lack of height, when compared with St-Etienne; the triforium is perfunctory, low blind-arcading; although above it the clerestory windows are very impressive. There is more ornamentation, however—geometrical in the nave arches, stylised foliage on the capitals. In the most interesting and beautiful apse the capitals of the quasi-ambulatory show representations of the mediaeval bestiary of oriental origin, perhaps inspired by booty brought back from the crusades by Robert Courteheuse, who also presented a Saracenic standard to his sister the Abbess Cecilia, which was hung here until it crumbled to dust. The vaulting is from an architectural point of view of very considerable interest; the covering of the nave shows how the Anglo-Norman builders of this time— c. 1130—were trying out methods of spanning these wide areas, here by what is known as false sexpartite vaulting. It was from such experiments that was eventually evolved the characteristic pointed gothic vault. This differs from that of St-Etienne by the heavier ribbing and by the fact that at every second column springs a rounded transverse arch which supports a wall upholding the vault. Both the aisles and the choir have their vaults of arris-work; the choir being very wide indeed to be spanned in this manner. The crypt, which is entered by an extremely low (and not a little dangerous!) doorway from the gothic thirteenth-century chapel off the right transept, retains its primitive solidity and simplicity, with its columns crowned by rude varioform capitals.

The early cloisters and conventual buildings were replaced in the seventeenth century by those we see, built in the classical style; these suffered grave damage in the last war and now form the Hôtel-Dieu, the hospital cared for by the nuns, who use the altar end of the abbey as their private place of worship. In the Place Reine Mathilde on to which open the entrance of both the Trinity and the Hôtel-Dieu are what little remains of an edifice which was the *paroissiale* for the ward of Bourg-l'Abbesse, the church of St-Gilles, founded by William and Matilda. The church's name is a reminder of the frequent travels which the Normans undertook at this time, mostly in the direction of Italy and the Holy Land, where they passed by St-Gilles de Languedoc. For nine hundred years the poor of this parish gathered each Sunday to hear a mass on their behalf and to receive a loaf of bread from the endowment of the founders. In the fifties of last century the Reverend Mr Musgrove wrote of St-Gilles: 'Without any exception, it is the most happily proportioned, and the most inviting in its general aspect, of all the rural houses consecrated to God I ever entered.' He had heard that the municipal authorities, for some reason known only to themselves, planned to pull down the apse of 'this little gem', and only hoped that an English architect would journey to Caen to draw plans of it before this act of vandalism was perpetuated. Alas, what was threatened took place in 1864, and the last war finished this needless act of destruction.

St-Pierre was the parish church of the burghers of Caen, their pride and their glory, in the beauty of its tower and spire and the magnificence of its flamboyant *chevet*. Like others of Caen's churches—the Trinity, Notre-Dame-de-la-Froide-Rue and St-Etienne-le-Vieux—St-Pierre does not follow the liturgical orientation, its apse not facing due east, but south-by-south-east. The present building, replacing a romanesque one, was raised between the thirteenth and the sixteenth centuries, being completed, that is, at the time of the full-flowering of renaissance flamboyant. It is a singularly beautiful church. The highly decorated *chevet*, which once was reflected in the still waters of a branch of the Orne (now filled in), was considered to be the work of the celebrated Caennais architect Hector Sohier. It is nowadays thought possibly to be attributed to other hands—Hugues Le Fournier and Jean Héroux have been mentioned, and even the famous Rouennais Rouland le Roux, although this last seems most improbable. The work was begun in 1518, and it ranks as one of the most beautiful specimens of renaissance gothic in Normandy, with its lacework tracery, its candelabra of pinnacles, its arabesques. In addition to the aesthetic satisfaction derived from the tapered elegance of the tower and spire, its construction is of great architectural interest. The hexagonal surfaces of the spire were raised with no internal supporting structure, simply the joining together of sheets of stone some sixteen centimetres in thickness. Apertures (in descending numbers of 'foils'—cinquefoil, quatrefoil, trefoil, etc., as the spire ascends) reduced the danger from high wind. The two first storeys of the tower were begun in the thirteenth century, the remainder after 1317, the latter being paid for by one man, the treasurer Jean Langlois. In the early hours of the morning of 9 June 1944 the spire was hit by a shell fired from H.M.S. *Rodney* and collapsed, but it has been perfectly repaired. The interior of the church is remarkable for the pendent vaulting in the apsidal chapels, possibly done by the school of Sohier in about 1520, and for the curious carving of capitals and spandrels of the nave, which depict scenes of popular mediaeval mythology and animals of the bestiary: Sir Lancelot crossing the lake on a sword-bridge to rescue Guinevere; Sir Gawain; two examples of the misery of senile love (the naked Aristotle ridden as a horse by Campaspe, and foolish Virgil strung up in a basket); the unicorn, the virgin, and others, all instructive and amusing to the worthy burghers of Caen.

Just off the Place St-Pierre in its courtyard stands the fine renaissance Hôtel d'Escoville, the town house built between 1535 and 1540 for Nicholas Le Valois d'Escoville, a rich burgher (considered one of the richest Normans of his age), a fastidious connoisseur and, according to reports, an alchemist. When one walks through to the courtyard, one is immediately reminded of the Hôtel de Bourgtheroulde in Rouen, both houses having been built by men who were influenced by Italian fashions. The architect and sculptor is not known for certain, but the work has been attributed by some to Blaise Le Prestre, who may also have executed the Henri II sculptures at the château of Fontaine-Henry. The hôtel has been judiciously repaired after war damage, and we may observe the fine adjustment of spaces—of windows and niches with the wall-surface—and the good statues of David (resembling so markedly the St George of Donatello), and Judith with Holophernes; above them the *bas-reliefs* of Andromeda delivered by Perseus and the Rape of Europe; all surmounted by ornate coats of arms of the d'Escoville, supported by the geniuses of the family.

The Rue St-Pierre, which runs from the church roughly eastwards in the direction of the Abbaye aux Hommes, is one of the principal shopping streets of the city. At Nos. 52–4, on the right, are two surviving examples of those mediaeval timber-framed houses which before the war gave characteristic picturesqueness to old Caen. And just beyond them is the church of Notre-Dame-de-la-Rue-Froide (wrongly known as St-Sauveur), a rather dark building of the fourteenth and fifteenth centuries, with some additions possibly at the hands of Hector Sohier or his followers. Its tower and spire, although modelled on those of St-Pierre, show how much depends aesthetically on proportion; in this case the spire sits rather squatly between the belfries which top its tower. Some little way on, in Place Malherbe, the street divides, the main thoroughfare being to the right, in Rue Ecuyère. At this point stands the house, rebuilt by Malherbe in 1582 on the site of the building in which he was born in 1555. It is rather shameful, when the house has survived the ravages of war, that its present condition should have caused so little concern to those interested in preserving places of historical interest. For François de Malherbe (1555–1628) was a very considerable man, who tried to purify, to systematise (and the ugly word is just), the French language from a foreign over-rankness imported by the poets of the *Pléiade*. The effect he had is well summed up by Boileau's famous words from his *Art Poétique*, '*Enfin Malherbe vint!*' It was said of him that he wished to make prose out of verse, verse of prose, working at this self-imposed task with 'the zeal, niggling but efficacious, of a policeman'. But he left us the well-known line, which La Varende possibly had in mind when he described the complexions of Norman girls:

> *Et, rose, elle a vécu ce que vivent les roses.*

And a few doors farther on, always on the same side of the street, a plaque on the dressed stone surface of an eighteenth-century house informs us that Rémy de Gourmont, that symbolist whose attention to style would render him suspect today, lodged there last century, while an undergraduate at the university. Before we reach the Place Fontette, an admirable example of eighteenth-century civic planning, an entrance at No. 42 (still on the right) leads to the small courtyard of the Hôtel des Ecuyers, a house of the fifteenth century, where once lived Bureau de Giberville, the lieutenant-governor of Caen under Charles VII. Today this has been converted into a pleasant little hotel, simple, quiet, clean—and cheap.

Another ancient hotel, the famous Hôtel d'Angleterre in the Rue St-Jean, unfortunately has not survived the war. The Reverend Mr Musgrove put up there in 1854, and complained of the noise from two trombones and a horn which daily regaled him at dinner and of the paucity of the courses of the *table d'hôte*, reflecting, on the latter point, that things must have been very different in Beau Brummell's day, when he sat down in the same dining room, with a peer or two for company, to a repast, he was informed, of upwards of twenty dishes, including three of fish. George Brummell died in Caen some fourteen years previously, on 30 March 1840. Musgrove visited the asylum of the Bon-Sauveur, where this greatest of all dandies spent his last days, cared (and paid for) by the people of Caen, and spoke with the gardener Pierre Dubois, who remembered Brummell well. He was so paralysed of body that he required two attendants to support him when walking in the garden; he seemed unaware of his mental condition, and assured his assistants that he had amply provided for them in his will; his appetite was good, even 'voracious', but he drank only barley-water mixed with a little wine. In 1816 Brummell, who had fallen from favour with the Prince Regent (it is said that his wit had cut too near the bone to be relished by his former patron) and found himself ruined by his gambling losses, took refuge from his creditors in Calais. There he remained for fourteen years, living in a style beyond his straitened purse, until in 1830 his friends in England secured him the post of H.M. Consul at Caen. Two years later he lost this position, and debts incurred both in Calais and Caen caused him to be imprisoned for a time, from which he was released by the assistance not of English but of French friends. Some years afterwards his mind and body both gave way, and he was committed to the charitable care of the nuns of the Bon-Sauveur.

In 1830 Barbey d'Aurevilly was reading law in Caen as an undergraduate at the university, with his rooms at No. 2 Place Malherbe, and he was much impressed by the ageing dandy, whom he seems to have met and who must have retained some traces still of 'that certain exquisite propriety' which Byron had observed. With the Count d'Orsay, Barbey d'Aurevilly did much to transplant in France this essentially English cult of the dandy, which the latter was to develop into something like a philosophy in his *Du Dandysme et de Georges Brummell*, published in 1844. The verisimilitude of his account of Brummell at the Hôtel d'Angleterre suggests that he may himself have been a witness of one of these distressing evenings.

On certain days, to the great astonishment of the hotel staff, he ordered his rooms to be prepared for him as for a reception. Chandeliers, candlesticks, lamps, a profusion of flowers, nothing was lacking; and he, under the blaze of all those lights, in the full-dress of his youth, the blue Whig coat with gold buttons, the piqué waistcoat, black trousers, close-fitting like the knee-breeches of the sixteenth century, in the centre of all, he waited. . . . He awaited an England dead! Suddenly, as if he had split himself in two, he announced in a clear voice the Prince of Wales, then Lady Connyngham, then Lord Yarmouth, and then all those notables of England, whose living law he had been. Believing that he saw them appear as he called their names, and changing his voice, he went to receive them at the door, flung wide open, of the empty room, through which no one, alas, passed that evening, nor other evenings; and he greeted them, these chimeras of his brain. He offered his arm to the ladies among all these phantoms whom he had just called up and who, certainly, would not have been willing for an instant to quit their tombs, to return to the rout of a fallen Dandy. This would continue a long time. . . . At last, when all was full of these phantoms, when all this world of the other world had arrived, then arrived also his reason, and the unfortunate man would perceive his illusion and his madness! At this point he would slump into his solitary armchair, and one would come upon him in floods of tears. . . .

The Bon-Sauveur was indeed not far away.

On the Conqueror's citadel is the chapel of St Georges, which has much of the charm of a small English parish church. Here on that saint's day, 23 April 1418, King Henry V created no fewer than twelve Knights of the Order of the Bath. In a new building close by is the Art Gallery, which, among a most representative and interesting collection of paintings, possesses the famous *Marriage of the Virgin Mary* by Perugino. The Reverend Mr Musgrove was delighted to be able to see in Caen the collection of paintings and prints brought together by M. Mancel, a publisher, connoisseur and city father, many of which came from the celebrated collection in Rome of the Cardinal Fesch, the Emperor Napoleon's uncle. Musgrove hoped that the British Museum or some rich patron would procure this precious collection of prints for England. In 1872 M. Mancel bequeathed them to the art gallery of his native city, where they can be seen and enjoyed today.

CHAPTER VI

Two Norman Women

IT SEEMS AT first sight as if some of the greatest of the regional writers of Normandy had entered into an open conspiracy to depict their countrywomen with similar characteristics, as if they had all declared their personal preference for a single type of young Norman womanhood—at once ardent and tender, loving and open in her desire to be loved, natural and responsive to the point of a warm, generous, laughing spontaneity. Barbey d'Aurevilly, Flaubert (even the crabbed misogynist Flaubert—in the springtime of his youth), Guy de Maupassant, Jean de la Varende—each of them in his turn praises, with a curious insistence, these country girls of Normandy, 'with the luminous complexions of roses, and freshness of mother of pearl'. La Varende becomes lyrical in describing the early loves (and they were many) of his maimed hero Nez-de-Cuir:

> And the race then was still purer; all had this complexion, so striking in its quality, which left an impression for life on those who admired it in their youth. How 'white' they were, these girls, how 'rosy', two attributes which come naturally to every Norman's pen, in spite of himself, since Basselin of Vire or Malherbe of Caen, who found in them his most celebrated 'effect', right down to Maupassant of Miromesnil, who based his aesthetics on them. Colour of rose, whiteness, flesh-colour, which Normandy with its blossoming trees seems still to extol in its meadow nosegays, its flesh-like forests. . . .

Perhaps, then, these general characteristics which have been given to their countrywomen by Norman poets and novelists reflect more particularly their own aesthetic predilections, and suggest the ideal rather than the actuality. But the type of colouring they depict does hold good for the two Norman women who are here presented— Charlotte Corday and Marie-Françoise-Thérèse Martin, the first sprung from the *petite nobleness* and the second from the *petite bourgeoisie*. Michelet describes Hauer's portrait of Charlotte Corday, painted at her own request in her death-cell, as 'sweet splendour of the apple-tree in bloom'; and Ste Thérèse is always portrayed as the epitome of pink and white, with her 'showers of roses' from heaven. Nor does the likeness end with their common Norman birth and colouring: both were prepared—desired even—to make a sacrifice of their lives in the furtherance of their faith.

Marie-Anne-Charlotte Corday d'Armont came of an ancient Norman family; her ancestors were known from the eleventh century, and she counted among her forebears the great Corneille and the philosophical Fontenelle. She was born on 27 July 1768 on the farm of Ronceray, in the little frame and thatched cottage still standing in an orchard near the village of Les Lignerits, in whose old church, St-Saturin, she was baptised. Opposite the church is the seventeenth-century house of Marie Corneille, daughter of the author of *Le Cid*. The Corday farm lies about a mile south-west of Les Champeaux, itself a village some two miles due west of Camembert, in the peaceful, rolling countryside of the Pays d'Auge. Her father farmed his own properties; of her mother and one sister we hear little, and little more of her brothers, who emigrated at the Revolution to enlist in the Royalist armies. An early record of Charlotte is of her refusal to drink the health of Louis XVI on the plea that 'a weak king cannot be good'. She was educated by the nuns of Queen Matilda's Abbaye aux Dames at Caen, and, on leaving school, went to live in the town with an aunt, Mme Coutellier de Bretteville. She kept very much to herself, an intensely earnest, thoughtful young person, occupying her leisure by a study of the classics and the *philosophes*, especially Voltaire and Jean-Jacques Rousseau. There seemed nothing fanatical about her, although she felt deeply the course that the Revolution, which she had warmly welcomed, was taking; to outsiders she appeared what she was—not strikingly beautiful, but a sincere, self-possessed, balanced, purposeful young woman, her nobility of birth and sentiment at once evident.

Like so many of the better spirits of her age, Charlotte was well read in the classical, republican authors; of political writers she knew Locke, Montesquieu, Helvétius and the encyclopaedists, and, above all, Jean-Jacques. And here, one imagines, she had proceeded to *Le Contrat Social* by way of *La Nouvelle Héloïse*. Nature (most of her contemporaries spent much of their time in the country), the finer feelings, virtue, reason and, in the sphere of the state, liberty—these were the concepts they habitually employed. Release man, they thought, from the shackles of obsolete laws and social conventions and he would stand forth free, virtuous, reasonable. It was beyond their imagination to realise that, the restraining hand once removed, men would behave like wild beasts. By mid-1793 Marat, leading the left-wing Montagnards, saw clearly, in the rapidly developing situation, that with the Parisian mob behind him, united in its Sections and in the Commune, he could rule France, either as a dictator or in a dictatorial triumvirate. (This was Marat's contribution to the theory of the dictatorship of the proletariat.) He was opposed in his plans chiefly by the provincial Girondins, who had reason to fear the predominance of Paris. On 31 May, Marat struck first and outlawed the Girondins, many of those who escaped finding a refuge in Normandy, and especially in Caen. A half-hearted insurrection took place in Normandy against the Parisian revolutionaries, but was put down on 13 July 1793. On that same day Marat was murdered.

It is not clear when Charlotte Corday arrived at her resolution to kill Marat and, in so doing, to save the Revolution, and France. In April, and therefore more than a month before the fall of the Girondins, she had acquired a passport for Paris from the authorities at Argentan. She saw little of the exiles in Caen, except for a visit she paid to the deputy Barbaroux, in order to secure introductions in Paris. Her ostensible reason for travelling was to seek repayment of the salary to her friend Mme de Forbin, wrongly withheld from her as a canoness of Troyes cathedral. She set out from Caen on Tuesday, 9 July, leaving a short letter for her father, containing her only known lie: 'I am leaving without your permission . . . without seeing you, because I should be so sorrowful. I am going to England.' Arrived in Paris, she put up at the Hôtel de la Providence, 19 Rue des Vieux-Augustins, and sought a meeting on the following day with the Minister of the Interior, on Mme de Forbin's behalf. On Wednesday, 12 July, she saw the minister, and that same evening sat down to write her moving *Address to Frenchmen who are friends to Laws and Peace*: 'Oh, my country, thy misfortunes wring my heart.' The next morning she bought for forty sous (about eight new pence) at a cutler's in the Palais Royal a table-knife with an ebony handle, encased in a sheath of imitation shagreen. Twice refused admittance to Marat's flat at 30 Rue des Cordeliers, she wrote a note by the ordinary post, and then presented herself again in the evening. This time she was admitted, and was shown in to the room where the sick Friend of the People sat in a shoe-bath. Taking a chair by his side, she answered quietly Marat's questions about affairs in Normandy. She gave him the information he required; and then stabbed him, killing him with a single blow.

At her interrogation and trial her attitude never wavered: she had come to Paris to kill Marat; her motive for killing him was his crimes. What crimes? 'The desolation of France, the civil war that he had kindled throughout the kingdom.' In killing him, what did she hope for? 'To give peace to my country.' Sentenced to death, she calmly prepared herself, wrote her last letters, had her portrait painted, refused the consolations of the Church, asked her small bills to be paid, and thanked her custodians. Then, conveyed by the tumbril, dressed in the scarlet chemise of a murderess, her auburn hair shorn, but wearing still her gloves on her pinioned hands, she indomitably went on her two-hour procession to the scaffold. Seldom could such high-minded resolution, such courage, such faith have achieved less. Within the short space of a year from the death of the perhaps already dying Marat, Charlotte Corday would be followed to the scaffold by the Girondins, by Danton, Robespierre and Saint Just—and by Charlotte Corday's panegyrist André Chenier. On 26 October 1795 the Convention Assembly was dissolved, to give place to the Directory. By the coup d'état of Brumaire 1799 Napoleon Bonaparte made himself dictator of France, and instituted a blood-bath for France and for Europe, which overwhelmed in horror (or, some maintain, glory) the excesses of the betrayed Revolution. What did it all avail?

Very different was the faith of the second of these Norman women, Marie-Françoise-Thérèse Martin, better known as Ste Thérèse of the Child Jesus, or of Lisieux, and more popularly in English-speaking lands as 'The Little Flower of Jesus'. She was born in Alençon on 2 January 1873 to Zélie Guérin, wife of Louis Martin, a prosperous watchmaker and jeweller of that town. Her parents were extremely devout, devout to the point of self-immolation, both having offered themselves for the conventual life and been refused by the superiors of religious houses. They regarded their meeting and marriage as providential. On their wedding night M. Martin informed his wife that he intended to live with her solely as with a sister; but the rigour of his avowed intention was relaxed, for we are told by a pious writer that 'nine flowers bloomed in this garden, of which four were transplanted to Paradise before their buds had quite unfolded, while five were gathered into God's gardens upon earth—one entering the Visitation Convent in Caen, the others the Carmelite Convent in Lisieux'. (This form of unctuous, devotional expression of extreme piety has plagued the literature of the devotees of Ste Thérèse.) Thérèse, the youngest of their children, was so delicate at birth that her life was despaired of; she was saved by being put out to nurse in the country with a Norman peasant woman, Rose Taillé. When Thérèse was only four-and-a-half her mother died of cancer of the breast; and her father, who already was rich enough to have retired, moved his family to Lisieux, where he could call on the help of his wife's brother and sister-in-law, M. Guérin, a chemist, and Mme Guérin.

It was in the house called Les Buissonnets (The Shrubbery), a comfortable, tasteless bourgeois house with a garden, that Thérèse grew up, surrounded by the loving care of her father and sisters. In this pious household (it is better admitted at the outset) there was more sweetness than intellectual light; everything was 'dear' or 'little'—Thérèse was her father's 'little queen', 'Sa Benjamine, sa petite reine'. The observances of the Church, the fasts and feast-days, were scrupulously followed; the reading was of improving books, the Liturgical Year or the Lives of the Saints. On her walks with her father Thérèse would be taken into churches to visit the Blessed Sacrament and to the chapel of the Convent of the Carmel: 'Look, my little queen, behind that big grating are holy nuns who constantly pray to God.' At home she had her own little altar which she tended daily; instructed in religious matters by her sisters Marie and Pauline, who both were to enter the Carmel, at an early age she began going to confession. The first word she learned to read was 'heaven', and she informed her father that her name was already written there, seeing the letter T in the constellation of Orion. At nine she persuaded Pauline to present her to the Mother Prioress of the Carmel as a postulant, only to be told that she must wait until she was sixteen. However, when shortly afterwards her sister entered the Carmel, Thérèse became so ill that her life was endangered. It was at this juncture that she was suddenly and completely cured, as she claimed, by a vision of Our Lady, who smiled on her. She bitterly regretted later having divulged this secret to her sister Marie and to the Mother Superior and nuns of the Carmel, regarding it as a betrayal which brought her great spiritual pain. 'Ah, if only I had kept my secret to myself I should also have kept my joy. . . . There are some things which lose their fragrance when exposed to the air. . . .' There is no denying the profundity of this last remark; how much of her own cult has suffered from this over-exposure.

At the Benedictine Convent which she attended she was shy and retiring, and her successes in class did not add to her popularity. On 8 May 1884, when she was eleven, she made her first communion, a day she had long looked forward to, and the language in which she described it gives some measure of the rapture she felt: 'Ah, how sweet was the first kiss of Jesus to my soul! Yes, it was a kiss of love! I felt that I was loved, and I said also, "I love you, I give myself to you for ever." Jesus asked nothing of me, He required no sacrifice. He and the little Thérèse had long since looked at one another and had understood. That day, our meeting could no longer be called a simple look, but a *fusion*. We were no longer two.' It was in language such as this that later, at the request of her Mother Superiors (first her own sister Pauline, and subsequently Mother Marie of Gonzaga), she wrote the *Story of a Soul* (*Histoire d'une âme*), the autobiography that has brought her life to the knowledge of millions. But first she was to reveal another side of her character, her extraordinary pertinacity, her refusal to be bent from the path that she had willed for herself. From the time of what she called her 'complete conversion' on Christmas Day 1886, a domestic occasion when she overcame her own self-will to do what would please her father, she had decided on and had set her course. Her resolution was to enter Carmel and there to achieve perfection. Nothing less. 'Reflecting then that I was born for glory,' she wrote, 'and searching for the means to attain it, it was inwardly revealed to me that my glory would never appear to mortal eyes, but would consist in becoming a saint. This desire might seem full of temerity,' she was careful to add, 'but I still feel the same audacious confidence that I shall become a *great saint*.' And she underlined the words. 'Searching for the means to attain it' she read with a new insight St Paul's *First Epistle to the Corinthians* (Chapters XI and XII), finding there that it is not given to all to possess a particular talent, but 'though I give my body to be burned, and have not charity, it profiteth me nothing'. Charity, love, was what she was seeking. 'My vocation is love,' she wrote. 'At last I have found it! I will be love itself! Oh, luminous lighthouse of love, I know how to reach even unto your fires. . . . But how shall I show my love, since love proves itself by deeds. I, the little one, will strew flowers. . . . I will sing Love's canticle in silvery tones. Thus will my short life be spent in Thy sight, Oh my Beloved! To strew flowers is the only means I have of proving my love, and these flowers will be each word and look, each daily sacrifice. I wish to profit by the slightest actions and do them all for Love. For Love's sake I wish to suffer and to rejoice: so shall I strew my flowers. . . . I shall scatter their petals before Thee. . . .'

She was fourteen when she sought out her father in the garden of Les

The cathedral,
Coutances

Bell tower, Langrune

Buissonnets at Whitsuntide 1887 (a hideous over-life-size marble group today marks the spot) and asked and received his permission to enter the Carmel. Her uncle, however, refused to agree, saying that she was too young, and that it would require a miracle to make him change his mind. Soon after, Thérèse relates, her prayers and his own enlightened him. But M. le Chanoine Delatroëtte, the Superior of Carmel, now intervened with the message that she could not enter before she was twenty-one. A meeting of Thérèse and her father with the canon evoked an unequivocal No, but he added that in refusing he only acted as the delegate of the bishop, who might see otherwise. So Thérèse, again accompanied by her father, journeyed to Bayeux to interview the bishop, Monseigneur Hugonin, who received them kindly (Thérèse putting up her hair for the first time that day, to appear older), but could say nothing more than that he would look into the matter and let her know on her return from the pilgrimage to Rome on which her father was taking her. At an audience of pilgrims in the Vatican, against all custom and despite a strict injunction to remain silent from the Vicar-General of Bayeux, who was standing at the Pope's side, and probably guessed her bold intention, Thérèse addressed her plea to Pope Leo XIII. She reports the occasion: 'Clasping my hands then and pressing them down on his knees, I essayed one last effort. "Oh, Most Holy Father, if only you would say yes, everyone would be willing." He looked at me very fixedly and pronounced these words, weighing each syllable in a penetrating tone, "Come now . . . come now . . . you will enter if God wills it." ' Returned to Bayeux, no message awaited her from the bishop. Characteristically she wrote him a polite note of reminder. Then on 9 April 1888, at the age of fifteen, Thérèse Martin entered the Carmel as Thérèse de l'Enfant Jésus.

When the gates of the convent closed behind her, shutting her off for ever from the outside world, it might have been thought that her lot would have been that of so many other young women who have devoted themselves to a rule of poverty, obedience and prayer—a life of austerity and abnegation, forgotten by most while living and by all soon after death had released them. On one so delicate and so used to the warmth and comfort of a bourgeois home the harshness of the Carmelite rule might have borne heavily, had she not so entirely willed it—willed it perhaps all the more strongly in her attempts to extinguish her own imperious self-will. Only on her death-bed did she once confess that for her the hardest to bear of all the discomforts of Carmel was the cold, the cold which penetrated her until she thought she would die of

E

it. She took her final vows on 24 September 1890; and, young as she was, it was not long before she was appointed Mistress of Novices, an office which she fulfilled with an exemplary care for the young women committed to her charge. As we have remarked, she wrote her book in obedience to her Superiors. She died of consumption, which had made her last months a long agony, in the infirmary of the Carmel on 30 September 1897, in her twenty-fifth year. The cause for her canonisation began in 1910, and on 17 May 1925 in St Peter's, Rome, Pope Pius XI proclaimed Thérèse de l'Enfant Jésus of Lisieux a Saint of the Church.

On a Sunday in the towns of Normandy—in the country towns and villages it is more strikingly noticeable—the visitor is aware of the hold the Church retains over the minds of all classes, all ages and of both sexes, when the crowds, dressed in their sober best, stream out from morning mass. It seems that only the anti-clericals, the irreconcilables, are playing cards over their drinks in the cafés on the square. In these churches it is rarely that the statue of the patron saint or of the national patron, St Joan of Arc, has fresh flowers before it; more often the pious attention of the faithful has centred on the figure of Our Lady—or on that of Ste Thérèse of Lisieux, so approachable in its sentimental, slightly vacuous modernity. It is to these undistinguished crowds that this young Norman woman appeals—these, and to others like them throughout the western world, to those who (one feels inclined to say) wish to keep cherished a little of the simple domestic virtues in a capitalistic, material, unfeeling civilisation. Ste Thérèse speaks directly to them, in the language they comprehend. Her cult is so readily accessible, popular, democratic, vulgar. To Lisieux the pilgrims come each year in their hundreds of thousands, to climb the hill to the aesthetically atrocious basilica, consecrated in 1954, past shops and booths which sell souvenirs, medallions, oleographs, artificial roses and knicknacks commemorating the Little White Flower, objects quite appalling in their mass-produced tastelessness, in their tawdry, trashy, gimcrack triviality. To enter this deplorable edifice, where mechanical music constantly blares, is to wonder how possibly any grain of true religion is engendered there. And yet this is a sanctuary dedicated to a saint. The paradox deepens into a seemingly impenetrable mystery, which is hindered, not elucidated, by the effusive exegesis of her devotees, by the reports of miracles, and graces received, the scattering of her thousands of rose petals.

A possible solution to one's difficulties may be sought in Ste Thérèse's book, *The Story of a Soul*, which was the way that her message has been divulged throughout the world, and brought these pilgrims from the ends of the earth to this Norman town. The sub-title is revealing: The Spring-tide Story of a Little White Flower (*Histoire printanière d'une petite fleur blanche*), which to some is quite exasperating in its sickly sentimentalism. The words *niaiserie* and *mièvrerie* have been used of Ste Thérèse by one of her French supporters—expressions perhaps untranslatable, but roughly paraphrasable as 'a silly infantile affectation'. The word 'little' she works to death: she refers to herself as 'the little Thérèse', 'the little flower'; the 'little ball for the Child Jesus to play with'; she is always too weak, 'too little'; she puts forward for 'little souls' her 'little way'. Her similes are often direct from the nursery; she has in a sense never grown up. To anyone educated in the western tradition, where the accumulated riches of unknown gothic builders, craftsmen and painters of stained glass, of sculptors, artists, architects, theologians, writers and musicians have been dedicated to the glory of God and the honour of the Church, the insipid, juvenile imagery of Ste Thérèse seems hopelessly inadequate and the vulgarities of her cult something of a profanation. Quite unbelievable to some minds is the lapse of taste of her famous *lettre à faire part*, the customary announcement of a forthcoming marriage in France, which begins: 'God Almighty, Creator of heaven and earth, Sovereign Dominator of the world, and the Most Glorious Virgin Mary, Queen of the celestial court, are pleased to inform you of the spiritual marriage of their august Son, Jesus, King of Kings and Lord of Lords, to little Thérèse Martin, now Princess and Lady of the Realms of the Holy Childhood and the Passion, brought her as her dowry by her divine Spouse, from which Kingdoms she holds her titles of nobility—of the Child Jesus and of the Holy Face. . . .' And then the carefully drawn and painted coat-of-arms, surmounted by JHS and FMT, with its childlike symbols; or the violently over-done references to the marriage *motif*—'Days of grace accorded by the Lord to his little wife'. The list of such *niaiseries* could be protracted; and yet it would lead us nowhere.

However repellent these aspects of the writings and cult of Ste Thérèse of Lisieux are to some finely attuned minds, they are assuredly beside the point. Whether we are believers or not, it would be a rash man who denied the power and majesty of the Church and its efficacy in moulding human minds. It was the publication of Ste Thérèse's *Histoire d'une âme* by the Carmels of Lisieux, first for other houses of the Order, then for a rapidly expanding public, and the fulfilment in the

eyes of the faithful of her promises, that brought the notice of the
ecclesiastical authorities on this obscure Norman nun. As she lay on her
sick-bed she said to her sister Mother Agnes of Jesus: 'I feel that my
mission is soon to begin—to make others love God as I love him . . . to
teach souls my *little way* . . . I will spend my heaven in doing good on
earth . . . I have never given to God anything but love, it is with love
He will repay. After my death I will let fall a shower of roses. . . . To
love, to be loved, and to return to earth to win love for our Love!'
What was her little way? she was asked. 'It is the way of spiritual
childhood,' she answered, 'the way of trust and absolute self-surrender.
I want to point out to souls the means that I have always found so
completely successful . . . to offer to Our Lord the flowers of *little
sacrifices* and win Him by our caresses. . . .' First Normandy, then
France, then soon the world responded; Cardinal Vico, Prefect of the
Congregation of Rites, declared that the Church had better hurry to
recognise the sanctity of Thérèse of Lisieux lest the voice of the peoples
out-strip it. On 18 May 1925 Pope Pius XI spoke to pilgrims from
Bayeux and Lisieux in Rome for her canonisation: 'Let your lives be
your thanksgiving to her who from the cloister offers us an example of
perfection that everyone can and should imitate. She desires to draw
us along *her little way*; she teaches us a childlike simplicity that is the
reverse of childish . . . *Spiritual Childhood* is the fruit of will—she is its
revelation.' Thérèse Martin might have been gratified to find where
her troublesome will had led her.

CHAPTER VII

The Châteaux of Normandy

IN HIS MONUMENTAL *Merveilles des châteaux de Normandie* M. Michel de Saint-Pierre, who writes in a spirit of familial piety and informed good taste, numbers over three hundred Norman country-houses and castles (for here the term 'château' covers not only these, but also the somewhat humbler manor-houses, and even fortified towers), and the list is very far from being exhaustive. Some, notably Balleroy, we have touched on elsewhere in this book (page 41); however, it would be quite impossible to describe within our present scope anything but the most limited number, fascinating as they all are from historical, architectural and aesthetic points of view. Many are still lived in by descendants of early families—for successive French governments (though some have not been at all favourable to the survival of the *noblesse*) have not sought by means of crippling taxation to deprive the owners of their and the country's heritage, in the way that has taken place in Great Britain. Others, such as Mesnières and Fervaques, have been adapted to serve various functions—as schools, orphanages, agricultural institutes, or for governmental, departmental, communal or commercial purposes. Since there must necessarily be omissions, I have chosen to say a few words here about some representative châteaux, taken from among those which are open to visits by the public—with the warning that the seasons, days and hours of opening differ, and are best ascertained from the *Syndicats d'Initiative*.

Of castles, military edifices properly so called, Normandy possesses numerous examples. Famous as the birthplace of William the Conqueror is the castle of Falaise, which appears to have been first strongly fortified early in the eleventh century by Robert, Count of Exmes. It was built on a lofty outcrop of sandstone, facing Mont Myrrha, and overlooking, directly below, the Val d'Ante, where Robert watched at the washing fountain the beautiful Arlette, who was to become mother of his son William. The square donjon, which we see today (alas, for romantics) was built about 1125 by Henry I Beauclerk, William the Conqueror's son, who had deprived his brother Robert Courteheuse of the Duchy of Normandy in 1106. It was here that King John Lackland imprisoned his nephew Arthur of Brittany, whom he caused to be put to death in 1203. At this outrage the Bretons rose in revolt against John; Philippe-Auguste invaded Normandy, and, securing the Château-Gaillard, made himself master of the duchy. It was the latter who added to the square donjon, the 'little donjon' next to it, and the curtain wall which connects it with the cylindrical tower, later known, after the English general of the Hundred Years' War, as the Tour Talbot.

Arques-la-Bataille has suffered much over the centuries, not least during the Second World War; and what remains of the castle building is still unsafe to enter. But the visitor may enjoy its site and the magnificent view which its lofty position affords over the valley of Arques. Built in the early eleventh century by William the Conqueror's uncle, Guillaume de Talou, the castle was held in September 1589 by Henry of Navarre, since the assassination of Henri III the rightful King of France. He was here besieged by the much superior forces of the Leaguers under the Duc de Mayenne, who were in possession of Normandy. On 21 September a mist prevented the effective use of Henri IV's artillery; suddenly the mist lifted; the guns opened fire on the massed ranks of the League, ploughing 'some fine streets in their squadrons and battalions'. The enemy were routed and Henri Quatre was no longer 'the king without a throne'. By the eighteenth century the castle had fallen into such disrepair that the masonry was used as building stone by the Bernardines of Arques. In 1836 the widow Reiset saved the castle from complete demolition, and her son sold it in 1869 to the state for 60,000 francs. I understand that the French Government have recently declared their intention, with the help of the Army, of starting work on its restoration.

Having employed in its building all the technical advances in the art of military fortification gained in the Crusades, Richard Cœur de Lion considered his Château-Gaillard a masterpiece—and impregnable. This castle was to be the linchpin of the defensive system by which he would defend the eastern borders of his Duchy of Normandy against the warlike intentions of his adversary, Philippe Auguste of France. It seems incredible to us today that all this excavation, the transport of stone, and the construction of chatelet, walls and donjon should have taken only a year to complete. Standing here in 1197, Richard could exclaim with delight: '*Qu'elle est belle, ma fille d'un an!*' The one flank alone that was open to direct attack, the south-eastern, was protected very skilfully by a triangular chatelet, which was separated from the castle proper by a huge ditch cut in the solid rock. Within the castle the attackers would have to gain possession of two further *enceintes*, before attaining to the cylindrical donjon on the cliff-top overlooking the Seine. Both the walls of the innermost *enceinte* and of the donjon itself have cleverly curved projecting surfaces as a further defence against missiles. It did indeed seem inexpugnable. Yet in 1204, Richard having died and been succeeded by the incompetent John, Philippe Auguste captured the Château-Gaillard after a siege of five months. In 1334 David Bruce, King of Scotland, was given refuge in the castle. Henri IV dismantled the fortifications in 1603, and finally the donjon was rendered useless by orders of Cardinal Richelieu.

Two other imposing ruins of this system of border fortification erected by the Dukes of Normandy can be seen at Gisors and Conches. Gisors was begun in 1097 by William Rufus, under the supervision of Robert de Bellême, a member of the Norman family famous as military engineers; it was added to by the Duke-Kings Henry I and II, and completed after his conquest of Normandy by King Philippe Auguste. Its donjon crowns with impressive grandeur the lofty *motte*. The castle was later used as a state prison, and there exist in the cells some touching graffiti and carvings done by prisoners, one of which reads: '*Mater Dei memento mei* (Mother of God, remember me)' and the initials 'N.P. 1575'. Conches, in the Pays d'Ouche, was long in the possession of the Courtenay family. Philippe Auguste had secured this important fortress before his successful siege of the Château-Gaillard in 1204. Today from the ruined castle or from the terrace which separates it from the beautiful apse of the church of Ste-Foy—the terrace which is occupied by an unseeing sentinel, a powerful wild boar in bronze—the panorama over the valley of the Iton and the bright green woods of the Pays d'Ouche is one of indescribable splendour.

In the peninsula of the Cotentin are three ancient castles, all of remarkable interest. Bricquebec had for its first lord the Viking Ansleck, grand-nephew of Duke Rollo; it later belonged to the Paynel family, then during the Hundred Years' War to the Count of Suffolk; reverting to the Paynel, it passed in 1450 to Louis d'Estouteville, one of whose descendants built in the sixteenth century the nearby *villa* of 'Les Galleries'. Inside the great mass of the polygonal thirteenth-century donjon, where the upper floors have collapsed, the greenish colouration of the rough stonework suggests some marine visitation, reminiscent of the sea-washed foot of the columns in Torcello Cathedral. The *corps de logis* has been in the last century converted into the Hôtel du Vieux-Château, which was visited on 18 August 1857 by Queen Victoria and the Prince-Consort, with their children, the Princesses Victoria and Alice and Prince Alfred.

The fifteenth-century castle at St-Sauveur-le-Vicomte, which suffered greatly from bombings in the last war, was begun in 1347 at the command of King Edward III of England. But it is still a grand pile of partly ivy-covered masonry, which today houses, besides its ancient home for old people, the Musée Barbey-d'Aurevilly. This museum was inaugurated in April 1925 by the faithful English friend of the writer, Miss Louise Read, and M. Louis Yver, and contained until the bombardments the furnishings of the flat in the Rue Rousselet in Paris, where he died on 23 April 1889. What could be recovered from among the debris, together with further gifts, have gone to refurnish this most evocative little museum. Beyond the main entrance a pathway leads down through an orchard to the charming, tranquil cemetery, where beneath the towering wall of the castle Barbey d'Aurevilly lies buried, and, in the grave next to him, his brother, the Abbé Léon d'Aurevilly.

At Pirou, about a mile inland from the sand dunes which form here the west coast of the Cotentin peninsula, stands perhaps the oldest castle in Normandy, in a romantic, abandoned spot, near a château of the seventeenth and eighteenth centuries, once belonging to the Boys-Pirou family. The *chateau fort* of Pirou was first raised by the Vikings, and must have been one of the very earliest of their strongpoints in this region which they soon made their own. Scandinavian blood runs very thickly in the veins of the inhabitants of the Cotentin. I was distressed to find that this most important monument, so rare in its simple veracity, was not better kept up, when I visited it a few years ago. Since then I have heard from M. Dupont-Danican that it is being restored slowly but with great care by its owners, the Le Vegard family. An ancient legend tells of the presence here of a flock of geese, 'the lords of Pirou', who, escaping the Vikings, came back each year for centuries to roost by its moat. Surrounded by the moat, its walls, some parts as early as the tenth century, rise sheer from the water, as if the whole edifice were afloat. It is curious to see in these walls the curvilinear irregularity of the surface planes and the apparent formlessness of the construction. How small, how silent it is today; its very appearance and utter tranquillity seem to deny that it was ever the scene of warlike preparations or resounded to the clamour of defence.

La Varende always insisted that one could not discuss the châteaux of Normandy without bringing up the subject of those who own or owned

Gatehouse of the Château Carrouges

St-Gervain de Livet, Calvados

Château de Brecy, Calvados

them—that is, the nobility. 'I remain perfectly persuaded,' he wrote, 'that the château was an organism necessary to the countryside, or better still, to society. In refining firstly a whole region, then in constituting hereditary élites, who cared, not only to preserve, to do justice to beauty, to appearances, but above all to establish that liaison between town and country, which tends more and more to disappear and to make of one and the other two blocs of strangers, unrelated, if not actual enemies. All the spirit of quality should see in the château a national heritage, whose effect is twofold: enriching, on the one hand, and civilising on the other.' He regarded the relation of the *noblesse* to the country folk on their estates as essentially natural, its growth being organic; and necessarily reciprocal, since the welfare or misery of one was equally the happiness or the concern of the other. The link, however real and natural, was at the same time ideal; this was by reason of the superior position of the noble, which therefore implied the necessity of acting in accordance with the maxim *noblesse oblige*. This feudal conception, if it sounds not only archaic but even revolting to modern democratic ears, was strongly held in Normandy, and is by no means dead today. Readers of La Varende's famous novel *Nez-de-Cuir* will recall that his hero slept with all the handsome country girls for miles around. This was not merely because it was his desire and pleasure to do so, but—and here the reciprocity comes in—because it was equally his 'victims' ' desire and pleasure that he should so do. Yet if calamity struck the *chaumière*, Nez-de-Cuir was the first to cross the doorstep. *Autres temps autres moeurs.* Among the peasants bastardy was not regarded with the same stigma as was customary among the bourgeoisie; perhaps in the fecund countryside of Normandy prolificacy both of animals and humans was taken as the natural course of things; the child was brought up by the mother's family and cared for in no way differently from the others.

The tenacity with which members of the nobility have held on to their ancestral estates is a remarkable feature of Norman life; they will do almost anything rather than dispose of family property, and this applies particularly to the château itself. Many peasants also feel similarly about their own land. It seems in some way symbolic of the nobility that the title should go with the property: for example, the king, to honour his subject, raised his *estate* (not him directly) into a marquisate. This pride in the continuity of family and property is shared, with obvious differences, by the land-owning peasant. In so many ways the Norman country gentleman partakes of essential characteristics with the peasants; they are both in the same boat; a fact which distinguishes the two classes most distinctly from the bourgeoisie. La Varende makes the archaeologist Le Prévost say in *Nez-de-Cuir*:

> 'This country has replaced the abbey by the factory. . . . The cycle is the monk, the gentleman, the workman.'
> 'And after?'
> 'Nothing . . . the barbarians.'

And if it is thought that the owners of the châteaux are all simply country gentlemen in time of peace—for their social function was always regarded by themselves as essentially martial—there is the Broglie family, Savoyard by birth, but long established in Normandy. In the three hundred or so years that the family has lived in the land of its adoption it has furnished seven dukes, three Marshals of France —and, in this century, two physicists of world-wide renown: Maurice, Duc de Broglie, famous for his work in crystallography; and his brother Louis (the present duke) whose researches in quantum physics were rewarded by the Nobel prize in 1929.

BAILLEUL, Commune of Angerville-Bailleul, Seine-Maritime.

Bailleul is one of the most beautiful renaissance-style country houses in Normandy, having suffered no alterations since it was built in 1550 by Bertrand de Bailleul. The family name of Bailleul recalls the Scottish Baliol, and although there may well be a connection, genea-logists are not in agreement on the matter. The present owners of the château are the heirs of the last Marquis de Bailleul, who died some years ago. It has never passed out of the family. The house is surrounded by a beautiful park in which stand statues and large urns of unusual quality. High above the main entrance, silhouetted against the blue of the sky, is a most charming leaden statue of the sixteenth century. The interior is furnished with great magnificence, the main drawing room containing busts and paintings, which include some good family portraits and excellent replicas. The dining room is hung with a collection of drawings of Italian and French masters from the seventeenth to the eighteenth centuries.

BALLEROY, Commune of Balleroy, Calvados. Described on page 41.

BEAUMESNIL, Commune of Beaumesnil, Eure.

'This kind of madrepore, this dream of stone'—it was Beaumesnil that La Varende had in mind when he described 'Mesnil-Royal' in

Nez-de-Cuir. 'It was the pride of the Pays d'Ouche, the question that one put to the newcomer: "Have you seen Mesnil-Royal?" At each fresh discomfiture the whole of the Ouche was cast down. In fact, there is no Louis-Treize dwelling in France of such beauty. Can one even compare a dwelling with it? All other châteaux appear but lodgings when they are brought in contact with its dazzling beauty, with its national lyricism. Where could one find its peer in architectural brilliance, a slenderness so proud, a colour as gorgeous, and such lavishness of decorative integument?' The house was begun in 1633 by Jacques Lecomte, Marquis of Nonant, who employed as architect the 'master-mason' Jean Gaillard of Rouen, and as landscape-gardener La Quintinie, the collaborator of Le Nôtre. The château passed by marriage to the Duc de Montmorency-Laval, and was the scene early last century of brilliant gatherings when the Duke entertained the Duc de Broglie and his Duchess, Albertine, daughter of Mme de Staël. In those days in Normandy it was the custom among noble families, who often drove long distances to attend such functions, to bring with them all their male servants in livery, some of which were very colourful and brilliant. The butler of the Broglie alone, as being above such vanity, was attired, following the English fashion, in sober black. When they had arrived at the château, the servants were detailed their duties by the butler: ' "You, the Montmorency, the dessert! You, the Dauger, the silver" (the Dauger silver was famous). "You, the Bernberg, you will announce the arrivals." ' And so on. Shortly before the last war the estate was acquired by M. Jean Furstenberg, the eminent biblio-phile, who is the present owner. Only the gardens may be visited, and these, as can be imagined, are meticulously maintained.

BIZY, Commune of Vernon, Eure.

Bizy belonged in the eighteenth century to the Marquis de Belle-Isle, the grandson of Fouquet, Louis XIV's disgraced superintendent of finances. Belle-Isle, who by his address and adroitness had won back the royal favour so long denied his family, exchanged in 1726 Belle-Isle for the county of Gisors, les Andelys, Vernon and the district of Longue-ville, which included the estate of Bizy. On his death without heirs, Bizy was left to Louis XV, who exchanged it against another property with the Comte d'Eu, and from the latter it passed to his cousin the Duc de Penthièvre, thus coming into the Orléans family. After the Revolution and Restoration it was in the possession of Louis-Philippe, who often stayed there. Napoleon III having confiscated the Orléans property, Bizy was acquired by the Baron de Schickler in 1858, who pulled down earlier buildings, with the exception of the stable block, and built the grandiose Italianate château which we see today. On his death in 1909 Bizy passed to his nephew, the Duc d'Albufera, whose family own it still.

Brécy, Commune of St-Gabriel, Calvados.

Brécy is a seventeenth-century Italianate gem in a Norman rural setting. As an ensemble it has notable charm: a great gateway, surmounted by a curved architrave of rich carving and flanked by lions; the court of honour and the house of simple, dignified proportions; the adjoining stone farm buildings; the church of the twelfth to fifteenth centuries; and behind the house, gardens laid out *à la française* in terraces, where stone steps lead up with a theatrical perspective to a delicate ironwork gate, preceded and supported by floridly topped stone pillars—and beyond, the open country. The tradition is that François Mansart, when he was building Balleroy, came to Brécy and had a hand in its planning, as a friend or at the request of its owner Jacques Le Bas. At the turn of this century it was owned by Mme Rachel Boyer, of the Comédie-Française, who used it as a summer residence. Subsequently it fell into lamentable disrepair, until it was bought and restored to its earlier beauty by its present owner M. Jacques de Lacretelle of the Académie Française.

Canon, Commune of Canon, Calvados.

The beauty of Canon lies in its charming site surrounded by immense trees with interlocking foliage, which give way to open spaces (one such enclosing a small lake in front of the house) and rides, somewhat neglected, but full of romantic rêveries. One of these avenues is roofed most picturesquely by a high leafed arch, and reveals at its end a pagoda-like kiosk. The walled gardens, also, are overgrown in a vegetative abandon; and everywhere the impression of time past is accentuated by lichened stonework and antique busts raised on high consoles. Canon was owned by the Bérenger family, one of whom, Robert, forced to flee to England rather than renounce his Protestant faith, sold it to Pierre de la Rocque, a tax collector from Valognes, who pulled down the earlier house and built the ground floor of the existing building. The niece of Robert de Bérenger, Mme Elie de Beaumont, successfully brought a case against La Rocque and in 1768 entered into possession of Canon. It was her husband who added the first floor and laid out the park and gardens in the English style. Both husband and wife possessed *âmes sensibles*; Voltaire wished the former might have shown a little better taste than to lard his *Mémoires* with schoolboy pathos; and Mme de Beaumont inaugurated at Canon what she was pleased to call Fêtes of Good Folk. An old man, a head of family, a mother and a maiden, all chosen for their virtue, sat down to supper between the chatelaine and the village curé in a pavilion open to the enchanted view of the assembled village. Canon remains in the possession of her descendants, in the person of Mme de Mézerac, *née* Elie de Beaumont.

CARROUGES, Commune of Carrouges, Orne.

To the English visitor, as he descends the hill from the village of Carrouges, the entrance pavilion of the château will appear unmistakably French in its twin *tourelles*, with their conical caps of slate, and the high detached central roofing also in slate; but the red-and-black lozenged brickwork will seem familiar to him from Tudor buildings. The gatehouse was, indeed, raised about 1530 by the Cardinal Le Veneur, the friend of Rabelais. This familiarity will be heightened when he crosses the moat and enters the vast mass of the château, built in Tudor fashion round a courtyard of glowing brick; and in ascending the staircase, again of rose brick and warm sandstone, which leads to the main apartments. Here the comparison is complete: in bare or panelled walls, hung with portraits of the period, and in the great open fireplaces and painted beamed ceilings. There was a castle at Carrouges in the days of the first Norman dukes, and the château we see today includes in its fabric buildings from the fourteenth to the eighteenth centuries. The history of the family of Carrouges, when it emerges from legend, such as that of Ralph and the Fairy of the Fountain, begins with Roger de Carrouges, who is mentioned in 1150, and continued almost until today; its members and those of its successors, the Le Veneur, playing so notable a part in the history of France that it plausibly might have been written around them. Tanneguy II, Comte de Tillières and Baron de Carrouges, as French ambassador to the English court arranged the marriage between the Prince of Wales, later King Charles I, and Henrietta-Maria, sister of Louis XIII, which took place in 1625. It was from his English sojourn that there came to Carrouges the portraits now there of James I, the Duke of Buckingham and Sir Francis Bacon. Towards the end, the family became so impoverished that it was forced to dispose of much of the furniture and pictures. Finally in 1936 Marie-Gaston-Tanneguy IX, Comte Le Veneur de Tillières, who was born at Carrouges in 1886, was obliged to sell his château to the state. His brother, Etienne-Marie-Denis-Alexandre, the last of the Le Veneur, died in 1963. The château is now cared for by the Beaux-Arts, who have furnished it with much of the original (or, at least, period) furniture and paintings.

LE CHAMP DE BATAILLE, Commune of Neubourg, Eure.

What we have said about the history of France and the Carrouges-Le Veneur family is even more appropriate to the family of Harcourt, of which there exist today both a French and English branch. The château's name derives, it is said, from a sanguinary battle that was fought here in 935 between the forces of Duke William Long Sword, commanded by Bernard the Dane, and the army of the rebellious Riouf, Comte de Cotentin. This Bernard Le Danois, the victor both here and on other fields, is claimed as the historical ancestor of the powerful Harcourt family. The original castle of the family, which was at Harcourt, a few miles to the west of Le Champ de Bataille, has been since 1828 the property of the Académie d'Agriculture de France. Although the buildings, which form an *enceinte* protected by eight towers, date mostly from the fourteenth century, a most interesting series of excavations still in progress has revealed strata of constructions going back possibly to the Carolingian era. The château of Le Champ de Bataille, however, was built between 1686 and 1701 for the Comte de Créqui, by an unknown architect who was influenced by the Italian style, as is clearly seen in the magnificent baroque gateways, which seem to have been imported into Normandy directly from the *palazzo* of some fastidious Roman cardinal. The count, dying in 1702, left his estate to a nephew, the Marquis de Mailloc, who had married Lydie, sister of the second Duc d'Harcourt, Marshal of France and Governor of Normandy. Childless, the marquise on her death in 1750 bequeathed her estate to her husband's nephew Anne-François d'Harcourt, Duc de Beuvron, the third Duc d'Harcourt's brother. Sacked during the Revolution, the château was re-acquired for the family through purchase in 1903 by the Comte d'Harcourt, but sold again in 1936. In 1947 Le Champ de Bataille, which had served as a prison during the war, was left abandoned, when the Ministries for Reconstruction and of Fine Arts effected its transfer to the present Duc d'Harcourt in compensation for the family château at Thury-Harcourt, completely destroyed in 1944 in the course of the war. The duke has brought together, with admirable taste, the priceless objects, many of them souvenirs of his family, which form its simple but quite magnificent furnishing today.

FILIÈRES, Commune of Gommerville, Seine-Maritime.

The château of Filières reveals itself as being very much of the eighteenth century, both in its exterior and in the *décor* of its beautiful interior. History and prudence have dictated the curious anomaly of its façade. The left wing was built in the late sixteenth century at the conclusion of the Wars of Religion, when an earlier château was seriously damaged or destroyed. Some few years before the Revolution, the Marquis of Mirville began to rebuild, engaging for the purpose, it is thought, Victor Louis, the architect of the Théâtre de Bordeaux and the arcades of the Palais-Royal; but, as if from premonition, the marquis only pulled down the older building as the new progressed. Lack of means, and then the Revolution, called a halt; and Filières has remained at the stage that had then been reached. The central block is an epitome of the late eighteenth-century style, with its shutters, fluted pilasters, cornice of triglyphs and rams' skulls, and in the pediment the Mirville arms between animal supporters and military trophies. The furnishings of the main apartments combine elegance with intimacy; everywhere there is light and colour; panelling, with medallions and plaques in low relief, and exquisite eighteenth-century Chinese wallpaper, decorated with flowers and birds, are the backgrounds for some most beautiful Louis Quinze sofas, chairs and footstools. Filières is still in the possession of the Marquis of Mirville's descendants, in the person of the Marquise de Persan.

FONTAINE-HENRY, Commune of Fontaine-Henry, Calvados.

Fontaine-Henry is built on foundations consisting of the vaults and cellars of a fortress built by Henri de Tilly in the thirteenth century, and possibly destroyed during the Hundred Years' War. A Jeanne de Tilly married a Philippe d'Harcourt in 1373, and Fontaine-Harcourt, as it became known, was held by the Harcourt family for five generations. Fontaine-Henry (reverting to the name derived from Henri de Tilly—'Henry' being the old French form) has never been sold, but has passed by inheritance, largely through women, to its present possessor, the Comtesse Pierre d'Oilliamson—whose name, even more curiously frenchified, comes from a Williamson, a Scottish gentleman who served in the famous guards of Louis XI. The house consists of a flat *corps de logis* preceded at right angles by an immensely lofty pavilion whose slate roof, rising at such an abrupt angle and to such a height, is widely known from photographs. Fontaine-Henry is well known also as an example of an early renaissance-style château, the bigger brother of the château d'O. Its building began at the end of the fifteenth century and continued until the middle of the sixteenth, the later, the Henri II portion, being attributed, at least in its sculptural decoration, to Blaise le Prestre, who possibly was also responsible for the Hôtel d'Escoville in Caen, where Italian influence is even more strongly felt. These attributions—and that of the beautiful '*pourtraict*' of Judith and Holophernes on the staircase within, thought to be by Philippe Delorme—should be taken strictly for what they are, informed guesses. Fontaine-Henry is reputed to contain good furniture and pictures. If this is so, then I was not shown them on a recent guided tour. It must be very difficult indeed, in these days of rapidly rising costs, for the owners of many of these châteaux to meet the increasing expenses of their maintenance. It must be said that Fontaine-Henry is far better appreciated for its architecture than for its interior —for those parts, that is, which are open to the public. And its architectural merits are of a very high order.

HÉBERTOT, Commune of St-André-d'Hébertot, Calvados.

The countryside round the château of Hébertot is rich and beautiful even beyond that so often seen in luxuriant Normandy; and nothing could be more delightful than the approach through the village, with its charmingly irregular church and the pretty cottages opposite it, where the road, ascending, becomes overhung with the tender, fresh foliage of ancient beeches, through which one glimpses the flank of the château. The visitor, standing back and facing the front of Hébertot, and overlooking the beautiful moat and lake, will immediately be aware that the pavilion on the left of the façade is anterior to the main body of the building. This pavilion was built in 1612 by Jacques de Nollent and was to have been one of four such pavilions at each corner of a square central court. The *corps de logis* of Hébertot was constructed at the beginning of the eighteenth century, and the pediment over the slightly projecting central section displays the arms of the de Nollent and d'Aguesseau families. The low pavilion on the extreme right was only built in the middle of last century—I should imagine by the architect Ruprich-Robert, who at that time restored the château. Hébertot has changed hands several times—the last occasion only recently.

MESNIÈRES, Commune of Mesnières-en-Bray, Seine-Maritime.

Today the château of Mesnières is occupied by a school run by the Pères du Saint-Esprit. The first written reference to the lords of Mesnières was in 1043; about the middle of the fourteenth century the fief passed to the Bailleul, one of whom, Henri, appears to have been cousin to King Edward de Baliol of Scotland and to have assisted him in his struggle for his kingdom; then at the end of this century Mesnières came into the possession of the Boissay. It was Charles de Boissay (or perhaps his father) who planned and carried out the building of the present château towards the close of the fifteenth and at the beginning of the sixteenth centuries. Its plan was inspired by Chaumont-sur-Loire, there being links between the de Boissay family and the Cardinal-Archbishop d'Amboise of Rouen, the proprietor of Chaumont. Originally the round towers on the side which faces the River Béthune were linked by buildings, but these were pulled down in the eighteenth century by the celebrated Président de Mesnières, and the beautiful peacock-tail entrance steps built. The sturdy round towers have what appear from a distance to be machicolations but are in reality corbels. Used as a prison during the Revolution, the château was restored to its owner, the Marquis de Poutrincourt, in 1799; and at the death of his son it narrowly escaped demolition, when it was reprieved in being bought by the Abbé Eude for use as an orphange. In 1878 it was taken over by the Pères du Saint-Esprit. The fine court of honour, which is built in a strictly classical style, opens at its farther end into an arcade which is decorated by renaissance statues of stags in stone, with the exception of the antlers, which are those taken from victims of the chase. The gothic chapel, which was consecrated in 1546, has also statuary of the renaissance and remains of stained glass of the period. The legend has it that Henri Quatre, 'le Vert Galant', kept and frequently visited at Mesnières his celebrated mistress Gabrielle d'Estrées.

MIROMESNIL, Commune of Tourville-sur-Arques, Seine-Maritime.

The château of Miromesnil is invariably associated in popular myth with the birthplace of Guy de Maupassant, which took place on 5 August 1850. However, if he was in reality born there (the actual room is shown—the bathroom on the first floor in the left-hand tower of the façade overlooking the park), he could remember nothing of his infancy at Miromesnil when years later he walked there in the woods with his friend Plinchon. The question of Maupassant's connection with Miromesnil has been raised on page 101. 'Miromesnil' is a corruption of

'Milonmesnil', from the name of a seigneur who built a fortress on the site in the twelfth century. The château, then in possession of the powerful Norman family of Dyel, was razed to the ground by royal troops after Henri IV's defeat of the Leaguers at nearby Arques in 1589. Jacques Dyel built the present house at the end of the sixteenth century and the beginning of the seventeenth; but in 1668 at the distribution of the Dyel estates Miromesnil came to Thomas Hue de la Roque, a member of a recently ennobled legal family. His grandson, Armand-Thomas Hue, Marquis de Miromesnil, the most remarkable of the family, was Keeper of the Seals to the young Louis XVI. It was he who abolished the preliminary investigation under torture, until then customary in criminal trials. The château, which is surrounded by magnificent beech woods, is constructed in most beautiful bright rose brickwork, heightened by the quoins, courses, and door and window jambs and lintels which are of pale golden stone; and surmounted by a high slate roof relieved with dormer windows. In the gardens of Miromesnil I saw many years ago a most beautiful climbing Etoile d'Hollande rose espaliered against the wall, its blooms splashes of dark liquid crimson against the dryness of red brick.

OMONVILLE, Commune of Tremblay-Omonville, Eure.

The château of Omonville was destined for demolition when it was saved, restored and furnished by its present owner, M. Manceaux. It was begun in 1750 by M. Le Carpentier des Longuaux, Seigneur de Glatigny, on plans drawn up by a local architect, one Chartier of Conches; but after only two years, when the central block and left-hand wing alone were erected, work was stopped. It was resumed and completed under the Second Empire, retaining the original design, by a linen merchant of Louviers, who laid out the gardens *à l'anglaise*—these last M. Manceaux has replaced by those foreseen in the original plan, *à la française*. The interior is distinguished by the beauty of its waxed oak panelling; in eight of the fourteen main rooms the early woodwork remained; the rest has been patiently collected by the owner.

PONTÉCOULANT, Commune of Pontécoulant, Calvados.

The château was left in 1908 to the Department of Calvados by Mme de Barrère, the last descendant of its former owner, the Le Doulcet family; and it has been preserved, with such of its furniture as escaped damage in the last war, as a museum. Without being grand in any way, Pontécoulant has great charm—there is something almost

Russian about it, and this is strengthened by the sight in the dining room of a heating-stove in beautiful white porcelain, its chimney having the form of the garlanded stem of a palm tree. The male members of the Le Doulcet family, which was of Savoyard extraction but established at Pontécoulant since the fourteenth century, usually followed a career of arms, and to this rule Louis-Gustave Le Doulcet, Comte de Pontécoulant, born in 1764, made no exception. The count lived, remarkable in those tumultuous times, to the venerable age of ninety-two, surviving the Revolution, the Empire and the Restoration, in all of which he played his part, and died on 3 April 1853, leaving his *Memoirs* and four volumes of his correspondence.

St-Germain-de-Livet, Commune of St-Germain-de-Livet, Calvados.

The small château or manor-house of St-Germain-de-Livet is a perfect work of art, an architectural jewel. Built between 1561 and 1578, incorporating parts of a house from a century earlier, it was paradoxically the fortified manor of a rude race of warriors, the Tournebu. Much of its charm derives, quite apart from its setting in this verdant and wooded landscape of the Pays d'Auge, from the materials used in the construction. Its walls are chequered with white stone and intervening brick—the bricks not only of the soft colour of rose, but—and these are very rare—of blue, green and turquoise enamels, the ancient prized bricks of Pré d'Auge. Seen reflected in the breeze-ruffled waters of its moat, the château is a harmony of palest colours, a Sisley of light, water, brick and stone, its tiled roof darker, but still of variegated reds and moss-green—a chromatic delight. Within the château the *salle des gardes*, with the open fireplace of the fifteenth century and the somewhat later carved or moulded decoration embellished by time-worn frescoes, gives one a lively impression of a typical seigneural room of the end of the Middle Ages. Some of the upstairs rooms retain their Pré-d'Auge tiling. St-Germain-de-Livet was passed down through marriage and succession until 1879, when it was sold; in 1920 it was bought by M. and Mme Pillaut, and finally bequeathed by Mme Pillaut in 1957 to the town of Lisieux. There are preserved some relics of Riesner, cabinet-maker to the Pompadour and an ancestor of M. Pillaut, and of the painter Delacroix, heirlooms of the last owners.

Sassy, Commune of St-Christophe-de-Jajolet, Orne.

Beautifully placed above terraced gardens on a hill overlooking the valley through which runs a tributary of the River Orne, Sassy is a well-proportioned building in eighteenth-century style. Begun in 1760 by the Comte de Germiny, progress was slow and was interrupted by the Revolution; it was continued, following faithfully the original plans, and completed by the Marquis d'Ormoy, who had bought the château from the Comte de Germiny in 1817. In 1850 Sassy came into the possession of the Duc d'Audiffret-Pasquier, descendant of a long line of eminent lawyers and administrators, and it has remained in the family ever since. The terraced garden, seen from above, with its meandering arabesques of clipped box, resembles the rich decoration of an oriental carpet. Sassy has some magnificent furniture of Louis XIV, XV and XVI styles and many family mementoes, in addition to a library of 20,000 volumes, many once owned by the famous sixteenth-century jurisconsult, Etienne Pasquier.

LE VAL-RICHER, Commune of St-Ouen-Le-Pin, Calvados.

Le Val-Richer was bought in an abandoned condition in 1836 by the historian and statesman François Guizot, and rebuilt and furnished by him as his home, where he lived when his duties allowed him until his death in 1874. It remains a splendid example of the standard and style of living of the cultivated high bourgeoisie at the time of the Second Empire. At Guizot's death Le Val-Richer passed to his daughter, Mme Conrad de Witt (who had married into the distinguished Dutch family), and from her to her descendants, who have maintained it as it was in Guizot's lifetime—the mahogany furniture, the pictures of famous contemporaries, even the billiard-table, are all evidence of comfort, studious pursuits, and considerable refinement of taste. Originally Le Val-Richer had been a Cistercian monastery, and it was here that Thomas Becket lodged for part of his exile in France from 1164 until 1170. When Guizot acquired the property for 85,000 francs, the seventeenth-century abbot's house, in a poor state of repair, alone remained, after the demolition of the abbey and expulsion of the monks at the time of the Revolution. About a mile to the north-west of Le Val-Richer, in a beautiful setting of water, trees and rich meadowland, is the manor of La Roque-Baignard, once the family property of the writer André Gide, who wrote of it in his novel *Isabelle*.

VAUSSIEUX, Commune of Vaux-sur-Seulles, Calvados.

The present château was built about 1770 in the neo-classical style, much in vogue at the period, by the Marquis d'Héricy, to replace a manor-house of the time of Henri Quatre. In 1778 the marquis lent his new house to the Maréchal de Broglie, for whom it served as the military (and, even more so, the social) headquarters of the so-called 'camp de Vaussieux'. Forty thousand men were gathered in this part of Normandy, officially for manœuvres to decide the efficacy of two opposing types of military tactics, 'thinly held' or 'in depth'. In fact, the purpose was political, to perplex the English, who were engaged in war with the rebellious American colonists. By this large-scale feint, English troops had to be maintained at home instead of being sent overseas, and a sizeable part of the Royal Navy was also neutralised. At night the château, illuminated by hundreds of candles, resounding to the strains of music, and brilliant with uniforms and court dresses, was the scene of sumptuous entertainments, for which the king sent a subvention of 200,000 livres. Since then the history of the château has been chequered; at one time it housed a *colonie de vacances*; but recently it has been acquired by M. Huntington-Wilson, who has gone to great trouble to restore Vaussieux to something of its past glory.

CHAPTER VIII

Marcel Proust at 'Balbec'

MARCEL PROUST WAS born at Auteuil on 10 July 1871; but the childhood of the Narrator of *Remembrance of Things Past* is invariably associated with the house and gardens of his Uncle and Aunt Amiot at Illiers ('Combray') on the edge of Beauce, the flat, featureless country-side around the cathedral town of Chartres. It was here that the family walks took them west towards the village of Méréglise ('the Méséglise' or 'Swann's Way') or northwards by the stream, the Loir, to St-Eman with its château ('the Guermantes Way'). From Illiers-Combray the nearest part of Normandy, here the foot-hills of the Perche, lies to the west, some twenty miles away as the crow flies. But *A la Recherche* is saturated with memories of Normandy: the church of St-Hilaire at Combray is an amalgam of Norman churches, those of Dives, Pont-Audemer, Jumièges, Evreux and others; and the name of Combray itself, although its suggestions are wide, is found as that of a hamlet some fifteen miles south of Caen, as well as of a Louis XIII château near the village of Norolles, just north of Lisieux. In the novel the Narrator visits Normandy only three times. Firstly, in his boyhood, with his grandmother, when he first meets 'the little band' of girls and its equivocal leader, Albertine. Secondly, a long stay with his mother, when take place his affair with Albertine, the dinners at Mme Verdurin's villa La Raspelière and the journey thither with the Baron de Charlus and 'the faithful'; the visit ending with the terrible 'agony at sunrise'. And thirdly, by himself very briefly, when he questions the hotel manager at Cabourg, Aimé, on the lesbian proclivities of the dead Albertine. In life Proust visited Normandy frequently, since the sea-air suited him, and he could find in the luxury of the Grand Hôtel at Cabourg much of the material and the surroundings that were favourable to the writing of his novel.

In the 1880s Proust, on account of his recurrent asthma, spent the summers at one seaside resort or another in Normandy; the composite picture of 'Balbec' is made up largely from his visits to Dieppe, le Tréport, Trouville and the recently-developed Cabourg. It was from this last that on 9 September 1891 he wrote nostalgically to his mother,

two summers after the death of Mme Proust's own mother, Mme
Nathé Weil, lamenting, 'How different it was from those seaside holidays when grandmother and I, lost in one another, walked battling
with the wind and talking.' And in a prose sketch written about this
time he mentioned 'some little girls I once watched at play by the sea'.
But it was in the first visit with his grandmother described in *A la
Recherche* that he refers to his disappointment at the appearance of the
romanesque-gothic church of Notre-Dame at Dives-sur-Mer. Very far
removed was the actuality of this mainly fourteenth-century building
from the picture so nursed in his imagination, so exotic 'that one is
tempted to describe it as Persian in inspiration'. Moreover, the little
market-town itself, its port long silted up, where William the Conqueror forgathered his invading ships, was far different from his
adolescent dreams, coloured by the reading of Renan, of the 'land of
the virtuous Armoricans, who dwell by a dark sea jagged with rocks,
beaten by everlasting storms'. When M. Durand-Morimbeaux and his
fellow Second-Empire financiers conceived the construction on the
coasts of Normandy of a luxurious brand-new resort for Parisians, they
preferred the desolate sand dunes and fine beach of Cabourg to the
'funereal coast, famed for the number of its wrecks, swathed, for six
months in the year, in a shroud of fog and flying foam from the waves',
which existed rather in the young Proust's imagination than in any
Norman reality. This confusion of Normandy with Brittany persists in
the novel, even if it is the Narrator himself who smilingly draws attention to it, as on the occasion when he is going on a day's excursion with
the little band. 'In the old days I would have preferred our excursion
to be made in bad weather. For then I still looked to find in Balbec the
"Cimmerians' land", and fine days were a thing that had no right to
exist there, an intrusion of the vulgar summer of seaside holiday makers
into that ancient region swathed in mist.' In the 1890s Proust spent
part of almost every summer in Normandy, mostly at Trouville, but
also intermittently at Cabourg and Dieppe. When he came to Trouville
alone or with his mother, he stayed at the Hôtel des Roches Noires,
overlooking the *chemin de planches*, which at that time was as fashionable
as the planks of Deauville were to become—'the summer boulevard of
Paris', as it was known to the society gossip-writers. It was at this period
that Proust was beginning to make his way through the drawing rooms
of the Faubourg St-Germain; and until the outbreak of the First World
War the villas and grand hotels of this stretch of Norman coast, from
Honfleur westwards beyond Cabourg, were occupied by many of his

fashionable and often aristocratic friends, and others 'as a rule mono-
tonously rich and cosmopolitan'. In 1891 he moved from Cabourg to
stay with Mme Baignières at her villa of Les Frémonts on the hills above
Trouville. This is the original of Mme de Cambremer's house let to
Mme Verdurin, La Raspelière, with the famous 'three views'—one out
over the turquoise Channel and estuary of the Seine, the second west
along the coastline as far as Lion-sur-Mer, the third inland over the
beech woods and orchards of Normandy, the valley 'changed by moonlight into an opalescent lake'. As late as the edition of 1926, Hachette's
Guide Bleu of Normandy had a map showing the environs of Trouville
and many of these luxurious houses owned by or let to Proust's friends.
One of these was Mme Aubernon's Manoir de la Cour Brûlée, rented
by Mme Straus for the season of 1892, when Proust most probably
stayed with her and met again the first model of Albertine, the pretty,
green-eyed Marie Finaly. Part, at least, of the descriptions of the Narrator's drives through the Norman countryside, at first as a boy with
Mme de Villeparisis and later at the time of his love with Albertine,
consists of recollections of this summer spent with his young companion
in driving through lanes of 'flowerless, fruiting' hawthorn and orchards
whose trees were already heavy with apples; or along Les Allées
Marguerite on the Honfleur road high above the sea, passing in their
carriage the old churches of Hennequeville and Criquebeuf (the latter
was the church at 'Carqueville', pointed out by the Marquise de Villeparisis to the boy opposite her as 'quite buried in all its old ivy').
Ever afterwards his memories of this summer were inextricably associated with the words of Baudelaire—'*le soleil rayonnant sur la mer*' and
'*J'aime de vos longs yeux la lumière verdâtre*'. Two years later Mme Straus
was in residence at the Clos des Mûriers, where her near neighbours
were the Princesse de Sagan at the Manoir des Roches and her friend
(and the Prince of Wales's) Mme de Galliffet. In August 1895 Proust
was in Dieppe with the musician Reynaldo Hahn, staying at 32 Rue
Aguado with Mme Lemaire, the rich hostess of one of the most brilliant
of bourgeois salons in Paris, who was to serve him with material for two
remarkable portraits, those of Mme Verdurin and of the Marquise de
Villeparisis, but chiefly of the former. The settings and figures for
Proust's great work were shaping; but he was not to visit 'Balbec' again
from 1895 (although he made a half-hearted attempt to drag himself
away from Paris in 1896 and did call briefly on Mme Straus at Trouville in 1902, accompanied by his loved Bertrand de Fénelon), until,
two years after his mother's death, in August 1907, he was back to stay

Château de Beaumesnil

Ornamental gardens at Sassy

Living arches—a country road

in Normandy; and from this time 'Balbec' centred on the Grand Hotel at Cabourg.

However, he paid a fleeting visit to Normandy in August 1904, travelling by train to Le Havre, to embark on the steam-yacht *Hélène* for a cruise along the Norman and Breton coasts, in the company of Robert de Billy and his wife Jeanne, and her father Paul Mirabaud, the yacht's owner. Proust wrote of his delight in this form of travel, describing their arrival at evening at Cherbourg, 'while a light breeze turned the sapphires of the sea to emeralds and set them in silver'. In 1906 he desultorily planned to take rooms at the Hôtel des Roches Noires at Trouville for his old servant Félicie and himself, but the memories of his dead mother and grandmother that would be awakened there, and the realisation that the thin partition of his bedroom would no longer resound to their gentle knocks, paralysed his will. The intervening two years, between his mother's death in September 1905 and his return to Cabourg in August 1907, were spent by Proust for the most part in bed in his Paris flat or in the valetudinarian luxury of a Versailles hotel. It had been his mother who tried to persuade him to go to Normandy—'You used to find it suited your health so well'—and now it was she who urged him from the grave: 'It was the memory of Mother, who continues to guide me rightly, that led me to Cabourg,' he confessed. Time Lost was about to be converted into Time Regained; but the process was a long and painful one, by means first of Normandy, and ultimately by the supreme work of expiation and purification that was his novel.

Cabourg is some 150 miles from Paris by train; and it was the advent of railways, about the middle of last century, that opened up this Norman coast to visitors from the capital. Proust could travel from the Gare St-Lazare, catching the 'beautiful, generous, one-twenty-two train', and arrive at the Grand Hotel in time to dress for dinner. At Mézidon (Doncières, the junction and garrison-town of *A la Recherche*) he would leave the Paris train, which went on to Cherbourg, changing to the small local 'Transatlantic', that linked Mézidon with Cabourg and 'Douville' (Deauville-Trouville). Just outside Cabourg it would stop at Dives, the equivalent of 'Balbec-le-Vieux' or 'Balbec-en-Terre'. This is the original of the 'Little Train', taken by the Narrator and Albertine, and joined at every small wayside halt by members of 'the faithful', on the way to dinner with Mme Verdurin, who had dispatched carriages to 'Douville' to meet and convey her guests to the heights of La Raspelière. For Proust place-names had a strong fascination; the

perusal of a railway time-table delighted him. The names he used for
the stops of the Little Train were sometimes taken (literally or with
slight change) from villages nearby, as St-Vaast, Douville, St-Pierre-
Azif; and sometimes from other places in Normandy, as Bricquebec,
Infreville, Fervaches. Rivebelle, where the Narrator dines with Saint
Loup, could be the Riva-Bella at the mouth of the River Orne; but as
a seaside resort that enjoyed a prolonged summer, because (seen shimmering across the bay from 'Balbec') it faced south, it would incorpor-
ate at least the site of the busy port of Le Havre. The restaurants of
Rivebelle may be taken as typifying those expensive eating-places in
which this tourist coast abounds. The farm-restaurants, like La Croix
d'Heuland and Marie-Antoinette, near St-Vaast, visited by the Narrator and Albertine for their calvados, cider and cherries, are still to be
found in the *clos* of the rich hinterland, where one can lunch or dine
delightfully secluded beneath the apple-trees. What could be pleasanter
for the hot, thirsty wayfarer than a 'bottle of cider drunk in the rough
coolness of a Norman farm'? The inn of Guillaume-le-Conquèrant,
prized above all by Proust for its cider, has, alas, put up its shutters, and
gone are its memories of Mme de Sévigné. Local place-names were
used also by Proust to designate noble families, like the Marquise de
Cambremer, to whom the lift-boy of the Grand Hotel in Cabourg, con-
fusing the name with the celebrated local cheese, invariably referred
as 'Mme de Camembert'.

Proust's pleasure in the euphony and etymology of Norman place-
names led him to make a systematic study of them, eliciting in 1919 the
help of the French authorities Louis Dimier and Henri Longnon. The
poor curé of Combray, who, Mme de Cambremer informs the Narrator,
has published 'a rather interesting little brochure' on the place-names
of Normandy, is cursorily dismissed ('the move to Normandy must have
made him lose his bearings') by the learned but vulgarly pedantic
Academician Brichot, one of the most faithful of 'the faithful'. But what
Proust, through the mouth of Brichot, tells us of these names is full of
interest, and not least historically, for evidence of the foreign invaders
and settlers in the ancient province of Normandy. Many of the etymo-
logical roots will be familiar from the English. At an evening of Mme
Verdurin at La Raspelière the Narrator asked Brichot the meaning
of Balbec and was told that it was probably a corruption of Dalbec.
' "Bec," Brichot continued, "in Norman is a stream; there are the
Abbey of Bec, Morbec, the stream from the marsh (Mor or Mer meant
a marsh, as in Morville, or in Bricquemar, Alvimare, Cambremer),

Bricquebec, the stream from the high ground, coming from Briga, a fortified place, as in Bricqueville, Bricquebose, le Bric, Briand, or indeed Brice, bridge, which is the same as *bruck* in German (Innsbruck), and as in English *bridge* which ends so many place-names (Cambridge, for instance). You have, moreover, in Normandy many other instances of bec: Caudebec, Bolbec, le Robec, le Bec-Hellouin, Becqueral, Varaguebec, from the old word *varaigne*, equivalent to *warren*, preserved woods or ponds. As for Dal," Brichot went on, "it is a form of *thal*, a valley: Darnetal, Rosendal, and indeed, close to Louviers, Becdal. The river that has given its name to Balbec, is, by the way, charming." '

The Narrator ' "had been delighted" ', he says, ' "by the 'flower' that ended certain names, such as Fiquefleur, Honfleur, Flers, Barfleur, etc., and amused by the 'beuf' that comes at the end of Bricqueboeuf. But the flower vanished, and also the beuf, when Brichot (and this he had told me the first day in the train) informed us that *fleur* means a harbour (like *fiord*), and that *boeuf*, in Norman *budh*, means a hut. . . . In almost all these names which end in *ville*, you might see still marshalled upon this coast, the phantoms of the rude Norman invaders. At Hermenonville . . . you might have seen the illustrious Herimund (*Herimundivilla*) . . . you have seen Incarville, or the village of Wiscar; and Tourville is the village of Turold. And besides, there were not only the Normans. It seems that the Germans (*Alemanni*) came as far as here: Aumenancourt, *Alemanicurtis*—also the Saxons, as is proved by the springs of Sissonne, just as you have in England Middlesex, Wessex. And what is inexplicable, it seems that the Goths, miserable wretches as they are said to have been, came as far as this, and even the Moors, for Mortagne comes from *Mauretania*. Their trace has remained at Gourville—*Gothorunvilla*. Some vestige of the Latins subsists also, Lagny (*Latiniacum*)." ' M. de Charlus interrupted to ask the meaning of Thorpehomme. ' "I understand *homme*," he added . . . "But Thorpe?" "*Homme* does not in the least mean what you are naturally led to suppose, Baron," replied Brichot. . . . "*Homme* is *Holm* which means a small island, etc. . . . As for *Thorpe*, or village, we find that in a hundred words. . . . Thus in Thorpehomme there is not the name of a Norman chief, but words of the Norman language. You see how the whole country has been Germanised."

' "I think that is an exaggeration," said M. de Charlus.'

The new Cabourg was laid out in a semicircular plan, with its diameter parallel to the sea-promenade, the Boulevard des Anglais, and its centre, its hub, the Grand Hotel and the adjoining casino, from which the streets radiate with the regularity of the spokes of a wheel. Old Cabourg was a village somewhat farther inland. It was near here, at the ford of Varaville, that on 22 March 1057 Duke William inflicted a devastating defeat on King Henri I of France, who from the high ground of Bastenbourg, overlooking Varaville and Cabourg, saw his troops cut to pieces by the Normans, as they struggled in the tidal waters of the River Dives. This is recorded by the Anglo-Norman minstrel Wace,

> *Monté fu de suz Basseborc,*
> *Vit Varaville e vit Caborc.*

Even in its pristine splendour the Grand Hotel must have been, more than a little, a brash and pretentious establishment—at once 'cruel and sumptuous', as Proust remarked; but for him it recalled so many conflicting, entangled emotions of grief, guilt and fugitive happiness. In the first volume of *Cities of the Plain* he remembered 'that Albertine whom I had known long ago beneath the sky of Balbec, when the waiters of the Grand Hotel, as they laid the tables, were blinded by the glow of the setting sun, when, the glass having been removed from all the windows, every faintest murmur of the evening passed freely from the beach where the last strolling couples still lingered, into the vast dining room in which the first diners had not yet taken their places, and, across the mirror placed behind the cashier's desk, there passed the red reflection of the hull, and lingered long after it the grey reflection of the smoke of the last steamer for Rivebelle. . . .' Today those windows are boarded up; it requires an effort of evocative concentration for the visitor to grasp the scene: the scorching sands, 'which the little waves come up one after another to sprinkle with their coolness'; the women's band thundering out excerpts from Bizet or Massenet from the rotunda on the beach; the promenade forming a 'seascape with a frieze of girls'; the small uniformed boy at the swing doors of the hotel, whose sole function is to raise his pill-box hat to visitors; the waiters in full organised movement, but passing on tip-toe the cane chair where sits a figure lost in cushions and swathed in thick rugs, showing only the battered top of his panama-hat. All has gone, a picture slipped away into the past. Next door, at the defunct casino, where Bloch's cousin showed her 'unconcealed admiration' for the actress Mlle Léa, where Albertine danced with Andrée, and Proust played baccarat and danced too from time to time 'to keep his joints from rusting up'—here shreds of tattered ceiling mark the side entrance, above which is now a faded notice, '*Calypsothéque*'. Deauville at least remembers Proust: a vast modern building of flats, timbered and plastered in the 'Norman' style to mask its reinforced concrete frame, flaunts its name in large letters to passers in the Boulevard Eugène Cornuche—'*Castel Guermantes*'.

The year 1907 formed a watershed in Proust's life, and his return to Cabourg marked a significant place in the sequence of events. It was at this time that he first hired his taxis, and was driven over the Norman countryside by Odilon Albaret and Alfred Agostinelli. The latter —compared by Proust, so incongruously as to be comical, with a 'young Evangelist bowed over his wheel of consecration', or even worse: 'his black rubber cape and the hooded helmet which enclosed the full-ness of his young, bearded face, made him resemble a pilgrim, or rather, a nun of speed'—drove him on a memorable visit to Caen. From the distance the spires of the Abbaye aux Hommes, St-Pierre, St-Sauveur and the towers of the Abbaye aux Femmes, displaced and re-united at every turn of the road, moved in a stately pavane which re-awoke from his unconscious memory an earlier dance-movement, when the youthful Narrator, seated in Dr Percepied's carriage, watched with delight how the twin spires of Martinville danced with the spire of Vieuxvicq in the countryside around Combray. Together, master and chauffeur visited the cathedral at Bayeux, the château of Balleroy (which became the Château de Guermantes of his novel), Falaise, Lisieux (whose porch was seen after dusk had fallen by the head-lamps of Agostinelli's taxi), and passed through the nearby village of Cam-bremer. Towards the end of September 1907, when the Grand Hotel was about to close for the winter, Proust and Agostinelli set off for Paris by way of Evreux, where in their nearby château of Glisolles the Clermont-Tonnerre hoped to welcome him. Instead, his asthma sud-denly returning after six weeks' absence, he put up at an hotel and booked the entire floor above him to ensure quietness. (This Hôtel Moderne was a victim of the last war.) It was while he was in Evreux that Proust visited the cathedral at dusk, from which the stained-glass windows 'contrived to steal . . . jewels of light'. It was on this occasion that he found the quality (which he transposed to St-Hilaire in Com-bray) of 'never shimmering more brightly than on days when the sun hardly showed itself, so that if it was dull outside you could be sure that there would be fine weather within'.

In the summer of 1908 in Cabourg Proust met the young girl whose

name, and characteristics even, have remained unknown to us, but who
played without any doubt an important part in Proust's life, and who
forms with Marie Finaly and Agostinelli the originals on which he
based his Albertine. This year, on his return to Paris, Agostinelli drove
him in the hired taxi through the Seine Valley, visiting Pont-Audemer,
where he took particular note of the mediaeval glass in the church of
St-Ouen; Caudebec, St-Wandrille and Jumièges, where in the ruins
of the abbey he saw the Merovingian crypt, which, with the St-Ouen
glass, was to reappear in St-Hilaire of Combray.

It is not clear when precisely Proust's affection for Agostinelli turned
into possessive love. Certainly, in July 1909 he could write to his friend
Comte Georges de Lauris, to whom (and to him only) he seems to have
confided his feelings for the young girl met in Cabourg and seen in
Paris during the winter of 1908–9: 'If I leave Paris [for Cabourg], it
will perhaps be with a woman'—*la femme* could equally read 'a wife'.
However, in the summer he was back in his attic room at the Grand
Hotel, hard at work on his novel, with Nicholas Cottin, his servant,
next door in a luxurious room with a private bath. (It was Céline Cottin,
Nicholas's wife, and a model for the family servant Françoise, who on
a cold night of the previous winter had given the shivering Proust an
unaccustomed cup of tea, in which he dipped a finger of toast, thus
setting in train the release of unconscious memory, accompanied by an
exalted pleasure, which was the origin of the famous tea and the
madeleine of *A la Recherche*.) However, this summer and those of 1910
and 1911, when amid the scenes of so much of what is the Balbec of his
novel, he worked at Cabourg, little seems to have been heard of his
young chauffeur. In 1912, when he arrived in Cabourg in August, it
was in pleasant anticipation of resuming his motoring in Normandy,
but a series of accidents, of which two were fatal, persuaded him to
hire the hotel 'bus and its 'careful' driver.

For reasons which must in part be attributed to his relations with
Agostinelli, Proust suddenly, late in August 1913, left Paris by motor-
car, driven by Agostinelli, for Cabourg and work on his novel. After a
few days, during which he frequently spoke of some mysterious un-
divulged necessity of returning at once to Paris, he set off for Houlgate.
From there he inexplicably fled with his chauffeur back to Paris, sending messages to his servants at Cabourg to pack and return as well.
Proust later told Lauris that it was Agostinelli's words, 'I can't bear to
see you looking so sad. You'd better take the plunge, and catch the
Paris train at Trouville . . .' which precipitated this sudden 'elope-

ment'. It does appear that Proust's accounts of his own dilemma—his love for the young girl of Cabourg and his love for (and growing jealousy of) Agostinelli—come very close to the events actually described in *A la Recherche*, when the Narrator calls Albertine early one morning to his bedroom in the Grand Hotel and explains to her: 'When I came here, I left a woman whom I ought to have married, who was ready to sacrifice everything for me. She was to start on a journey this morning, and every day for the last week I have been wondering whether I should have the courage not to telegraph her that I was coming back. I have had that courage. . . .' Later, he continues to Albertine: 'You see, I came very near to marrying her. But I dared not do it, after all, I should not like to make a young woman live with anyone so sickly and troublesome as myself.' Those words are almost verbatim the ones used in letters of Proust to Lauris, and, in all likelihood, to Agostinelli. This was the Agony at Sunrise of *A la Recherche*. Furthermore, the Narrator makes Albertine his mistress and captive in Paris, and when at length she escapes from captivity it is to meet her death in an accident. The parallel is there in Proust's own life after the flight from Cabourg to Paris, Agostinelli's captivity in luxurious dependence, then his escape and death, when his aeroplane crashed into the Mediterranean off Cagnes on 30 May 1914.

At the outbreak of war in August 1914 Proust was in Paris, where he remained, until on 4 September, with Céleste Albaret, he set out on the weary twenty-two hours of the wartime journey, to visit Cabourg for the last time. The Norman coast was full of memories and ghosts, particularly of poor Agostinelli. It was full too of wounded and the disorientated rich. He did arrange to go again on 15 August 1919 in a friend's car, but, as was usual with him, he changed his plans at the last minute. In Paris during the war years he continued to enjoy a habit, learnt in Normandy, of supping alone or with friends on fried potatoes served on a silver dish, and washed down with beer or cider. In November 1916 he wakened the Quatuor Poulet at midnight from his taxi and took them off to his cork-lined room, to play the Franck quartet in D Major—with its hints of the 'Vinteul Sonata'. When they had finished, he thanked them; and then inquired with extreme politeness if they would be so kind as to play it all over again. Strengthened by a curious repast of Norman fried potatoes and champagne supplied by Céleste, they did so. Proust died on 18 November 1922, without revisiting Balbec and the Norman coast. So many of the scenes and events of his life, those closest to his innermost being both as man and supreme artist, centre on Balbec, that it is difficult to imagine *Remembrance of Things Past* without summoning up this setting, the seascape and landscape of Normandy.

It was all these memories that Proust carried with him, stored in his unconscious memory, but there, potentially dynamic, ready to be released by some fortuitous, some even trivial, happening in the external world. In the last volume of the novel the Narrator was waiting in the Prince of Guermantes' library for a piece of music to end before entering the drawing room, when 'the strident sound of a water-pipe' brought flooding back to him the remembrance of a late afternoon in Balbec, the long screeches of the excursion steamers, 'the sun slowly setting on the sea with its wandering ships', and he felt that he had only to step across the window-frame no higher than his ankle 'to be with Albertine and her friends who were walking on the sea-wall. It was not only the echo,' the Narrator continues, 'the duplication of a past sensation that the water-conduit had caused me to experience, *it was the sensation itself.*'

CHAPTER IX

Norman Ecclesiastical Architecture

UNDOUBTEDLY THE OLDEST Christian building that exists in Normandy is the *martyrium* which forms the crypt of the church of St-Gervais in Rouen. This was possibly built at the beginning of the fourth century and has been considered the earliest Christian edifice to remain north of the Alps. Not far from the ancient crumbling church, the romanesque Notre-Dame, built on the tidal estuary at Portbail in the Cotentin, M. Michel de Bouard discovered and excavated some few years ago a polygonal baptistery of pre-Carolingian times, perhaps as early as the sixth century. On Mont-St-Michel a Carolingian church, Notre-Dame-sous-Terre, as its name partly indicates, has been built over, so that now it forms a crypt to the west end of the great romanesque abbey church—to the last three bays, that is, which, becoming unsafe, were demolished late in the eighteenth century. It may be claimed that the two oldest existing churches in Normandy are the little St-Germain on the hilltop at Querqueville, near Cherbourg, and the chapel (much restored) of St-Saturnin, in the woods of St-Wandrille, near Caudebec-en-Caux. The dates of these two churches have been variously given; we have the authority of the Norman scholar M. René Herval for assigning them roughly to the same period, the eighth century. However, it seems more likely that they were later; that they were popular shrines, which had been, perhaps, destroyed and then rebuilt in their original trilobate form, possibly in the ninth century.

In Normandy the Carolingian revival, when several monasteries and many churches were built, was almost entirely obliterated, destroyed in the incursions and ravages of the Vikings in the ninth and early tenth centuries. By the time the Duke Rollo had established his power, monasteries as famous as Jumièges, Fontenelle (St-Wandrille) and Fécamp lay abandoned and derelict, quarries for building stone. It was the purposeful alliance of the first Norman dukes with the great Benedictine Order that gave stability to their administration and favoured the construction of those rich and celebrated abbeys whose majestic ruins—the sterile heritage of Revolutionary vandalism—we see today everywhere throughout the fertile lands of Normandy. The monastic

F

foundations were for the most part the work of the dukes, their families, or of feudal magnates, who in this way supported the civilising mission of the Church, at that time a powerful factor in economic and intellectual advance; the cathedrals in Normandy, unlike those in England, where they were often joined to an abbey, were the work rather of the richer townsfolk, gathered round the Bishop and Chapter. In both cases they had the willing co-operation of the artisan and peasant classes. We are fortunate in having a letter written by the Abbot Haimon to the religious house of Tewkesbury in England, giving a graphic account of the rebuilding of the abbey church of St-Pierre-sur-Dives, after it had been destroyed by fire in the early years of the twelfth century. The abbey had been founded as a retreat for nuns by the Countess Lesceline, wife of Guillaume, a bastard son of Duke Richard I; but for some reason unknown, it had been taken over later by the Benedictines. The monastery was entirely burnt to the ground in the fratricidal struggles between William the Conqueror's sons. The Abbot Haimon describes the work carried out by bodies of volunteers, men and women of all ages, in dragging for long distances wagon-loads of building stone, timber and provisions.

> When they halt on the road, nothing is heard but the confession of sins and pure and suppliant prayer to God to obtain pardon. At the sound of the priests preaching peace, hatred is forgotten, discord thrown aside, debts are remitted, and the unity of hearts is established. But if someone is so advanced in evil as to be unwilling to pardon an offender or to obey the pious admonition of the priest, his offering is instantly thrown from the wagon as impure, and he himself is ignominiously and shamefully excluded from the society of the holy. There, as a result of the prayers of the faithful, one may see the sick and infirm rise whole from their wagons, the dumb open their mouths in praise of God, the possessed recover a sane mind. The Priests who preside over each wagon are seen exhorting all to repentance, confession, lamentation, and the resolution to a better life, while old and young, and even little children prostrate on the ground, call on the Mother of God. . . . All the faithful resume their march to the sound of trumpets and display of banners; the journey is so easy that no obstacle can retard it. When they have reached the church, they arrange the wagons about it like a spiritual camp, and during the whole of the following night the army of the Lord keeps watch with psalms and canticles; tapers and lamps are lighted

on each wagon, and the relics of the saints are brought out for the relief of the sick and the weak, for whom priests and people in procession implore the clemency of the Lord and of his Blessed Mother. If healing does not follow at once, they cast aside their garments, men and women alike, and drag themselves from altar to altar . . . begging the priests to scourge them for their sins.

Such was the faith that moved mountains of stone and erected these monuments of soaring masonry.

Normandy is fortunate in its building stone, of which the finely-grained Caen stone, the limestone quarried just south of the city, is famous, much having been exported by the Normans for the cathedrals and castles of England. Again, Rouen and the towns of the Seine valley have at their disposal the excellent local stone; in the northern parts of the Pays de Caux *grès* is used, a stone akin to granite, but always in combination with brick; to the west, in the Cotentin and the Bocage, the grey granites, immensely hard to carve, have been employed; and in those districts where the rust-brown schist is readily available it also has been used with pleasant chromatic effect. The romanesque architecture of Normandy has characteristic differences from the romanesque of Provence and Languedoc, territories more accessible to the influence of classical building and decoration, so that 'Norman' is often applied to the eleventh- and twelfth-century style of church building common to Normandy and Norman England. The word 'romanesque' (*roman*) was first employed early in the last century by the Norman archaeologists, Charles Dehérissier de Gerville and Arcisse de Caumont. Norman is distinguished from southern French romanesque chiefly by its comparative lack of decoration and its freedom and grandeur of form. In this latter respect the Benedictine builders owed much to the general development of Carolingian construction, itself based on classical building proceeding by way of Ravenna, Lombardy, and the Rhine. The credit for beginning the building or the re-building of the abbeys and churches of Normandy is usually given to Duke Richard I (942–96) whose abbey church at Fécamp was dedicated in 990; but little or nothing of this remains. The next stage seems to have been marked by the most ancient parts of the church of St-Pierre at Jumièges, Carolingian in style, which was begun in the closing years of the tenth century or the opening of the eleventh. The Benedictine reconstruction grew apace: before the mid-century work was begun on the great abbey churches of Jumièges and St-Wandrille (as from now on Fontenelle was called, after its founder), the cathedrals such as Rouen and Bayeux, the abbey church of Bernay (now in process of restoration) and the nave of the abbey church at Mont-St-Michel. Soon the distinguishing characteristics of Norman romanesque become apparent: the clear-cut and beautifully dressed masonry, the blocks not too large or yet too small (the use of the saw came later); the simple capitals—often but cushions with rudimentary curved or scrolled design—and likewise the mouldings of chevron, billet, nail-head, cable, embattled or beak-head design. Above all, attention was given to the strictly architectural, constructional elements—the flat buttresses, the rounded columns and piers (like those at Lessay), the circular arches, the large triforia, and the lantern at the 'crossing'; in a word, the harmonious relation of volumes, of stonework and openings.

However, this was but the beginning; it was henceforth, in the generation of William the Conqueror and Lanfranc of Bec-Hellouin, at the time of the conquests of South Italy, Sicily and England, that was seen the wonderful flowering, the full measure of the skill of Norman ecclesiastical architects, of these Benedictine monks who gave such majestic form to the Norman conception of Church and State. The eleventh century marked the apogee of Norman romanesque. This is the period of the great abbeys and their churches: Bec-Hellouin, St-Ouen in Rouen, St-Georges-de-Boscherville, Montivilliers, Ste-Honorine de Graville, Cerisy-la-Forêt, Lessay, and in Caen St-Etienne (Abbaye aux Hommes) and La Trinité (Abbaye aux Dames). The plan was most usually basilican, with transepts; the wide central nave being flanked by two narrower aisles. At first the ceiling of the nave was of timber, the aisles of groined vaulting; then attempts were made to cover the nave with crossed barrel-vaulting, as can be seen in the great Caen abbeys, where different methods have been tried out. It was at Lessay that the first steps were taken to solve the problem of spanning oblong spaces by the use of pointed arches: this is 'officially' held to have originated at Durham, a revolutionary step forward that was to be developed in the Ile-de-France and to culminate in the glory, the aerial verticality, of French gothic architecture. The twelfth century added mainly refinements, mostly in decoration, to the magnificent drive, the impulse towards grandeur and constructional simplicity of the Benedictine builders of the eleventh century—for these abbey churches were nothing if not grand, a grandeur of conception and of execution, a simplicity robustly religious. The western façade of the Abbaye aux Hommes, with the two flanking towers and their octagonal

spires forming the letter H, was the prototype for much of later romanesque and gothic building. The north tower and spire, the change-
over from square to octagon masked by *clochetons* at the four angles,
was to be the model for many church spires in the neighbourhood of
Caen and in the Bessin.

If there is a homogeneity in the construction of the great abbey
churches (which is a reasonable conjecture, although much has been
obscured by rebuilding and, alas, by the vandalism of the Revolution),
the parish churches of Normandy, whatever their size or period, present
a bewildering multiplicity of styles, although many reveal a regional
family-likeness, that resemblance which comes from an important
stylistic ancestor. Until recently it had been thought that those churches
which exhibited, not the regularity of ashlar, but the use of small stones
or brick in chromatic designs—geometric, reticulated or *opus spicatum*—
were necessarily of great antiquity. In the rebuilding of Normandy after
the Viking devastation, the constructional methods and styles from
nearby Touraine and Poitou influenced the Normans, as can be seen in
parish churches in the Pays d'Auge and the Pays d'Ouche—at Vieux-
Pont-en-Auge, d'Ouilly-le-Vicomte and Notre-Dame at Rugles. These
churches and others like St-Martin-de-la-Lieue and St-Jean-de-Livet in
the diocese of Lisieux, and Reuilly in that of Evreux, are all perhaps
from the last decades of the tenth century or the first of the eleventh.
At Vieux-Pont an inscription reveals that it was built at the time of the
Viking raids, but its style is still Carolingian. The church of Norrey-en-
Auge, although its design is very primitive, was built about 1045.

Few regions of France can boast of such richness of romanesque
architecture as that lying between the River Orne and somewhat to the
west of Bayeux—this episcopal town which has, furthermore, a unique
example of romanesque art in the famous Tapestry. The reason for
this primacy is the political and economic prominence of town and
district at the time of William the Conqueror and his half-brother, the
notorious Odo of Bayeux. Within a matter of a few miles from each
other are three most beautiful and interesting churches: Thaon (the
French pronounce it '*Tan*'), Secqueville-en-Bessin and the priory
church of St-Gabriel. All lie a short distance to the north-west of Caen,
in this white, featureless plain—as it seems, until we come on its sur-
prising green valleys. At the bottom of one of these, in meadows by the
little River Mue, surrounded by cypresses and poplars covered with
ivy and mistletoe, the church of Thaon stands undisturbed and
neglected, remote in its idyllic beauty. When Charles de Gerville

'discovered' Thaon early last century, he is reported to have exclaimed, with the fervour of the contemporary Romantics: 'I could never bestow a finer compliment on my Dulcinea than by saying—"You are beautiful, you are pure, you are charming, like the church of Thaon!"'
At Gabriel-Brécy you enter under the twelfth-century portal into the garden of the priory, now an apprentice-school for horticulture, with gay flower beds between the apple trees. At the end of the orchard rises the choir, all that remains of the early twelfth-century priory church—but, nevertheless, it is architecturally outstanding. At Secqueville the visitor is aware of the purity of line of this Norman style, with its soaring tower and spire (the latter of the thirteenth century), so clearly modelled on that of the Abbaye aux Hommes. Other examples of these towers and spires may be seen at Bèrnieres-sur-Mer, Huppain, Bény-sur-Mer, Ouistreham, Rots, Norrey-en-Auge, Rosel, Vienne-en-Bessin, Meuvaines and Colombiers-sur-Seulles. The churches in this area are too numerous to recount individually, but their variety is as astonishing as is their quality.

However, no visitor to Normandy should overlook, if he is anywhere in the locality, such fascinating romanesque churches as St-Martin at Tollevast (carving), Notre-Dame-sur-l'Eau at Domfront, St-Céneri-le-Gérei (sculpture and thirteenth-century frescoes), Alleaume (carving), Barneville (also for carving), Bully (carved doorway), Goult (capitals of doorway), Orglandes (tympanum), Ouézy (figure on tympanum), Rucqueville (marvellously carved capitals), St-Evroult-de-Montfort (leaden font), St-Sauveur-de-Pierrepont (carved Christ in Glory) and Savigny (magnificent Christ in Glory). Not much early frescoing remains, but vestiges may be seen, besides those of St-Céneri-le-Gérei, at Norroy-en-Auge, St-Evroult-de-Montfort, and Ste-Marie-aux-Anglais. And, of course, no one will willingly miss the celebrated Bayeux Tapestry, to which no pictorial reproduction can ever do justice.

At the Revolution, under the Civil Constitution of the Clergy, the seven dioceses of the province of Normandy were reduced to five, and this was the administrative shape retained at the Concordat between Pope Pius VII and the First Consul in 1801. The bishoprics of Avranches and Lisieux were abolished, but subsequently their titles were added to those of the Bishops of Coutances and Bayeux respectively. The Cathedral of Avranches, placed high on its hill like some northern Albi, where on 22 May 1172 King Henry II, in penitent's shirt and barefooted, knelt to seek the forgiveness of the Church for the murder of Becket—this church no longer exists; neglect, not Revolutionary outrage, caused part of it to collapse in 1796, and by 1836 only vestiges of it remained. At Rouen, Coutances, Bayeux and Lisieux portions of the original romanesque edifices of the Norman ducal days have been retained in varying degrees in the present buildings. Rouen's Cathedral we have already noticed (pages 73ff).

In Bayeux the church that was said to have been erected by Duke Rollo seems to have been destroyed by fire in 1046. It was the formidable Odo of Bayeux, William the Conqueror's half-brother, who built the romanesque edifice that was consecrated on 14 July 1077, in the presence of the Duke-King and his wife Matilda, Archbishop Lanfranc of Canterbury and the Archbishop of York, a former canon of Bayeux. Odo's building was partially destroyed by the army of Henry I in 1105. It is to Bishops Philippe d'Harcourt, Henri de Beaumont ('the Englishman') and Robert d'Ablèges that we owe much of the present cathedral, built between 1142 and 1231, incorporating in it what remained of Odo's romanesque building but recasing it in early gothic. Externally, to many eyes, which include my own, Bayeux's beauty is sadly vitiated by the incongruous lantern and flèche over the central tower and octagon of Philippe d'Harcourt's beautiful first storey. This is the work of one not inappropriately named Crétin in the sixties of last century. The south transept is a fine example of the purity of thirteenth-century gothic—the period which gave us la Merveille of Mont-St-Michel. In the tympanum over the doorway are representations of scenes associated with St Thomas Becket, which are peculiarly fitting in this place, since Henry's hasty words which led to his murder were spoken nearby at the castle of Bur-le-Roy. On the west front Odo's towers (these and the crypt are the remaining portions visible of this romanesque church) have been subsequently strengthened, in the thirteenth-century, and the spires added. However, within the church the decoration of the nave has confounded archaeologists for more than one hundred and thirty years, and the problems are not yet solved to everyone's satisfaction. About 1200 Odo's nave pillars were encased in engaged columns, with beautifully crisp-cut capitals and archivolts. Above them the walls of the nave below the carved course supporting the balustrade of the triforium are covered with a tapestry of carving of varied interlaced work; and in the spandrels have been placed (in mitred frames) curiously stylised figures of bishops and mythological animals. The carving was possibly done about the middle of the thirteenth century. All this would have been picked out in colour, to resemble a tapestry or rich carpet, similar to examples in the nave at Secqueville-en-Bessin and formerly in Rochester Cathedral. The figures in the spandrels present greater difficulties: they have been attributed to influences as disparate as mediaeval bestiaries, oriental (Chinese, Persian, Indian) sculpture, Irish or English illumination, and ancient Scandinavian (even earlier than Viking) wood-carvings! Professor Lucien Musset of the University of Caen sees influences nearer to home than these—in those figures at St-Gabriel-Brécy or on the west front of Le Mans Cathedral, where two dragons are associated with similar decoration and even with the *arcs en mitre*. In Bayeux these figures appear to have been put in place at a date later than their surroundings; may they not have been simply *jeux d'esprit* of some master-mason? But, if so, this still leaves unsolved the original provenance of these exotic art-forms.

John Ruskin, visiting Normandy in 1848, with his newly-married wife Effie, found the cathedral of Coutances, placed high on its hill, 'marvellously interesting, a pure and complete example of the very earliest French Gothic'. It seems that in the declining years of the Empire a Roman basilica had been raised on the site of the present cathedral, and that the church was added to by the fifth (or third) bishop, the famous St Lô, who died in 566. This building was in the ninth century destroyed by the Northmen. The present structure was begun by Bishop Robert I, and carried on by his great successor, Geoffroy de Montbray, who travelled out to Southern Italy, mitre in hand, to collect funds from former parishioners, the Hautevilles, now princes of Apulia and Sicily. In this he was successful, and Geoffroy was able to complete nave, choir, ambulatory and transepts and to crown his work with lantern and the two west towers before his death in 1093. Geoffroy's episcopate extended over sixty-four years, but he seems to have achieved much of the rebuilding before he accompanied William on his conquest of England, where his brother Robert was created Earl of Northumberland. Until the nineteenth century the church we now see was regarded as that of Geoffroy de Montbray; only gradually did archaeology assert its authority and show that the cathedral of Coutances is early gothic, begun in the first third of the thirteenth century; it was at this period that the builders had with a skill that still staggers one clothed the whole romanesque structure in its gothic coat. This work appears to have been undertaken by Bishop Hugh de Morville (1208–38). In its severity, its vertical austerity, Coutances is most impressive; although one may feel that the addition of the lateral corner towers on the earlier towers of the west front has the effect of retaining the eyes at the level of their pinnacles, and thus not allowing them a full majestic sweep from ground level to the tapered points of their spires. Referring to the central lantern-tower, the celebrated seventeenth-century military engineer Vauban asked: 'Who in the world was the sublime fool who had the hardihood to launch into the air such a structure?' '*Le Plomb*', as it is known locally, which is a masterpiece of strength, grace and dignity, became the model for Norman lanterns; in 1479 Bishop Geoffroy Herbert wished to surmount it with a stone spire which would dominate the two western spires (like Lichfield), but he was overruled by the Chapter; and the money went to build the nearby parish church of St-Pierre. From within, at the beginning of the choir, one can more fully appreciate the immensity of the lantern, the four arches composed of sheaves of slender columns supporting its octagon of windowed galleries—all flooding the great church with light. The cathedral contains some good glass, although much was smashed by Montgommery's Huguenots; and of considerable interest are the windows of the north transept, forming a triptych—those of St Thomas Becket, St George and St Blaise. The ascent to the upper parts of the building well repays the effort: in towers and triforium is revealed the romanesque masonry of Geoffroy de Montbray's church; and a closer inspection of the stained glass and the work of the lantern is most rewarding. The view of the countryside of the Cotentin, and away to the west the little group of the Isles of Chausey and the outline of Jersey, is quite magnificent.

On 6 May 1152 in the damaged Cathedral Church of St Peter of Lisieux the marriage was celebrated by Bishop Arnoul between Henry Plantagenet, son of Geoffrey, Count of Anjou and of Henry I's only daughter the Empress Matilda, and Eleanor of Aquitaine, the divorced wife of Louis VII of France. In this way there came about the creation of the Angevin Empire (Henry succeeding Stephen as King of England in 1154), an inevitable increase in the fears and hostility of the French Crown, and the subsequent wars between France and England, which were so ruinous for Normandy. The town and church of Lisieux had been badly burnt by the Breton troops of Geoffrey of Anjou only a few years before, in the episcopacy of Arnoul's uncle, Jean I. It was Bishop Arnoul who set about rebuilding his cathedral in the gothic style already being employed at Paris, Laon, Noyon and Senlis; but Lisieux is a *heavy* building, lacking in the *élan*, the verve of many of its contemporaries. The two great piers just within the west door, and forming part of a narthex (rare in Normandy), are the chief relics of the earlier romanesque edifice of Bishops Herbert (*d.* 1050) and Hugues d'Eu (*d.* 1077). The western façade, raised on its plinth, lacks unity, and has suffered at the hands of Huguenots, Revolutionaries and others. The south-western tower came crashing down on the afternoon of 16 March 1553, and was rebuilt in 'romanesque' style (how much more effective are the elongated lancets of the north-western thirteenth-century tower), and capped with a spire in the following century. Whatever is claimed about the architectural influence of the Ile-de-France, the transepts, the fine lantern and the beginning of the choir seem typical Norman work of the period, the early thirteenth century. The beautiful flamboyant Lady Chapel is the creation of the notorious Pierre Cauchon, formerly Bishop and Count of Beauvais, who was rewarded by his English masters for his sorry part in the condemnation and execution of Joan of Arc with the bishopric of Lisieux. In April 1931 his body was found buried in his chapel, and, replaced in an oak coffin, it has been reinterred there. The fourteenth-century choir stalls of Lisieux are of great simplicity and distinction.

A history of the Cathedral of Our Lady of Evreux reads like an epitome of the devastation suffered by Normandy since Roman times, so that one may with reason consider the church's survival as something not far short of a miracle. The Gallo-Roman town was, as the ruins of nearby Vieil-Evreux show, a place of importance and prosperity, and appears to have had its first Bishop (St Taurin) in the fourth century. It was utterly destroyed in the following century by the Vandals. Rebuilt on its present site on the pleasant River Iton, Evreux was pillaged and burnt in the ninth century by Vikings returning from an unsuccessful attempt on Paris. In the comparative peace which followed the establishment of the Norman Duchy, the Bishops Guillaume Flertel and Gislebert (*d.* 1112) erected a great romanesque church, which was overwhelmed in the conflagration of the town deliberately ordered by Henry I of England, at the time of his struggles with his brother Robert Courteheuse and the Count of Evreux, Amaury de Montfort. This took place in 1119, with the unwilling complicity of Bishop Ardouin. A fresh undertaking was then begun, as an act of atonement by Henry and Ardouin; and the result was that by about 1160 there had risen a cathedral, judged by William of Jumièges to 'surpass almost all the churches of Neustria'. Then in 1193 Philippe Auguste, in reprisal for a crassly cruel act of treachery on the part of John Lackland, gave the town over once again to the flames, and the cathedral suffered great damage. After 1204, when Normandy was united with the Crown of France, its rebuilding under Bishops Raoul de Clévrey and John de la Cour d'Aubergenville began, using in this the arcade of Ardouin's nave; and it fell to Bishops de Bar and des Essarts to complete soon after 1300 the glorious choir, one of the finest creations of this finest period of gothic architecture in France. But Evreux had not told all the beads on its chaplet of horror. In 1356 Jean II besieged the town in revenge for the murder of the Constable of France by Charles of Navarre, and in the fighting the town was again set on fire and the cathedral with it. Only thirteen years later the restored town suffered severely from the troops of Charles V. To pass over destruction by Huguenots and Revolutionaries, and the ravages of time, in June 1940 German aerial bombardment began fires which lasted nearly a week. The enormous damage then done was completed by the Allied bombers in June 1944. It seems unbelievable that today we can enter by the north portal (that flamboyant masterpiece of Jean Cossart) into a church filled with light from its magnificent lantern and clerestory windows, and still enjoy the stained glass of the fourteenth to the sixteenth centuries. The windows in the apse have been described by Emile Mâle as 'the most beautiful of the fourteenth century and of a delicious limpidity'—or, as some others go so far as to say, 'the most beautiful in all France'. It would require a volume in itself to recount the beauties of Evreux, not only of this glass, which Marcel Proust made a special journey to see; but of the north porch, the choir, ambulatory and chapel of the Mother of God, the eighteenth-century choir-grill, and the beautiful carved wooden panels of the late gothic and renaissance periods in the ambulatory chapels. Even the somewhat clumsy west front, mirrored in the waters of the Iton—the cold incongruous classical styles of this are owed to Bishop Le Veneur and his successors in the seventeenth century—even this cannot prevent our doing reverence to the beauty of Evreux. And, on the other side of the town, in the old abbey church of Bishop St-Taurin, is the *châsse*, the saint's silver-gilt reliquary, presented by St Louis, a masterpiece of the thirteenth-century goldsmith's art in France.

Today Sées is a sleepy old country town on rising ground above the winding River Orne, a place that is at once market-town and small commercial depot for the rich countryside, whose cornfields stretch away to the horizon, undulating in their folds of chalk. The town is inescapably ecclesiastical—but, if it were not for its cathedral, rather with the atmosphere that might be expected from a centre principally providing a retreat for superannuated priests and elderly Sisters of the Poor. Far from being disparaging, this may suggest the restful, even slightly timid or prim quality of ancient, episcopal Sées. It has not always been thus. Originally a Gallo-Roman town, it was first destroyed by the onrush of the barbarians; then, having been rebuilt, it was, as so many Neustrian towns, sacked and burnt by the Vikings. At the close of the tenth century Bishop Axon raised a romanesque cathedral, dedicated to the popular Milanese martyrs St Gervais and St Protais. In 1048 the bishop—one Yves de Bellême of that belligerent race of marcher-lords who were some of the finest military engineers of the age—was in Rouen, when he heard that a band of adventurers led by the sons of Guillaume Soreng (whose surname suggests his Viking descent) had seized the town and fortified the cathedral. He returned forthwith, and unable to expel the intruders acted, in a way which was only too customary at the time, by setting fire to the place. Pope Leo IX, who was at a Council held in Rheims, ordered him to rebuild the cathedral at his own charge, which he could well afford. The new church was consecrated in 1126, in the presence of the Duke-King Henry I, the Papal Legate, the Primate of Normandy (the Archbishop of Rouen), and the Bishop of Sées, Jean de Neuville. Five years earlier, in part of the older building, there had taken place the marriage of the Empress Matilda, the only surviving child of Henry I, with Count Geoffrey of Anjou. Before a century had elapsed their grandson Richard Cœur de Lion was to present himself in the cathedral to seek absolution from the Primate of England for having drawn sword against his father. Then for long afterwards history is sketchy or silent; but it was during this interval that the building we see today, a fine example of early Norman gothic, was raised. From internal evidence this must have been, in the main, from about 1250 to 1300. The nave is remarkable for not having been touched from the time of its inception. At first the interior strikes the visitor, like that at St-Ouen in Rouen, as being rather cold and austere; but, if my own experience is a guide, it will grow on him, and he will become aware that its simplicity and nobility are reciprocal. The choir is very beautiful, with its gabled arches and regularly receding archivolts, and the graceful intervening columns soaring unbroken to the carved capitals, whence

spring the fans of the vaulting. And how beautiful is the entirely inte-
grated composition of triforium and clerestory. It is hard to imagine
the western front of Sées without its sixteenth-century buttresses,
necessitated by weaknesses caused by subsidence; but the very deeply
recessed main doorway, with its archivolts resting on slim columns
with crocketed capitals, is most impressive. The spires were modified
in their design when they were rebuilt early in the last century. After
other Norman cathedrals one misses the central lantern tower—even
to the extent (I will avow it) of thinking that Sées's Cathedral would
have been fortunate had some daring bishop, with funds at his disposal,
crowned it with central tower and spire.

This early gothic period of cathedral building in Normandy was
accompanied by the rebuilding of the destroyed abbeys and the
foundation of others: Jumièges, St-Wandrille, Fécamp, Bec-Hellouin,
Valmont, Cérisy-la-Forêt, Lonlay, La Lucerne, Ardenne, the Abbaye
Blanche at Mortain, Mortemer, Hambye, Fontaine-Guérard, St-
Evroult-Notre-Dame-du-Bois; and the establishment of priories, such
as Beaumont-le-Roger, St-Gabriel-Brécy and Ste-Gauberge. The list
is a formidable one, even when not exhaustive. Some notable rebuilding
of abbeys took place later; in the eighteenth century, for example, rose
Mondaye near Bayeux and the Abbaye aux Hommes in Caen. The
absence, which is very noticeable, of the *rayonnant* gothic style in
Normandy is explained by the Hundred Years' War (1337–1453);
when peace came, gothic had passed into its last phase, that of *flamboyant*, and in this remarkably decorative style Normandy is particularly rich—St-Maclou in Rouen, St-Pierre in Caen, the Notre-Dames
of Alençon, Louviers and Caudebec-en-Caux, to name but a few
examples, all of great beauty. In this only too cursive and desultory
account of the ecclesiastical architecture of what is recognised as one
of the richest provinces in France one could perhaps hope to be com-
pendious, but not much more. To supplement my inadequacy I append
below a short list of churches not mentioned above or previously remarked on in any detail in the text, all of which—among so many
impossible even to name—are for one reason or another of outstanding
interest.

SEINE-MARITIME:
Allouville-Bellefosse. An oak, reputed to be ten centuries old and one of
the oldest in France, contains two chapels one above the other. The
lower was dedicated to Notre-Dame-de-la-Paix in 1698.

Les Andelys. At Grand-Andely the sixteenth- and seventeenth-century church of Notre-Dame has a thirteenth-century nave. Stained glass, paintings and statuary. At Petit-Andely St-Sauveur was built by Richard Cœur de Lion.

Duclair. St-Denis. Parts, including tower, from the twelfth century. Statues of fourteenth century, coming from Jumièges, and remains of glass of the same period.

Eu. Notre-Dame et St-Laurent. The collegial church dedicated to Our Lady and St Laurence O'Toole, Primate of Ireland. Gothic of the twelfth and thirteenth centuries, with apse rebuilt in the fifteenth. A fifteenth-century *Entombment* and figure of Christ. The Chapel du Collège in the Rue du Collège, founded by Catherine of Cleves in 1620, has within the mausoleum of Catherine and her husband the murdered Henri de Guise, known as the Balafré.

Fécamp. The magnificent church of the Trinité was part of the ancient abbey founded by Duke Richard I. Gothic of the twelfth and thirteenth centuries, with western façade of 1748. Stained glass and statuary.

Gisors. The church of St-Gervais and St-Protais is of different periods: the central tower twelfth century, the choir thirteenth century, the aisles early sixteenth-century gothic, and the west front sixteenth-century renaissance. *Descent from the Cross* and *Tree of Jesse* in stone, *Pietà* in polychrome wood, and beautiful *grisaille* window of *Life of the Virgin* (sixteenth century). Column decorated with dolphins.

Moulineaux. Charming country parish church of the thirteenth century.

Ry. The sculptured wooden porch (renaissance) of the parish church is reputed one of best of this period in Normandy.

Varengeville-sur-Mer. Simple parish church (eleventh, thirteenth and sixteenth centuries) in beautiful site has stained glass by Georges Braque, who is buried in the churchyard overlooking the sea.

Yvetot. A circular church in concrete and glass, replacing the former parish church of St-Pierre, destroyed in the last war. Stained glass by Max Ingrand.

EURE:

Bourg-Achard. The parish church, a former Benedictine priory, has some early sixteenth-century glass and beautiful woodwork of fifteenth and sixteenth centuries, including a rare specimen of celebrant's chair.

Broglie. The parish church of St-Martin is eleventh-century romanesque, parts being rebuilt in the fifteenth and sixteenth centuries. It was a stopping place for English pilgrims on their way to the shrine of St James of Compostella. Built mostly in the brownish-red ferruginous local stone known as *grison*. *Chaperons* of the confraternities of Charity. Painting by Georges de la Tour (1593–1652).

Le Chamblac. Simple country parish church near château. Beautiful vestments given by the La Varende family.

Conches. Church of Ste-Foy. Lofty flamboyant apse. Early sixteenth-century stained glass. English alabaster reliefs of fifteenth century, *Scenes of the Passion* and the *Trinity*.

Louviers. Built in the thirteenth century, this church of Notre-Dame was refaced in its beautiful flamboyant gothic at the end of the following century. The porch has been said to resemble rather the art of the gold-smith than of the mason. Fine statuary from the fifteenth to the eighteenth centuries, and some renaissance stained glass.

Pont-Audemer. Begun in the eleventh century, nave refaced at end of the fifteenth century, unfinished façade of sixteenth century. Triforium. Early sixteenth-century stained glass, which inspired Marcel Proust. Modern glass of Max Ingrand.

Verneuil-sur-Avre. The church of the Madeleine. Its tower resembles the Butter Tower of Rouen Cathedral. Romanesque nave arcading, re-modelled gothic. Choir rebuilt sixteenth century. Statuary. David d'Angers' monument to the Comte de Frotté, the Chouan leader, shot at Verneuil on the order of Bonaparte. Stained glass. The church of Notre-Dame in *grison* of the twelfth century, but several times rebuilt. Collection of early sixteenth-century statuary by local sculptors.

ORNE:

Alençon. The church of Notre-Dame. In predominantly flamboyant style, the building was completed by 1444, except for the magnificent porch (reminiscent of Rouen's St-Maclou), the work of Jean Lemoine from 1490 to 1506.

Autheuil. Romanesque church. Fine apse. Carved capitals.

Mortagne-au-Perche. Church of Notre-Dame illustrates the linking (1494–1535) of flamboyant gothic with renaissance. Fine woodwork. Ancient Convent of the Sœurs Clarisses has sixteenth-century cloister.

Moutiers-au-Perche. Romanesque parish church (eleventh century).

Rémalard. Parish church, with portions of the eleventh and fifteenth centuries.

CALVADOS:

Aubigny. In the parish church are six kneeling figures of seigneurs of nearby château.

Dives-sur-Mer. The church of Notre-Dame-de-Dives, a former pilgrimage place, dates from the fourteenth and fifteenth centuries, with remains of eleventh-century romanesque building at the crossing of the transept. Choir and Lady Chapel of the fourteenth century, examples of *rayonnant* style rare in Normandy.

Guibray. The romanesque church of Notre-Dame-de-Guibray, although much rebuilt, conserves its main and subsidiary apses in their early purity.

Honfleur. The church of Ste-Catherine and its free-standing belfry (in this showing Scandinavian influence) are masterpieces of the joiners' craft, built on the conclusion of the Hundred Years' War by local shipwrights. The carved panels are of the sixteenth century. Ancient and modern statues in wood. The seventeenth-century chapel of Notre-Dame-de-Grâce, on the hill above the town, in a wood planted by the 'Grande Mademoiselle', is the seaman's church. Statue of Our Lady.

St-Pierre-Azif. The parish church, standing in a beautiful wooded position, contains paintings by van Helmont, Jordaens, two by van Cleef and a triptych by Lucas van Leyden.

St-Pierre-sur-Dives. (See page 162 above.) The present building of the abbey church goes back to the twelfth century. The lantern tower is of the thirteenth century. The lower parts of the edifice show vestiges of the twelfth century; much of the upper work is of the fifteenth century. In the *salle capitulaire* is a beautiful floor of enamelled tiles of the thirteenth century, resembling in their patina the later bricks of Pré-d'Auge.

Ste-Gertrude. In the village of that name near Caudebec-en-Caux. A small flamboyant parish church, consecrated in 1519, in a most beautiful setting.

LA MANCHE:

Carentan. The large parish church of Notre-Dame was built from the twelfth to the fifteenth centuries. On a gable on its south side a charming angel sounds its trumpet.

Granville. This parish church of Notre-Dame, high in the old town, overlooking the port, is typical of the granite-built churches of La Manche. West front and nave of the seventeenth century; older portions going back to the fifteenth century. Venerated thirteenth-century statue of Notre-Dame-du-Cap-Lihou.

CHAPTER X

Painters' Impressions

ABOVE THE CHARMING old port of Honfleur, as picturesque in its high houses faced with slate and its shiplike church of Ste-Cathérine as the most romantic of us could wish, rises the hill of the Côte de Grâce, its slopes covered with woods and apple orchards, so thick, when seen from below, as to obscure the low Norman farmhouses, thatched, wood-framed, and washed over with white. From these heights we can look out, northwards and west, over the estuary of the Seine, which appears beneath us as a pale fabric of watered silk, turquoise or opalescent, to where Le Havre shimmers in a haze, punctuated here and there by the orange tongues of flame, like Roman candles, coming from its oil refineries. Only since the war has the great span of the Pont de Tancarville bridged the Seine so near its mouth, and brought the inhabitants of Le Havre and Honfleur, as it were, within hailing distance, so appreciably nearer as to be almost neighbours. At the beginning of last century it was otherwise; to travel from one to the other required a long detour, or a voyage. Le Havre for the Honfleurais might have been the Channel Islands to the inhabitants of Granville. In the 1820s the towns were connected by a primitive paddle-steamer, which was piloted across the treacherous waters of the estuary by a Captain Boudin, a native of Honfleur. In 1824 a son, Eugène, was born to the pilot and his wife; and it was only natural that, when the boy was old enough, he should join his father, first in the lowly capacity of cabin-boy. Some years later the elder Boudin, having saved some money, set up as a stationer and picture-frame maker in Le Havre, where he moved his family from Honfleur; and the young Eugène left the sea to help him in the shop.

Any spare time that he had Eugène Boudin occupied in drawing; maritime subjects particularly pleased him—ships and their sails and bunting, the quays and the shorelines. Normandy was becoming known to the Romantics and to artists, like the Englishman Bonington; Alfred de Musset and Sainte-Beuve stayed with their friend Guttinguer above Honfleur; the fashionable court painter Isabey was discovering the romantic beauty of the Norman coast, and Troyon the placid charm of the valley of the River Touques. These last two painters and Millet, the Norman from the Cotentin, visited the shop of Boudin *père* to buy materials and were shown Eugène's sketches. Their words of praise and advice encouraged the boy to further progress, with the happy result that the town council of Le Havre made their adopted son a grant to enable him to continue his studies in Paris.

Géricault, a native of Rouen, and Eugène Delacroix had been among the first to lead the romantic revolt against the classicism of David and the academic schools; painters began to leave their studios, setting up the easels in the open air; and these were soon to found a 'school' in Barbizon, the village in the forest of Fontainebleau, frequented by Corot, Rousseau, Millet, Daubigny and others. Considerable interest was shown from this time by French artists in the work of Bonington, Constable and Turner. Bonington had hung paintings of Lillebonne and Le Havre at the Salon of 1822. In 1824, the year of Boudin's birth, Constable aroused great admiration when he exhibited at the Salon, and his picture *The Hay Wain* was sold to a Frenchman for £250, a large sum for the period. Bonington visited this Salon, perhaps with his friend Delacroix, and the next year on a visit to England they sought out pictures by Constable. Delacroix had the highest opinion of his friend's ability. 'I knew Bonington,' he wrote, 'and was very fond of him. . . . As a young man he developed an astonishing dexterity in the use of water-colours, which were in 1817 an English novelty. . . . No one in the modern school, perhaps no earlier artist, possessed the lightness of execution which makes his works, in a certain sense, diamonds, by which the eye is enticed and charmed independently of the subject or of imitative appeal. . . . Not that he was easily satisfied; on the contrary, he often began over again perfectly finished pieces which seemed wonderful to us. His dexterity was, however, so great that in a moment he produced with a brush new effects which were as charming as the first, and more truthful.' Bonington's paintings of Normandy had all the freshness of a *pochade*; he was a precursor, in more ways than one, of Boudin.

If Normans claim the greatest French painter of the seventeenth century as their own, it must be in default of a stronger claim from elsewhere. Nicholas Poussin was born in 1594 at the village of Villers, outside Grand-Andelys, to (it is said) a Norman mother, but of his father—except that he was a soldier, and apparently not a Norman— nothing is known. In the church of Notre-Dame at Grand-Andelys are two paintings by Quentin Varin, the artist from Beauvais, who gave

Poussin his first lessons in drawing—and in this very church. But as a young man Paris attracted him, and then Rome, where he settled in 1624 in the household of the Cavalier Marini, the Neapolitan *seicentisto* poet and friend of Milton; and in Rome he stayed, except for a short intermission in Paris between 1640 and 1643, until his death in 1665. Poussin is frequently likened to his great contemporary Pierre Corneille, born under the same skies; and undoubtedly there are some points of comparison in their characters and work—both indeed were imbued with a strong classical spirit, the desire to achieve power of expression through form—in this they may be seen as Normans who were at the same time sons of antique Rome. Another of Poussin's early Norman masters was Noel Jouvenet who, according to family tradition, came of Italian stock settled in Rouen since the sixteenth century. Noel was the grandfather of the celebrated Jean Jouvenet, born in Rouen in 1644. Later, drawn, as most men of ambition were, to Paris, he attracted the notice of Le Brun, with whom he worked at Versailles. Jouvenet produced much of his native province, including a great allegory for the Parlement of Normandy, the *Triumph of Justice* (now destroyed), which he painted with his left hand, having in 1713 suffered paralysis of the right side. For his best known work, the *Miraculous Draught of Fishes*, now in the Louvre, he made the journey to Dieppe, to study at first hand the movements of fishermen, their nets and fish. He died in 1717.

In 1685 the marriage took place at Rouen between Jouvenet's sister Marie-Madeleine and a painter—one of another dynasty of artists, the Restout of Caen—Jean Ier Restout. Jean Ier's father, Marc Restout, himself a painter, had several sons, of whom Jean Ier was the eldest; two entered the Premonstratensian Order—Jacques, who wrote about art rather than practised it, and Eustache (1655–1743), the architect and decorator of the baroque rebuilding of the Abbey at Mondaye (1706–95), south of Bayeux. Jean Ier and Marie-Madeleine had a son, Jean II (1692–1768) who, left an orphan at the age of ten, worked with his uncle Jouvenet, and is the most widely known of the family, many of his paintings finding their way into Norman churches. The family of Restout remained in the public eye until the overthrow of the *ancien régime*, when Jean-Bernard (son of Jean II), who had been appointed to an official position by Roland, nearly lost his life during the Terror, on account of this enviable patronage.

Théodore Géricault, born in Rouen in 1791, was a painter of great verve and talent, but his premature death in 1824 prevented its full development. His best known work, *The Wreck of the Medusa*, which was exhibited at the Salon of 1819, excited discordant comment—some saw in it the 'renewal of the school and the manner of Jouvenet', but others, chiefly among the younger painters, hailed it as a source of liberation, with its fresh directness and breadth of treatment. When Delacroix exhibited at the Salon of 1822 his work was greeted with the same chorus of approval and dissent, one critic going so far as to suggest that Géricault had had a hand in it. It is perhaps not too removed from the truth to say that from Géricault stemmed important elements of both the Romantic and the Realist schools of painting—if these terms may be meaningfully used. One of the greatest of the French Realists was without a doubt Jean-François Millet, the peasant son of peasants from that austere yet imaginatively suggestive northern coast of the Cotentin, where Atlantic waves break against the granite cliffs, and in summer the crops are stirred noiselessly by the salt-bearing breeze. Millet was born at Gruchy (the cottage is still there), a hamlet west of Cherbourg, in 1814. His self-taught talent was early recognised, and he went for instruction in drawing to Cherbourg; but, shortly after, on the death of his father in 1835, he returned to work on the farm; and it was only when his own family added their behests to those of others that he accepted a scholarship from the communal authorities and went to study in Paris at the Beaux-Arts. Although Millet returned to La Manche and painted in Normandy, his work is principally associated with Barbizon; and it was there, and not in his native province, that he painted his popular masterpieces, *The Gleaners* and *The Angelus*. On his visits to Le Havre he met Eugène Boudin—as we have seen— admired the boy's talents, and bolstered in him his ambition to paint. Millet lived to achieve widespread acclaim and official recognition before his death in 1875.

Towards the middle of last century the number of artists who visited Normandy to paint its seascapes and landscapes grew apace. Leprince exhibited at the Salon views of Honfleur; and his pupil Charles-Louis Mozin, who was one of the first to discover Trouville, painted many scenes of the valley and mouth of the River Touques, ending his days in Trouville in 1865. These artists, with Isabey, Troyon, Huet and Flers, were followed by Courbet and the Dutchman Jongkind, who both showed a preference for the localities about Honfleur and Le Havre. Barbizon sent its own contingent, perhaps spurred on by Millet: Daubigny painted especially the majestic Norman coast; Rousseau favoured the sombre seascapes of Granville; and Corot, more eclectic in choice of locality, has left us his evanescent impressions of St-Lô, Honfleur and Rouen. Stanislas Lépine, a native of Caen, who was Corot's pupil, made numerous studies of the beautiful banks of the Seine. But fine as some of these artists were, none captured and rendered so well the fleeting play of light on the Norman sea and shore as Eugène Boudin.

So it came about that by the 1850s each summer brought these painters to Honfleur. On the Trouville road, below the Côte de Grâce, but still high above the sea, stood the Ferme St-Siméon, a characteristic wood and plaster Norman farmhouse, with its half-timbered outbuildings, set among the apple orchards and their emerald carpet of grass, as close-cropped and luxuriant as an English lawn. At this friendly establishment many of these painters found their board and lodging, always welcomed by the large and hospitable Mère Toutain, who provided at small cost abundant, wholesome fare, and flagons of excellent Norman cider. The painters rose early, and by five o'clock were at work, since one did not have to go far to find 'subjects'; they merely put up the easels on the beach or on the quays, or simply, not moving at all, beneath the apple-trees on the cliff-edge of the Ferme St-Siméon. In 1859 Courbet painted there his *Garden of Mère Toutain*. Lunch was taken at the scrubbed-wooden *tables d'hôte* in the orchard, where you only needed to lift your head from your plate to watch the swift passage of clouds and light changing the tones and colours of the sea below—a lunch of *batons* of crisp, fresh bread, a huge bowl heaped high with the black-blue shells of *moules marinières* or a *soupe de poisson* —the Norman *bouillabaise*, made of fish caught the preceding night— or a *gigot* of lamb; then, cheese from Camembert or Pont-l'Evêque, fruit—and gallons of cider. And all the while the talk. Boudin wrote of the huge, genial Jongkind at Honfleur, '. . . the great Jongkind, another excellent fellow that, who came here many times to get drunk on our view of the Seine estuary, as well as on our friendly chat and our good Norman cider'. By the late sixties Boudin had become something of the 'master' of this St-Siméon group, although he had gained little by way of reputation in the world—he remained for years a painter's painter, recognised only by connoisseurs like Corot and Baudelaire, who considered him unrivalled in the depicting of the passing moods of the sky.

It was the peculiarly northern quality of Normandy that drew these painters there—the conjunction of land and restless sea, the incessant alterations of the skies, and the resultant changes in colour—the fleeting, fugitive interplay of all these lights and shades, these exquisite shifting colours. Only new methods of painting could adequately capture the subtleties, revealed sometimes only for an instant, of these chance combinations. Boudin was for ever obsessed by the challenge which they presented to the painter. In 1854 he wrote:

> I still feel this abundance, this delicacy, a shining light which trans-forms everything before my eyes . . . and I simply cannot put that across with my grubby palette. It must be twenty times now that I have started all over again to try and capture that delightful quality of light which plays on everything around. What freshness there is about it, at once soft, fugitive, a shade pink. Objects become dis-solved, so that there are only variations in density everywhere. The sea was marvellous, the sky mellow, velvety; whereupon it changed to yellow, became warm, then as the sun began to set the loveliest shades of violet crept over everything. The shore as well as the dykes took on the same tone.

This was written as early as 1854. To acquire that accuracy of vision, and to render it in pigment with all its natural freshness and nuances retained, Boudin had found that what was demanded was painting *en plein air*. 'Everything that is painted directly on the spot,' he wrote, 'always has a strength, a power, a vividness of touch that one doesn't find again in the studio.' It is interesting to note a parallel here with the different methods in the fifteenth century of the Flemish and Italian artists in their desire to render in painting the solidity of material objects. The Flemings—Van Eyck is a good example—achieved their representation of form by an intense study of the effects of light, 'the flood of light which penetrates all nature'. The Italians, on the other hand, were more *a priori*, painstakingly building up their material objects according to the newly discovered laws of linear perspective. Impressionism was evolved through this outdoor study of the power of light to affect colour; it was later *theory* that produced pointillism.

It seems that about this time Boudin met Claude Monet, for the latter's family had been settled in Le Havre since 1845, and the youth had gained some reputation for his skill in caricature. In 1858, when Monet was seventeen, he became Boudin's pupil, and the two were often seen sketching and painting together on the beaches and cliffs of Ste-Adresse. Monet, who was also helped by Jongkind and Courbet, later admitted his debt to Boudin: 'If I have turned into a painter, it is to Boudin I owe it.' After being invalided out of the army Monet, who was working in Paris in the studio of Gleyre, met Manet, Sisley, Renoir, Bazille, Camille Pissaro and others, who were to form the group known as 'Impressionists' (a name employed as much to distinguish their technique as to abuse them), possibly from Manet's use of the word 'impression' in his catalogue of 1867, or from Monet's painting of a sun rising over the sea, which he entitled *Une Impression*. Monet persuaded his Parisian friends to accompany him in the summer to Normandy, to paint in the open air with Boudin at the Ferme St-Siméon. In 1864 Bazille wrote home to his parents: 'As soon as we arrived at Honfleur we looked for landscape *motifs*. They were easy to find because the country is heaven. . . . We are staying in Honfleur itself, at a baker's, who has let us two small rooms; we eat at the Ferme St-Siméon, situated on the cliff a little above Honfleur; it's there we work and spend our days. The port of Honfleur and the dress of the Normans, with their cotton caps, interest me greatly.' In 1870, during the Franco-Prussian war, Monet and Pissaro were in London, where they studied with increasing admiration the work of Turner from whom they gained confirmation of their ideas—in the high pitch and the range of his colour, with the infinite suggestiveness of his use of it, not in flat brush-strokes, as Manet painted, but broken up into tiny touches of glowing pigment. Boudin, meanwhile, went on in his own way, producing the delightful paintings of beach scenes, fresh and vibrant with aerial luminosity, with sunlight and sea breeze, where boats sail off-shore or lie drawn up on the sand, and fashionable women saunter, their crinolines and parasols brilliant patches of white, yellow, or clear red.

In 1874 the impressionist group (with the exception of Manet, who continued to fight for acceptance at the Salon) first exhibited together as *l'Exposition des Impressionistes* at Nadar's gallery in the Boulevard des Capucines, and included with them in the show were Boudin, Lépine and the Southern Italian De Nittis. Thenceforth their paintings were taken up by the Parisian art-dealer Durand-Ruel. It was Monet who perhaps carried farthest the light-and-colour-theories of what only for convenience can be called the school. In 1874 he exhibited his series of *Cathedrals*, with those celebrated views of Rouen cathedral in varying lights, times of day and seasons. He invariably worked out of doors and in the presence of the object which he was representing; and this, too, only at that brief moment whose evanescence he wished to fix on his canvas. He strove to catch the fugitive colouration of the atmosphere by broken touches of pure colour, using a high register of tonality, so that solidity of form became dissolved and material objects melted into a suffused iridescence. These theories of light and colour led—in other hands, and in an attempt to render them more 'scientific'—to *pointillisme*—to Surat, Signac and (for a while) Pissaro, all of whom painted in Normandy. In 1883 Monet settled at the village of Giverny, near Vernon, at the junction of the River Epte with the Seine. There, across the road from his charming house, he built himself a garden, still to be seen brilliant with the floral gaiety of summer. He became fascinated with the reflections of sky and flowers in his ponds of water-lilies, exhibiting first some paintings called *Le Basin des Nymphéas* in 1900, two years after Boudin's death. He continued to paint there until his own death in 1926. Of Monet's Norman followers perhaps the best known is Albert Lebourg of Monfort-sur-Risle.

It was this Norman town of Honfleur, which Alfred de Musset, Baudelaire and Proust so loved, which gave to the world Boudin, the poets Henri de Régnier and Lucie Delarue-Mardrus and the musician Eric Satie—this little fishing port of some 9,000 inhabitants, that can justifiably make good the claim, which today is made by the lavishly spruced-up Ferme St-Siméon, of being the *'berceau d'Impressionisme'*. The Musée dedicated to Boudin at Honfleur has some examples of his work, and of his followers'; but the finest collection is at Le Havre. No one should miss this. There also is a good selection of the work of Raoul Dufy. But artists have flocked to many others of these Norman seaside towns: to Etretat, Cabourg, Trouville, Deauville, Varengeville, Dieppe—above all, to Dieppe. Vuillard and Helleu made Cabourg their headquarters; later, when impressionism had developed into post-impressionism, Othon Friesz came to Honfleur, Paul Signac to Barfleur, and Raoul Dufy, Valloton, Marquet, all painted in Normandy. Van Dongen, whose superficial facility went well with the *mondaine* vulgarity he depicted, was a familiar figure on the *planches* of Deauville. And at Varengeville, not far from Dieppe, lived for years and died in 1963 Georges Braque, who perhaps will be judged by posterity one of the finest painters of his time. At Dieppe—and what modern artist has not painted in Dieppe?—the doyen of all painters was Walter Sickert, in whose work the houses, churches and streets of old Dieppe take their place beside the music-halls of Edwardian London as characteristically part of his iconography. Jacques-Emile Blanche, who always looked on Sickert as *'the* greatest painter of Dieppe', lived in the neighbouring countryside, at the village of Offranville, where he painted for the village church, as a memorial of the First World War, a large canvas in which the crowd of figures are portraits of the villagers. And nearby, at Auppegard, two Englishwomen, friends of Henry James—Miss Hudson and Miss Ethel Sands—in the twenties did up the old manor-house opposite the church. They themselves painted and entertained artists at Auppegard, among them Vanessa Bell and Duncan Grant, who repaid some of their hospitality by painting frescoes on their drawing-room walls. But Dieppe can only be a lesser rival to Honfleur. In another part of Normandy, the Vallée d'Auge, inland from the coast, lived the cubist painter Fernand Léger, whose farmhouse at the village of Lisores, not far distant from Vimoutiers, has been since his death in 1955 converted into a museum, with a permanent exhibition of his work.

CHAPTER XI

Dieppe

ON THE CLIFF top above the village of Puys, which lies something under two miles north-east of Dieppe, undulations in the green turf over a wide area of the meadows suggest the presence here of the foundations or ramparts of some ancient habitation, which the local people refer to as Caesar's Camp. In reality it is all that remains of the Cité de Limes, a spot rich in legends of wild nocturnal dances in midsummer, of beautiful maidens who lured young men to their deaths over the cliff's edge, and of the appearance of phantom ships with pitch-black sails on the sea below. Excavations have revealed that the site was at a very early period inhabited by Gallic peoples, by the Romans after them and perhaps even by the Normans; but by about the tenth or eleventh century many of the inhabitants had dispersed —it may be to Arques, or to Dieppe, which it seems they founded. In the fifteenth century there was still nominally a *curé* of Limes, although he had no duties, having no longer any parishioners. Before the rise of Dieppe, Arques was the main port for this part of the coast, salt-pans separating it from its neighbour and eventual successor. Dieppe, the name itself, comes from the same Germanic root as the English *deep*, a reference to the harbour, which can be used by vessels even at the lowest tide. Like St-Malo in Brittany and Honfleur at the Seine's mouth, Dieppe owed its prosperity to the skill of its sailors, nursed in the Atlantic fisheries off Iceland and Newfoundland. Realising the value of the maritime power built up by the Dieppois, particularly as a bulwark against the English, the Kings of France from Philippe Auguste to François Ier granted the town important immunities and privileges. It was under François Ier that Dieppe reached the apogee of its power and splendour.

The most famous of the merchant princes of the period, these *armateurs*—that is, both shipowners and privateers (for in these times when the Pope had divided the recent territorial discoveries exclusively between Spain and Portugal any interloper had to fight his way)—was the Dieppe-born Jean Ango. His father, who came of a rich bourgeois family enobled in 1408 by Charles VI, had made his fortune at sea, and was well enough off in 1508 to equip two vessels on an expedition which attempted to colonise Newfoundland. Jean was born in 1481; he spent some years at sea, but on his father's death he stayed at home in Dieppe, where he built up a fleet of merchantmen, with which he traded to the four quarters of the globe, protecting his ships with his own men-of-war. His commercial connections with the merchants of Rouen, Honfleur and the new port of Le Havre brought him ever-increasing financial returns, and his wealth became fabulous. One of his captains, Jean Fleury, in 1521 captured three caravels off the Azores laden with the plunder from Montezuma. Among his shipmasters were two brothers, the Florentine exiles Giovanni and Girolamo da Verrazano, one of whom (Giovanni) in 1523 discovered the bay of Manhattan and the site of the future New York. Others were the Parmentier brothers who sailed round the Cape of Good Hope and reached Sumatra and Java in 1529, being the first to stage the burlesque ceremonies of King Neptune as their ship crossed the equator.

In Dieppe Ango built himself a beautiful house of exquisitely carved oak, which he named, after the humanist style in vogue, La Pensée, and filled it with Italian paintings, sculpture, precious furnishings and plate of a grandeur and good taste that amazed even visiting Italians, who had known the collections of the Medici. As a *maison de plaisance* in the country he built the manor-house at Varengeville, five miles west of Dieppe. On the stone gateway to the Manoir d'Ango have been set medallions in low relief, very much after the antique; and similarly they appear in his arcaded *loggia* at one end of the interior court, the whole building a charming mingling of the style of the Italian renaissance with the more homely fashion of Normandy. In this gracious dwelling of rose brick and stone, built around the large paved and grassed court, Ango entertained François Ier in 1532, when the king raised him to the rank of *vicomte*. The dovecote, at that time a privilege of the nobility alone, is one of the most beautiful in Normandy, a miracle of fretted and patterned stone and brickwork, comparable with (if it is not even more perfect than) that of the château of Launay. It was here in his manor at Varengeville that Ango received the ambassadors sent by King John of Portugal. Granted letters of marque by François, Ango fitted out fleets to challenge Portugal's pretensions off the coast of Africa and on the maritime routes to the Indies and the New World. He was reported to have captured in all, Portuguese and those of other nations, some three hundred vessels, with their cargoes and crews. When two of his own ships were seized by the Portuguese, by way of reprisal he dispatched fourteen men-of-war to the Bay of Biscay, burnt and destroyed some villages on the coast, then posted his vessels off the entrance to the Tagus and threatened to blockade Lisbon. King John forthwith sent ambassadors to François to protest. The king received them coldly, saying, '*Messieurs, ce n'est pas moi qui vous fais la guerre. Allez trouver Ango et arrangez-vous avec lui.*' They came to Varengeville, and Ango, having obtained the reparations he considered due to him, entertained the embassy so sumptuously that they might have believed they were being regaled at the expense of François himself.

Ango was indefatigable in the service of the king in his relations with Henry VIII of England, and when in 1535 François came to inspect the troops gathered in the Pays de Caux he entertained the court lavishly in Dieppe and Varengeville. This munificence put at the disposal of his sovereigns contributed largely to his ruin. Henri II showed no alacrity to repay the debts contracted by his father with Ango, who was then the governor of Dieppe. His hauteur and his successes caused much jealousy among his fellow citizens; and when one former partner named Morel brought and won a legal suit against him, this was the beginning of several similar actions, which also went in favour of his adversaries. Some unfortunate speculations hastened his fall. Dispersed were valuable pictures, his works of art, his silver and gold plate, when, a prematurely old and embittered man, he died in 1551 at his manor of Varengeville, the scene of so much past splendour. His tomb is in the church of St-Jacques in Dieppe, which he embellished at his own expense with the beautiful apsidal chapels, enclosed by open-work doorways, finely carved with renaissance decoration in low-relief.

His town house of La Pensée (he must have liked the name, since his flag-ship also bore it) unfortunately did not survive the Anglo-Dutch action against Dieppe in 1694, when Admiral Berkeley poured fire-bombs into the town, which was almost entirely destroyed in the conflagration that followed. The two churches of St-Jacques and St-Remy, surrounded as they were by cemeteries, alone escaped destruction. Louis XIV ordered plans to be drawn up for the re-building of so important a town, but the charge was given not to the great Vauban, but to a subordinate named Ventabren, whose work so displeased the leading Dieppois magnates that many of them moved their businesses elsewhere. Vauban is reported to have said to the incompetent architect, 'Monsieur, you could do much better, but you could never do worse.' The castle and these two churches are all that remain of the most glorious period of Dieppe's history; yet the reconstruction begun under Louis XIV has given the town much of its characteristic appearance, so well conveyed by Sickert, the unrivalled painter of old Dieppe, as Boudin is of the Norman coastline and Monet of its rivers and gardens. When reports came through of the Dieppe raid by the Allies on 19 August 1942, many must have feared that the streets, squares, churches and houses so cherished from their youth would have been perhaps irretrievably damaged, if not entirely destroyed. War has extinguished the heart of old St-Valéry-en-Caux, but it has left Dieppe virtually intact.

This raid in force ('Jubilee'), carried out by 7,000 men, mostly Canadians, was made at dawn on eight points of the coast between Berneval-sur-Mer to the north-east of Dieppe and the lighthouse of Ailly to the west. The cumbersome Churchill tanks, put ashore at Dieppe on the gravelly beach near the casino, came under murderous artillery fire from entrenched positions and had to be sacrificed in effecting the re-embarkation of the troops. At Puys, where the narrow valley comes down to the beach, there is a moving memorial in French and English to those who at dawn on that 19 August lost their lives 'that we who came after them might enjoy in freedom the beauty of the place'. This costly raid was not without results. The Allies drew the conclusions (rightly) that ports would be strongly held, but that shipping losses might be comparatively light; the Germans (wrongly) that a landing on the continent would be attempted only at the ports nearest England. The operation 'Overlord' of 6 June 1944 was carried out in Lower Normandy. St-Lô perished, as did much of Le Havre, Cherbourg, Caen, and numbers of small towns and villages—but Dieppe has survived.

Most visitors arrive in Dieppe by sea; the astonishing figure of over half a million is given for those who pass through its port annually. As the Newhaven ferryboat approaches the French coast, the cliffs, white laced with green, seem replicas of those of the South Downs, cleft from the same chalk as the Sussex hills left not three hours before. Yet something very different from the tight-laced propriety of the English south-coast ports is the scene, when the boat enters the dredged channel of the River Arques which forms the harbour of Dieppe. To the right, the shallow sickle of the gravelled beach, backed by lawns and an unbroken line of hotels and rather nondescript houses, ends in the new casino, tucked away below the cliff on which rises, with its cylindrical tower and conical cap, the mediaeval bulk of the castle. To the left, on the hilltop stands the modern brick chapel of Notre-Dame-de-Bon-Secours, the church of Dieppe's fishermen, above their own ancient

quarter of Pollet. Ahead, and the boat advances rapidly as if to drive
straight through the centre of it, lies the town, faced by the prominent
early eighteenth-century arcades. However, the ferry slackens speed
and berths right alongside the busy street, in which the boat-train for
Paris is drawn up, waiting; and behind this rise houses whose fronts of
cream stucco, drab brick, or frame and plaster reveal, above the cafés
and restaurants, the predominance of the architecture of the eighteenth
and early nineteenth centuries. All this evokes a sense of that intimate
immediacy of historical setting, which Aubrey Beardsley and Charles
Conder had in mind when they described Dieppe as 'Balzac-ian'. The
epithet and the atmosphere it conjures up are exact. Without intro-
duction, and (if we did not feel the ticket and passport in our pocket)
almost as intruders, we enter into the everyday life of an old historic
town and its inhabitants. The dockers, clumsy in baggy blue denims,
hands in pockets, the inevitable Gauloise dripping from their lips, the
police and uniformed customs officials also all smoking on duty, the
black-shawled women with their string shopping bags, the fair-haired
children returning from the boulangerie with the long *baguette* of fresh-
crusted bread—these have no precise Anglo-Saxon counterparts. To
the newcomer this is Normandy; it is unmistakably French. And in the
savour of this lies part of the charm of Dieppe.

The visitor may leave the Gare Maritime on the Quai Henri IV and
walk into the town, passing at the end of the quay the fish market, a
marvellous display of the sea's harvest to delight the eye of the icthyo-
phagous gourmet. The market here is best seen early on a summer's
morning, and one feels inclined then to credit the story that French and
English trawlers are accustomed to meet in mid-Channel, where an
exchange takes place, the English transferring the best species of the
catch (to be taken to Dieppe) for an equivalent value of the coarser
varieties, which find their way to the fish shops of Southern England.
One may well be disposed to believe it. . . . Leaving on the left the
arcades of the Quai Duquesne, with its many restaurants, one enters
the Grande Rue, Dieppe's main street, lined with a variety of good
shops, some pleasantly old-fashioned, and one comes almost immediately to the open space of the Place Nationale, with its eighteenth-
century buildings and, at the farther end, the northern flank of the
church of St-Jacques. In the centre of the square is a statue of the
brilliant seventeenth-century sailor, Admiral the Marquis Abraham
Duquesne (1610–88), a native of Dieppe, whose undying hatred for
the Spaniards (they had killed his father, also a distinguished naval

officer), led to a long series of successes against them, culminating in the great victory over the combined Hispano-Dutch fleets in the Mediterranean off Catania, when their admiral de Ruyter was mortally wounded. Duquesne refused to change his religion, although his doing so would have made him a Marshal of France, and retired from the navy in 1684, possibly foreseeing the revocation of the Edict of Nantes, which occurred in the following year, with such dire results for Normandy.

St-Jacques is a structurally beautiful gothic church, with many additions and alterations to the original early thirteenth-century fabric, particularly to be observed in the door and rose-window of the west front (fourteenth-century), the tower (fifteenth-century) and Jean Ango's contribution of the flamboyant and renaissance *chevet* (sixteenth-century). From the *place* the stonework of St-Jacques (beneath the rather anomalous seventeenth-century slate roofing and lantern, which cover its squat central tower) appears as if its surfaces have undergone something of a sea-change, a pitting and mouldering produced through the centuries by sun and hail and the caustic action of the salt-bearing winds. From a distance it has a soft mellowness and great charm; close to—if, for example, one walks around Ango's *chevet*—the battering it has received from time and tempest is only too clearly visible in the scarred and crumbling masonry. At an angle on the left of the west front project two curious gargoyles, one of a bearded triton and the other of a siren from whose breasts stream jets of rainwater. Within the church, seen from the thirteenth-century nave the effect is sombre, suggestive of neglect, an absence of aesthetic if not religious feeling —and yet the church is well-attended, its congregation including the well-to-do. St-Jacques was the principal church of the Dieppois *armateurs*, the rich shipowners who here have raised their memorials. Particularly fine are the dedicatory chapels, which are faced with bold open-work (some of it modern)—the renaissance carving is of great delicacy—and which are covered by flamboyant groined vaults; one such chapel is that dedicated to St-Sépulcre in 1612, off the right-hand aisle. Ango's chapel of the Treasure (today used as the sacristy) is entered by a doorway which incorporates sculpture from his destroyed Dieppe house, a frieze of exotic faces, suggesting tribesmen of Africa or perhaps of Brazil. The *armateur* lies buried in the chapel of St-Yves, built by him as an oratory.

The second of Dieppe's two main churches, St-Remy, has nothing architecturally comparable with St-Jacques, the rebuilding (1522–1640) of an earlier church being interrupted by the Wars of Religion, which as we have seen were bitterly contested in these parts of Normandy, where many of the more enterprising of the upper and middle classes were Huguenots, who on their defeat were forced to leave the country. The castle of the governors of Dieppe was in the parish of St-Remy, and several of them have their tombs in the church. And here again we find, contemporary with the Ango frieze in St-Jacques', carvings of armed tribesmen, one with an assegai, further evidence of the hold those foreign voyages had on the imagination of the Dieppois.

The castle (picturesque, even elegant despite its mass, with its cylindrical towers and its pointed roofs of grey slate) dominates both town and coast—the view from it is particularly fine. This typically feudal structure of flint and sandstone was begun by Governor Desmarets in 1435, the year that the English were finally driven from Dieppe, five years after their decisive defeat at Formigny. Today the castle houses a well appointed museum and art gallery. The maritime history of Dieppe is recorded in models of ships, figure-heads, maps, charts, navigational instruments, engravings and arms. Of outstanding interest is the collection of most beautiful examples of the carving of ivory, an art brought to perfection by the Dieppois sculptors. The direct importation of elephant tusks from Africa and India led early to the establishment of schools of craftsmen and to the pre-eminence of the Dieppe ivory-carvers. By the seventeeth century 350 highly skilled artists were employed, where today only two remain. Medallions, figurines, boxes for patches or snuff, objects which lend their surfaces to the carving of exquisitely delicate figures and scenes—these may have their polished whiteness accentuated by backgrounds of the purest deep blue. Furthermore, there is a permanent collection of paintings, of great value in their evocation of the peculiar colours and light of Dieppe, as seen through the eyes of nineteenth- and twentieth-century painters: Courbet, Isabey, Le Poittevin (who was connected with both Flaubert and Maupassant), Boudin, Lebourg, Bertin, Pissaro, Sisley, Van Dongen, J.-E. Blanche, and, perhaps above all, Blanche's life-long friend, the Englishman Walter Richard Sickert (1860–1942).

Abroad, away from the Victorian and Edwardian London which provided him with models and subjects for so many of his finest *genre* paintings, Sickert preferred to paint in Venice or in Dieppe. He seems first to have visited Dieppe about 1884, becoming in time something of a local curiosity, the well-known and much loved figure, which was seen each morning descending the hill from his house at Pollet and greeting all acquaintances with the perfect politeness that was his

Charlotte Corday:
engraving by Lefrancq after Desandré

Ste Thérèse (of Lisieux) with
her father

Gustave Flaubert

Marcel Proust

armour. (Once, it is said, that irascible baronet and connoisseur Sir William Eden, stung by some of George Moore's ill-natured remarks, turned on him with fury: 'Sickert boasts of being middle-class, but he has the *manners* of a gentleman!') After the First World War he returned and lived with his recently-married wife at the village of Envermeu, a few miles to the south-east, near the Forest of Arques, but also renting a secret studio in Dieppe. He painted the town in all its moods. In one canvas he shows a street slatey after rain, reflecting the blue of the sky, the bright flowers of public gardens and the multi-coloured dresses of the women. But chiefly it was the surfaces of buildings that affected him most, the crumbling stone of St-Jacques', eroded by sun and salt wind, and the fronts (time-scarred and peeling) of old houses. Today many of these houses are to be seen, much as they were in Sickert's time, between the church and the quays, particularly in the Place Louis Vitet and the little streets off it. Sickert often employed in these Dieppe paintings the deep tones and colours which are so associated with him, those variations of burnt brown, red, maroon, blue, green and yellow, marvellously controlled. If Sickert 'explains' Dieppe, Dieppe in turn 'explains' Sickert—they are inseparable.

Jacques-Emile Blanche in his memoirs *More Portraits of a Lifetime* gives a poignant if macabre picture of his friend at the funeral of his wife Christina at Envermeu in the early 1920s. Sickert had wired to Blanche, telling him of Christina's sudden death. A few days later a message gave notice of the funeral in Envermeu cemetery, where the remains would be brought from the cremation in Rouen. It was a cold but sunny October day, with a strong wind blowing, as the mourners gathered by an open grave to await the hearse, which had been de-layed. When it finally arrived, Sickert was given the casket which contained the ashes of his wife, clasped it reverently to him, with his head bowed over it. Then, instead of placing the casket, as everyone expected, in the prepared grave, he suddenly opened it, plunged in his hand, and flung the ashes into the air. A gust of wind carried them away like a cloud against the blue sky, not before part of them had covered those who stood nearby with a fine coat of white dust.

Dieppe is the doyenne of all French bathing resorts. It was at the time of the restoration of the Bourbons after the fall of the First Empire that the Duchess of Berry made fashionable the sea-bathing here, thus antici-pating by some decades the rise of Trouville-Deauville. Lusty local fisherwives carried the ladies, secluded from male eyes in box-like sedan chairs, between the bathing huts and the water. From the outset until the First World War the tone of Dieppe society, with the annual influx of rich and distinguished visitors from Paris and abroad, was un-ashamedly aristocratic, but there was a healthy leavening of the arts —painters, writers and musicians. A season of stage performances and musical concerts by international artists added variety to the play for high stakes at the tables of the casino, a Kublai-Khan construction of glass, with oriental domes and minarets, surrounded by extensive gardens bright with flowers. The Reverend Mr Musgrove described the original buildings in 1854 just after their opening: 'This delectable rendezvous . . . is now complete, and forms a vast improvement upon the shingly beach, where a thousand ladies in their morning or evening costume may sit at their ease, with book, crochet, or fan in hand, in a long gallery of glass, like fair flowers in a conservatory, awaiting notice and admiration.' Unfortunately this charming absurdity was replaced in the twenties by the concrete edifice destroyed in the Allied raid of 1942, but it has since been rebuilt in stone.

The Prince of Wales (later Edward VII) would come ashore from his yacht anchored in the roads to visit incognito his intimate friend the Duchessa Caracciolo, whose daughter Olga was the prince's god-child. It was of Olga that Henry James remarked, 'That charming Olga learnt more from Dieppe than my *Maisie* knew.' Later, as the Baroness de Meyer, she served Proust as a model in his account of Swann's love affairs, and Dieppe too became part of the composite Balbec in *A la Recherche*. Although Cabourg figures mostly as the setting for his *jeunes filles en fleurs*, each summer brought to Dieppe a crowd of notables from the Faubourg St Germain, who, transposed, were to appear as characters in his novel: Polignac, Greffulhe, Caraman Chimay, Broglie, Clermont-Tonnerre and the exquisite 'chief of fragrant odours', Count Robert de Montesquiou. Many writers frequented Dieppe about this period, among them Dumas *père et fils*, Strindberg, Henry James, George Moore, Proust and Max Beerbohm. Oscar Wilde, released from prison, retired there, but feeling himself followed he moved to an hotel at nearby Berneval, not before he had sampled the pleasures of the local brothel. He was urged to do this by the advice of his friends, particularly the poet Ernest Dowson, who thought the publicity might do his name good in England. A large crowd escorted him there, and awaited his reappearance. He came out and the expression on his face explained his deep sense of failure—'It was like cold mutton.'

Another of those faithful to Dieppe was Lady Blanche Hosier, Sir

Winston Churchill's mother-in-law, whom J.-E. Blanche remembered 'marketing of a morning, proudly marching from shop to shop, her snow-white hair below her lace-edged handkerchief, her billowing skirts brushing the pavement of the Grande Rue, or the floor of the casino, which she, an impenitent gambler, frequented.' Musicians also came to Dieppe: Saint-Saëns—who conducted his own music at the casino, and bequeathed to the museum his collection of autographs of famous composers—as well as Debussy, Fauré, Grieg, Percy Grainger, and the ballet impresario Diaghileff.

But above all Dieppe, since the time of Delacroix, has attracted artists, great names among lesser ones and those now forgotten—Corot, Puvis de Chavannes, Boudin, Whistler, Dégas, Monet, Vollon, Pissaro, Beardsley, Sargent, Braque, Vanessa Bell, Duncan Grant—and, deserving a place among them, the portraitist-writer Jacques-Emile Blanche, who seems to have known and painted everyone of note. He lived in or near Dieppe for seventy years, dying at Offranville during the Second World War. Some of his pictures hang in Dieppe castle, and there is a large war memorial in the Offranville church, but one must journey to Rouen to see his portraits, representative of much that is best in French twentieth-century culture.

To enjoy the sight of the Dieppe crowds, the visitor must sit down in front of the ancient Café des Tribunaux, opposite the flower-covered well-head, which gives its name to the Place du Puits Salé, the open triangle formed by the intersection of six streets. (On Saturday mornings the Dieppe market is held in the two streets which join at the Tribunaux—the Grande Rue and the Rue St-Jacques—and in the Place National, all traffic being stopped there while it lasts. If anyone doubts the richness of Normandy, the culinary material on which the Dieppe chefs and housewives work, let him wander between the market stalls and gaze his fill on all the richness of produce from Cauchois farms and prolific sea.) For the lover of old Dieppe the Café des Tribunaux presents something of a pantheon of vanished figures, of pale wraiths, of voices now silent. No longer does Roger Fry sit there with Jacques-Emile Blanche, puzzling over the secrets of Sickert's genius; or Oscar Wilde, bravely failing to notice that a former friend has just cut him; or the opulent Sir William Orpen; or Diaghileff; or Augustus John . . . The aristocrats are gone, the numbers of artists diminished; today the crowds are mostly Franco-British, democratic, chiefly young, gay, noisy, very colourful and very much alive. How pleasant, how charming Dieppe is still on a sunny August morning.

CHAPTER XII

The Norman Cuisine

The pleasures of the table are common to all ages and ranks, to all countries and times; they not only harmonise with all the other pleasures, but remain to console us for their loss—
Brillat-Savarin

THE REVEREND GEORGE MUSGROVE describes a Norman meal that he witnessed on an August day in 1854 on board the river-steamer *Courrier*, which was taking him and a number of very ordinary Normans down the Seine from Rouen to Quilleboeuf. It will be appreciated that the cooking facilities offered in the stifling galley, five feet by three, of a small steamer are limited; nevertheless we have the worthy parson's word for what he saw:

Close alongside of me stood for some time, till a shower displaced them, a remarkable couple, whom, in respect of physiognomy, I might have designated (after the style of our old Nursery Book) 'The Beauty and the Beast'. One was a strikingly pretty woman, fashionably dressed, all smiles, grace and good humour; the other a coarse, gross, unwieldy and dirty-skinned man, bearded like the pard, gloveless, graceless, witless—what the French call *'un gros animal, et très bête'*. . . . This Caliban-like worshipper of the fairest daughters of Eve prevailed upon his gentle companion—I believe she was his bride—to go below and breakfast. The French seldom take that meal before ten or eleven o'clock. I was sketching on the hatchway . . . but the flavours from below seemed to invite me to put on record . . . that prolonged and mighty meal, to every single portion of which the lady addressed herself with an energy and impetuosity of appetite compared with which the fabled feats of schoolboys or aldermen would sink into tame insignificance. I witnessed the first onslaught (when the soup was disposed of) upon the fried mackerel: it was a vigorous attack; but the fish-bones, at any rate, were removed. Two relays of beefsteak, ditto of French beans and fried potatoes followed, with an omelette *aux fines herbes*; flanked immediately by a *fricandeau* of veal and sorrel; and these (or rather, I should say the dishes that had contained all this) were supplaced by a roast chicken, garnished with mushrooms, and commended to the gentle senses by a hock of ham, served upon spinach. This engrossed an interval of twenty-five minutes—the chicken having become invisible in the first ten; but the salted meat demanded more laborious manducation. Then came an open apricot tart, three custards, and an endive salad, which I felt sure was the precursor, as it proved, of a small roast leg of lamb, with chopped onion and nutmeg-powder sprinkled upon it. All, except the joint, was consumed; and then came the coffee and two glasses of absinthe and *eau dorée*, a Mignon cheese, pears, plums, grapes, and cakes—two bottles of *petit Bourgogne* and one of *Chablis* having been emptied between eleven and one o'clock. This was a breakfast . . .

And if we would prefer now to call it lunch, it is still pretty good going.

Before we come down to our own degenerate days, we have the authority of the great gastronome Curnonsky for the description of the form of any important meal in Normandy in the days before the Second World War. It was inevitably arranged in this way: '*bouillon* and *pot-au-feu*, after which a glass of wine is taken; then tripe; then leg of mutton. Here a halt is called for the *trou normand*. We fall to again with roast veal, then fowl, then the desserts, coffee, and again Calvados.' This is still something of the pattern followed at a Norman wedding-breakfast, which takes place often in a large barn open to the green freshness of a Norman apple-orchard, or, in summer, in the orchard itself; a joyful *kermesse* that continues, with music, songs and dancing, and frequent libations, late into the night, or rather morning, only perhaps to be resumed with renewed ardour on the following day. But this is for high days and holidays, exceptional junketings; still for all that, the Norman eats exceptionally well; no puritan disposition prevents him from enjoying the fruits of the earth and sea with which a bountiful nature has blessed Normandy in such prodigal abundance.

The traveller has only to enter Normandy to be aware of the luxuriance of its countryside, its fields, meadows, orchards, farmyards, gardens; its woods replete with game, its streams with speckled trout. He observes the quality of the sleek cattle, the plump sheep, well-fed pigs, the prime geese, ducks and farmyard cocks; even the domestic goats and rabbits. Then let him be present at the quayside, when the

fishing boats return to unload their prolific catch. Or better still, let
him visit the early morning market in, say Rouen, or those held weekly
on Saturday mornings in towns like Dieppe and Honfleur; and he will
see the excellence of the raw material on which the Norman cook
executes, with devotion and skill, those transformations which constitute in their regional peculiarities the distinctive *cuisine normande*.
Worthy to be noted is the presence of *boucheries, charcuteries, laiteries* and
poissoneries around the market itself, a fact which goes a long way to
explain the general superiority, at all levels, of French cooking, since
it presupposes *choice* (and its corollary, competition)—for no self-
respecting French housewife would forgo the privilege and prerogative
of selecting, of choosing—and no salesman could ignore the custom,
and survive. What first strikes the eye in Norman markets are the huge
blocks of fresh dairy butter and those cavernous bowls of thick, velvety
cream, *onctueuse*, the colour of ivory; and it is these two ingredients that
form the essential groundwork of typically Norman cooking. They are
used lavishly; and both seem to have some miraculous quality of con-
verting with apparently little effort into the most perfectly smooth and
rich sauces, which may be blended and enlivened by the addition of
cider, wine or Calvados. Then there are the heaps of cheeses, most now
from factories, but not a few brought to market by the farmwife herself—Camembert, Pont-l'Evêque, Livarot, Neufchâtel, the *petit-
suisse, demi-sel* and *double-crème* of Gournay, and other local varieties
without number. And the vegetables, all cleaned and neatly displayed:
the white-green cauliflowers, slim young carrots, crisp radishes, arti-
chokes, slender leeks, baby turnips, asparagus, tomatoes (with the ample
flesh beneath the skin, not like the miserable, tasteless Canary Islanders),
savoys, onions (both Spanish and spring), endives, lettuces—all of a
tantalising freshness. Then there is the poultry, both alive and dead;
the kids, rabbits, game, the brown and white eggs, all straight from the
farm. Every market seems to have some old black-shawled women who
specialise in fresh herbs from their gardens, carefully tied bunches of
chervil, chives, parsley, sorrel, chicory or other seasonal necessities for
delicious salads. If one chances to enter a *boucherie*, immediately one is
aware of the cleanliness and the skill, worthy of a surgeon, with which
the meat is prepared—the bone, sinews, gristle and surplus fat are all
removed; there is no waste anywhere in the *faux fillet* or in the boned
and rolled shoulder of lamb, that delicious *pré-salé* lamb from pastures
by the sea in the Cotentin. And of the veal and pork their wholesome
pinkness reveal their tenderness and quality; even the pig's head in the

window, with the whole lemon in his mouth and the chaplet of parsley encircling his head, seems smiling, as if from a succulent reverie.

It is difficult to decide which gives the greater pleasure—the *poissoneries* or the *charcuteries*. Here again the fish is so fresh, so translucently fresh, redolent of our pale grey northern seas: the great flat turbots and their cousins the brill (*barbue*), the fearsome skates and John Dorys, and beside them the slippered elegance of the soles; the thick cod and slimmer haddock; the silvered mackerel, striped with its blues and blacks; the angry pink gurnet; the dark-red lobster (*homard*), crayfish (*langouste*) and the delicate prawns (*langoustines*); heaps of pale shrimps and boxes of pearl-like smelts; scallops in their reddish-brown shells, and brownish crabs, and the paler reds and browns of the mosaic of little shell-fish; and, their colour the foil to all this chromatic kaleidoscope—huge baskets, overflowing with tiny black-blue-black mussels. In aerated tanks swim the quite delicious Norman trout—delicious, that is, if you have them cooked in any way save that of the ubiquitous *truite aux amandes*, where the almonds roughly overpower the delicacy of flavour and of texture of the fish.

Ah, but the *charcuteries*. It is no easy matter to decide here, for the Norman *charcutier* holds a very high place indeed among other regions in this particular branch of the culinary art, which is raised to such perfection by the French. In any sizeable town there will be an astonishing number of *patisseries* and *charcuteries*; this again illustrates the element of choice (and competition). The French housewife is not fond of the baking of cakes or tarts (unlike her English or American counterparts), nor does she very often cook *pâtés* or *terrines*. She will go out and buy what and when she pleases; but she *knows*. She knows just who provides the best *pâté de campagne* or *rillettes d'oie*, the same way as she will know on what days Lemaistre's bake their excellent open apple tart or Dupont the *petit fours* in which he excels. If I had my way, I would seldom lunch at a French restaurant; I would walk round to my favourite *charcuterie*, and there make, after quite difficult deliberation (it takes thought and time), my purchases; and then stopping at the *boulangerie* and again next door, where I had noticed a perfect *doyenne du comice*, make my way to a café in the *place*, where I knew *on peut apporter son manger*. And how could deliberation have taken less time, when there is such abundance to choose from?—hams, cooked or smoked both local and from Auvergne; varieties of sausage too lengthy to be listed, but including *boudin*, *andouillette*, plain garlic sausage and the excellent *andouille de Vire*, black, made of lightly smoked chitterlings.

Of the *pâtés* and *terrines*—where possibly could we begin—*pâté campagne* (*de maison*), *pâté de foie gras* (with or without truffles), *pâté de canard*, or for a change *pâté de canard au porto*, both Rouen specialities; *terrine de gibier*, *terrine de lièvre*, *pâté en croûte*, *pâté de foie de volaille*, and *rillettes*, those soft, stringed, delicious kinds of potted pork, so good in Normandy; the numerous *galantines*, and sausage and chicken in aspic. Then all those marvellous made-up dishes from *coquilles St-Jacques* and stuffed pig's trotters to feather-light *vol-au-vents*; and ready-prepared salads—prawn, Niçoise, potato, *celeri rémoulade*, fennel, tomato, olives, anchovies, herrings in brine, smoked salmon and trout. . . . And then about mid-day the hot dishes arrive from the oven. . . .

As may well be imagined, the *cuisine normande* is based firmly on the excellence of the meat and fish, the prodigious use of beautifully fresh butter and cream, and the flavour imparted by cider (although many cooks, particularly in restaurants, use white wine in preference) and Calvados. For those who require some ready means to counteract all this richness there is the unfailing recourse at hand—the *trou normand*. By way of *hors d'œuvres* the Normans recommend, and rightly, their *rillettes*, the moist and delicate shredded pork *terrine*, the various *andouillettes* and above all the *andouille de Vire*, which despite its slightly off-putting appearance is delicious. Dieppe claims to be the place of origin not only of *sole dieppoise* but also of *coquilles St-Jacques*—and *moules marinière*. Mrs Elizabeth David, in her wholly admirable *French Provincial Cooking*, confesses that one of the first things she eats on landing in Northern France and the last before she returns across the Channel is a dish of mussels; nowhere else, she writes, do they seem 'to have quite the *cachet*, the particular savour, of those mussels of Normandy, so small and sweet in their shining little shells'. The simplest (and in so much cooking the simplest is the best) way to serve mussels is *moules marinière*, a plate heaped high with black shells, open to reveal the little saffron-coloured fish in their beds of sky-blue—which have been cooked in a *bouillon*, with cider (or white wine), shallots, chopped celery tops, lots of parsley, and some freshly ground black pepper. A somewhat grander version of this is *moules à la normande*, the mussels, which have been cooked similarly, being served in a thick sauce, made from the fish stock, to which cream and butter have been added. And then there is the quite delicious fish soup, *potage crème normande*, which has as its ingredients good white fish, crayfish and prawns, vegetables, garlic, herbs, mace, cider and cream.

The three ways of cooking sole which are most closely associated

with Normandy are *sole dieppoise, sole à la normande* and *sole deauvillaise*.
A simpler, and perhaps a much older, method of preparing sole than
these is that sometimes known as *sole en matelote à la normande*, which
may have been the primitive version from which *sole à la normande* was
evolved—perhaps not by Norman chefs, by the way, but possibly first
by the Parisian Carême and then modified by Langlais, the famous
chef at the Rocher de Cancale restaurant in Paris early in the last
century. The *matelote* is usually of fish cooked in red wine but here, in
this case, it refers to a sole baked in the oven, with mussels, cider, an
onion, butter and parsley. There is no one generally recognised version
of *sole normande*, and one needs to beware. And even with *sole dieppoise*
it is foolish to ask for it in an ordinary restaurant, perhaps crowded in
the season; it requires careful and individual treatment to avoid disappointment. It seems that this has been so for a long time, since John
McNeill Whistler used to go to a particular restaurant in Dieppe run
by the Veuve Bellet (alas, no longer there), who prided herself that the
painter had told her that nowhere else could he get a *sole dieppoise*
really well cooked. The sole is first poached in cider (or white wine),
with butter, salt and black pepper; meanwhile prawns and mussels
will be prepared separately, and poached in water. When all are
cooked, the fluids in which they have been poached are amalgamated,
reduced, butter and cream added, and brought slowly to the velvety
consistency of thick cream. This sauce is poured over the sole, and the
prawns and mussels added. This can be a beautiful dish. In *sole deauvillaise* the fillets of fish are poached, then a sauce prepared of onion,
cider, butter, cream, French mustard, nutmeg, lemon, salt and pepper
is poured over them, bread-crumbs are sprinkled over the dish, and it
is browned before serving. Norman chefs often use any good white
fish, such as turbot, brill or John Dory, in place of sole, and cook them
either as in the *matelote* or *à la deauvillaise*. The shrimps and prawns of
Honfleur are highly praised, as well as the mussels of Villerville nearby
and of Isigny, the oysters of Courseulles (bought for 50 *centimes* the
dozen in 1914!) and St-Vaast, and the magnificent lobsters (*homards*)
of Cap de la Hague and Barfleur in the Cotentin. Although Normandy
has no wine, from neighbouring Maine comes the excellent Muscadet,
which is a perfect wine to drink with fish. This comes from the *melon*
vine of Burgundy, which, transplanted to the pebbly soil around
Nantes on the Loire, is dry and has an attractive bouquet.

For the main course I must limit myself to mentioning *poulet Vallée-
d'Auge, tripes à la mode de Caen, faisan à la cauchoise* and *canard* (or *caneton*)

à la Rouennaise or *au sang* or *à la presse* or *à la Duclair*. The Vallée d'Auge, being one of the richest districts in Normandy, famed for its cider and Calvados as well as for its cheeses, has given its name to this extremely rich way of serving a chicken in a thick sauce made from fresh cream and Calvados. Here again one does well to know one's restaurant. *Tripes à la mode de Caen* is a most formidable dish for anyone to prepare, since it is best cooked in quantity and consists of the stomach of an ox, its four feet, onions (four pounds of them!), carrots, leeks, herbs, cider and a half-pint of good Calvados. In Normandy *tripes* are sold cooked in little brown earthenware bowls at most reputable *charcuteries*. This is an excellent dish when it has been carefully compounded, as it is at Le Rabelais restaurant in Caen, the flavour being most distinguished; but I for one find it so glutinous that my lips have frequently to be unstuck by recourse to the *trou normand*—but then, one reason is as good as another. The famous duck or duckling of Rouen (and of Duclair, which is a few miles down the Seine from Rouen, and is also celebrated for its own variety of *canard* and *caneton*) is a cross between the domestic bird and the wild variety from the Seine valley, which accounts for its distinctly gamey flavour. In order to retain the blood, the duck is strangled; it is stuffed and partly roasted, the breast then being cut in long slices and *flambéed* in Cognac or Calvados; the thighs are grilled, and the carcass pressed to extract the blood and juices, which form the basis for a rich sauce. Perhaps the best place to try the different ways of cooking Norman duck is at Duclair at the Parc restaurant, where Mme Schmitt can also offer you duck *pâté* and her version of *sole normande*. The Normans serve their pheasant with apples—this is the well-known dish of *faisan à la cauchoise* or simply *faisan normand*. The pheasant is cooked gently in butter in a *cocotte*; when it is ready it is carved and kept warm, while the juices are put into a pan into which Calvados is poured and set alight, then cream added, and the thickened sauce is poured over the pheasant pieces. This is served with sweet apple fried in butter until golden.

As we should naturally expect, apples figure prominently in Norman puddings: there is delicious *soufflé* flavoured with Calvados and served with macaroons and apple, a speciality of Rouen, which also has a sweetmeat which goes by the name of *sucre de pommes*; and then there is *tarte aux pommes normande*. But all the fruit tarts are delicious, the pastry rich with fresh butter; I remember a *tarte aux prunes*, which I tasted in Dieppe in 1939, whose memory will remain with me until my dying day. Equally attractive can be the sweet *fromage à la crème*, accompanied by a plate of fresh strawberries or raspberries. And another word, while we are on the subject of Norman dishes—the famous omelettes of Mère Poulard in Mont-St-Michel, which are quite unlike any other you have tried, as light as air, tasting of the fresh eggs, the butter and cream, with which alone they are made. Colonel Newnham-Davies wrote about the numerous Poulard restaurants at the Mount in 1903, and there are still two today, both claiming to be the 'original house'.

In that gourmet's guide to the eating places of Europe—surely he must have been unique in being English, military and a gourmet—the colonel writes of a meal eaten in the Norman countryside at the village of Martin-Eglise, a few miles south-east of Dieppe:

> A Norman gate has above it a thatched roof, and the long roof to this gate also shelters an array of white clothed tables. Beyond is an orchard where wooden tables are set under the trees. . . . We go through the orchard to the trout-stream which, with a pleasant gurgle, runs between grass-covered banks. The water is crystal clear, and moves the long green weed in it softly to and fro. The shadows above the pebbles are trout, which are rarely to be caught at this point with a fly, but which by some means or another are regularly transferred from the stream to the tank in the barn. Hidden by trees, but its presence made clear by the clack-clack-clack of its wheel, is the mill driven by this stream. Across the water are meadows in which placid cows graze, and in the shadow of a pollarded willow an old peasant sleeps. The apple trees by this brook shelter the most favoured tables, and one of these we secure and sit on rush-bottomed chairs to look at our neighbours while the trout are being cooked. . . . A little flock of geese take to the water and swim upstream, keeping just level with our tree, their beady eyes on the alert for any crumbs that may be thrown them. . . . A waiter in shabby dress clothes . . . presently comes shuffling over the grass with his arms full of hot plates, two bottles of cider, and a covered dish in which sizzles the trout. . . .

Such in 1903 was the beautiful and peaceful setting of the Clos Normand at Martin-Eglise. It is there still.

Like other provinces of France, Normandy has many inns and restaurants set in *clos* or in picturesque spots by rivers or the sea, or which retain their Norman furnishing of former times. It would be invidious in a book of this kind to single out restaurants or inns as being superior to others which cannot be named here; however, I am giving a list of some places which are most attractive—with the warning that there are so many others, perhaps even superior to these:

Les Andelys, *La Chaine d'Or*, inn on the Seine.

Avranches, *Croix d'Or*, garden.

Caudebec-en-Caux, *Le Manoir de Rétival*.

Clécy, *Le Moulin de Vey*, inn on the Orne.

Commes, *Hostellerie du Bosc*, eighteenth-century country house.

Conteville, *Auberge du Vieux Logis*.

Duclair, *Le Parc*, on the Seine.

Fécamp-St-Lionard, *Auberge de la Rouge*.

Fourges, *Moulin de Fourges*, old mill on the Epte.

Gisors, *Hostellerie des Trois Poissons*.

Honfleur, *Ferme St-Siméon*, view over Seine estuary.

       Ferme de la Grande Cour, farm in orchards.

       Roche Vasouy, view over Seine estuary.

Houlgate, *Ferme des Aulnettes*, farm in orchard.

       Ferme Vimard, Norman *chaumière*.

       Ferme du Lieu Marot, in orchards.

Ivry-la-Bataille, *Moulin d'Ivry*, on the Eure.

Lyons-la-Forêt, *La Licorne*, garden.

Martin-Eglise, *Auberge Clos Normand*, rustic interior, on stream.

Mesnil-Val, *La Vieille Ferme*, Norman farmhouse near sea.

Orbec, *Au Caneton*, old Norman setting.

       Equerre, old Norman setting.

Pins-au-Haras, *Hostellerie Tourne-Bride*, on edge of wood, old furniture.

Pont-Audemer, *Auberge Vieux Puits*, seventeeth-century inn.

Pont-l'Evêque, *L'Aigle d'Or*, ancient coaching inn.

Port-Villez, *La Gueulardière*, setting.

Rouen, *La Couronne*, claims to be oldest exsisting restaurant in France (1345).

St-Adrien, *Manoir de Becquet*, ancient priory with view over Seine.

St-Ouen-sous-Bailly, *Prieuré Bailly Bec*, old house and garden.

Tôtes, *Hôtel du Cygne*, ancient inn, literary associations.

Varengeville, *Les Sapins*, garden.

Villequier, *Le Grand Sapin*, on the Seine.

Villerville, *Manoir de Grand-Bec*, terrace overlooking sea.

       Chez Mahu, to eat outside.

Vironvay, *Les Saisons*, garden.

Yport, *Le Deun*, overlooking sea.

As a museum piece it is amusing to read the menu for dinner at the Hôtel de Normandie in Le Havre before the First World War; this is not, by the way, *à la carte* but *table d'hôte*, and a *maigre* one at that, its having been a fast day, Good Friday.

Bisque d'Ecrevisses
Reine Christine
Filets de Sole Normandie
Nouillettes Napolitaine en Caisse
Saumon de Loire Tartare
Sorbets Suprême Fécamp
Coquille de Homard à l'Américaine
Sarcelles sur Canapé
Salade panachée
Asperges d'Argenteuil Mousseline
Petits Pois au Sucre
Glace Quo Vadis
Petits Fours   Corbeille de Fruits
Dessert

'Garçon, please, another *trou normand*, and quickly!'

CHAPTER XIII

Barbey d'Aurevilly, Chouans and Legends

LATE IN THE year 1829 Jules-Amédée Barbey, twenty-one years old and fresh from the Collège Stanislas in Paris, arrived in Caen, where he took a room in the *pension* of Mme Lefoulon, No. 2 Place Malherbe, and entered the faculty of law at the university. At this time Barbey was fired with republican ardour, at odds with the inherited ideas and aspirations (limitations, in his eyes) of his conservative family, spurning the addition of the 'd'Aurevilly' to which, in the rather curious usage of the French nobility, he was entitled as a member of the *petite noblesse*, the squirearchy of the Cotentin. He was born in 1808 at St-Sauveur-le-Vicomte, and was brought up there and at the neighbouring town of Valognes, the centre at once somewhat pretentious and not a little absurd of a provincial, lesser aristocracy, which is well summed up in the expression sometimes used of the town and its society—'*le petit Versailles normand*'. Devoted to the causes of Monarchy and Church, those latter-day cavaliers of La Manche had still strong memories of the *Chouannerie*, the insurrections, which spread to these parts from La Vendée, against the Revolutionary government in the years after 1789; and it was here in 1832, following the exile of Charles X two years earlier, that the Duchess of Berry turned, when she tried to rouse the countryside in support of the restoration of the Bourbons. The young Barbey would have none of all this; his mind at the time was on other matters. In Caen he met a learned, crippled antiquarian book-seller, Guillaume-Stanislas Trebutien, and the two had much in common in their views on literature and politics, which they wished to publicise by founding a paper, *La Revue de Caen*, aided financially in their venture by Barbey's cousin, the well-to-do Edelestand du Méril. But what engrossed his whole being, almost to the exclusion of liter-ature, the *Revue* and certainly the law, was his love for du Méril's sister-in-law, '*Elle*', Louise des Costils, who in 1830 had entered into one of those frequent *mariages de convenance*, arranged in families of their class and time, with a man considerably older than herself, Alfred du Méril, from Valognes. The love of Barbey and Louise was mutual and violent; Barbey spent much of his time at his cousin's château of

Marcelet, which is some few miles west of Caen, near what is today the Carpiquet aerodrome; and Louise frequently visited him in his Caen *pension*. It appears that some scandal was on the point of breaking out, when in 1833 Barbey, having taken his degree and seriously quarrelled with his family, left Caen for Paris. It seems that there was little love between Louise and her husband, but on both sides the families were shocked, fearing their good name; Edelestand withdrew his money from the *Revue*, and Barbey's quarrel with his family, although in part caused by their reluctance to make over to him a legacy legally his, must be seen as the result of conduct which appeared to these conservative souls as nothing less than scandalous.

The impossibility of Barbey's passion for Louise du Méril, a love which tortured him for some eight years, left its mark for life; his experience, coloured as it was by his sense of failure to achieve happiness with Louise, became with the passage of years generalised into an ineradicable pessimism, a conviction of the hopelessness of all love, a deep and confirmed misanthropy, which he extended to himself as well as to others. With the years, the only solution short of suicide that lay to hand was the relief that he obtained from the actual working out of his own personal problems in literature, by the projection in his writing of his own imagined predicament in the events and characters of his stories and novels. It was at this time, the first period of his living in Paris, when he was obliged to eke out his meagre monetary resources by the wretched profession of miscellaneous journalism, that he adopted, as an armour to protect his pride and heart against the harshness of his view of the world, the fastidiousness of dress and the supercilious manner of the accomplished dandy. Visitors to the Barbey d'Aurevilly museum in the castle of St-Sauveur-le-Vicomte may see to what fantastic lengths he carried this narcissistic splendour. In Caen Barbey seems to have met Beau Brummell, who had held the appointment of H.M. Consul there from 1830 to 1832; and Brummell, even in his reduced condition, weighed down in body and spirit by his accumulated debts, who was to end his pitiful career in the asylum of the Bon-Sauveur, made a powerful impression on Barbey d'Aurevilly, as he was to style himself thenceforth. From that time he adopted the tightly-waisted frock-coats, the elegantly slim trousers strapped under the instep, the cravats of *point de Venise*, the exquisite lace handkerchiefs, the capes with linings of coloured silk, in which, unless he exchanged the latter for the rough waggoner's cloak, the *limousine* from his native Cotentin, he was to adorn himself until his death in 1889, the familiar

figure, becoming increasingly anachronistic, of the Paris boulevards.
Sainte-Beuve wrote of him: 'At a time when nothing any longer
appeared ridiculous, he found the means of appearing so. An intelligent man would blush to cross Paris with him, even during the Carnival.'

Restless and wretched in Paris, harassed by the persistent need to
earn enough money even from the most sordid journalism (he descended
to writing fashion notes) to pay for his extravagances and the de-
bauchery (if it was that) in which he tried to forget himself, Barbey
seems seldom to have revisited the Cotentin, perhaps not until the early
fifties, when Mme de Bouglon, whom he thought he might marry,
persuaded him to become reconciled with his family. And yet the
settings and much of the plots of his stories and of his three best novels
are firmly placed in Normandy—his writings are, in fact, redolent,
saturated with the scents and 'feel' of the Norman countryside and of
the life in its small towns, places like Valognes, Coutances or Avranches.
The region of La Manche has been considered one of the most super-
stition-ridden in France at the time when Barbey grew up there—in
these towns which were so open to, so encompassed by, this strange
haunted country of heaths, marshes, hidden, almost buried tracks; of
close woods and hedge-bound fields. Barbey himself tells us that 'the
little poetry that has ever haunted his brain' was imparted to him by
the family servant Jeanne Roussel, a country woman herself, and one
steeped in the oral tradition of tales, historical incidents and fantastic,
diabolical legends, that were told in the cottages by the fireside on the
long winter evenings, when the gales tore inland from the Atlantic and
roared in trees and eaves. It was from members of his own family that
he heard of the historical details, become in time legendary, of heroic
actions performed by the Chouans of the district. Two of his relations,
his great-uncle Lefèbre de Montressel, and his grandmother Lucas-
Lablairie, had been involved personally in the troubles following the
Revolution; and their stories had conjured up in the boy's imagination
a whole world of mystery, heroism, cruelty and underlying tragedy
that was to form the background of his stories and novels.

The *Chouannerie* in the Cotentin was associated with the rising in La
Vendée, which in origin was a protest of the peasants against the
bourgeoisie and the ideas of the Revolution, and in support for those
priests who had refused to submit to the civil constitution of the clergy.
In February 1793, when the Convention ordered a levy on the whole
of France for the defence of the Republic, the Vendéans rose in insurrection, and in this they were joined increasingly by members of

the nobility (Louis XVI had been executed in January), both those who had gone into hiding in France and *émigrés* from the Channel Islands or from England. In that year the royalist leader La Roche-jaquelein attempted to capture Granville, but failed, and the troops fell back on the Vendée. The revolt again spread to Brittany and to Normandy, after Hoche's defeat of the rebels at Quiberon Bay in 1795; there the members of the 'Catholic and Royal Army' were known by the Bas-Breton word *'Chouans'*, 'screech-owls'. Their supporters wore a white cockade, until its wearing was made punishable by death; and the republican soldiers sent against them were known from the colour of their uniforms as the 'Blues'. An insurrection of this kind presented great difficulties for the government; soldiers were sent to rout out men who knew every inch of the district, who were impelled by fierce loyalty to their priests and those nobles who lived among them, who wore no distinguishing uniform—and who, on the word being passed of the coming of the Blues, were given the order to scatter (*'Egaillez-vous, mes gars'*) only to re-form and to attack where least expected. In such circumstances of guerrilla warfare, it can easily be imagined that many acts of cold-blooded cruelty were perpetrated by both sides; the atrocities were the product of both loyalty and fanaticism—and of revenge. One of the most popular (and still remembered) leaders of the Norman Chouans was Count Louis de Frotté, of the family who still own the château of Couterne near Bagnolles, who was betrayed with seven of his companions, and fell before the firing squad at Verneuil, on the orders of Bonaparte.

L'Ensorcelée, The Woman Bewitched, is the first of Barbey d'Aurevilly's three Normandy novels; the others are *Le Chevalier des Touches* and *Un Prêtre Marié. L'Ensorcelée* is a work of great originality and imaginative power, in which the force of Barbey's thought and the intensity of his writing overcome the reader's rational incredulity, so that he finds himself accepting as fact such unlikely themes as the *reality* of super-stition, of bewitching, sorcery and diabolical possession. The tales and legends of the Cotentin and its haunted landscape are not merely the background to the novel, but are essential to the unfolding of the plot; they are woven into the very texture of a book which affects us simul-taneously on several levels. In all Barbey d'Aurevilly's stories and novels, and likewise in his criticism, he refuses to be bound by a straight-forward narration or judgement of the facts; he is absorbed by the irrationality of passion, which grasps us with such overwhelming strength, when we are in its grip, that it does appear that we are truly *possessed.* He was a Freudian before his time. In his view, any strongly held emotion, if worked out, may (*will*) lead to tragedy; similarly, if it is repressed, the end is equally tragic. This pessimistic view, the outcome of his personal experience, is central both to his own life and to his work. On the surface, at least, *L'Ensorcelée* seems a common enough story of sexual frustration and jealousy, bringing suicide and murder in their train.

However, no account of the novel must omit the leading character —Normandy, the Normandy of legends and superstitions, those beliefs, of a people who inhabit the isolated backwater of the Cotentin, where history has for long periods stood still, and men and women have turned in on themselves and gone back for spiritual nourishment to those primitive ideas which were formed in the infancy of the race—and are not the less powerful for that. But this Normandy is a country very different from 'the fresh, smiling, fecund landscape' that we know. It is the province in the aftermath of revolution, when all that is most primitive in the people comes to the surface; and it is seen through the perfervid imagination of Barbey d'Aurevilly.

CHAPTER XIV

The Battle of Normandy

IN JUNE 1944 the Normans, like so many other European peoples, had endured four years of German occupation, but for them there were certain mitigating features that others lacked. After the fall of France, when so many of the young men were held prisoner by the Germans, and the subsequent deportation of others to work in the factories in Germany, the Norman peasant farmers took stock of the situation—and went on working as before, assisted by all the able-bodied members of their families. While the coastal areas were guarded mostly by divisions of static troops, more inland areas were used as training grounds for the panzer divisions. On the whole the Germans behaved 'correctly', and the Normans were spared the worst brutalities of the SS troops in their treatment of the conquered populations, so that over the years they had reached some practical *modus vivendi*, which was far from being without material advantage to them. This needs to be understood, in order to explain the attitude of the Normans to the Allies. The rich, fertile countryside yielded its abundance as before, and the peasants did very well in selling their butter, cheeses, milk, cream, eggs, chickens, and the rest of their produce to the occupiers, finding a certain pleasure, and indeed a pride, in cheating the Germans at every turn. Some collaborated with the enemy, but mostly they treated their enforced guests with a sullen resentment and passive resistance, while they continued to profit by their presence. After the Dieppe raid of 1942, the German staff considered that any main invasion attempts by the Allies would be in the Pas de Calais, although there might be diversionary raids elsewhere, some in force. They therefore disposed their armoured divisions to meet the requirements of the supposed eventuality, in which supposition they were encouraged to believe by the deceptive movements and stratagems of the Allies. However, in the autumn of 1943 Hitler appointed the former Afrika Corps commander Rommel as Inspector-General of Defences in the West, serving nominally under Field-Marshal von Rundstedt as Commander-in-Chief Forces West with his headquarters in Paris, although as a field-marshal Rommel had direct access to Hitler.

Rommel strengthened the coastal defences of the so-called Western Wall and incorporated Caen, as a most important centre of communications, in this system, moving there in May 1944 the 21st Panzer Division. The Normans accepted the Germans' assertion that the Western Wall was impenetrable by a sea-borne landing and that any forces that did get a temporary foothold would be speedily met by the movement of armoured divisions, held in reserve farther inland, and cast back into the sea. In Rommel's own words, 'the first twenty-four hours would be decisive'—decisive, that is, in the complete defeat of any Allied landing. In spite of the increased tempo of Allied bombing, not only of the coastal areas, but of railway marshalling yards, radio and radar stations, communications and bridges deeper into the country north of Paris, Rommel left Normandy on 5 June to visit Hitler at his headquarters in East Prussia. He did not know that just off the Norman coast were already lying in position, one opposite the mouth of the River Orne and one farther to the west, two small submarines, the markers for the landing craft of operation 'Overlord'.

In the early hours of D-day, 6 June 1944 (bad weather had delayed the assault by twenty-four hours), parachute troops dropped at the eastern and western extremities of the planned landing area, capturing the bridge over the Orne, which is now known as Pegasus Bridge, and destroying the powerful enemy battery at Merville; and taking the small town of Ste-Mère-Eglise at the foot of the Cotentin peninsula. Then at 7.25, preceded by a cataclysmic barrage against the shore defences from waves of heavy and medium bombers and fighters, from battleships, cruisers and destroyers, and from guns and rockets mounted on landing craft, the first troops came ashore and the liberation of France began. The landings were effected at five points: the American 1st Army under General Bradley at Utah Beach, opposite St-Martin-de-Varreville in the Cotentin, and at Omaha Beach, just east of Vierville-sur-Mer; the British 2nd Army under General Sir Miles Dempsey at Arromanches (Gold Beach), Courseulles (Juno Beach) and about Luc-sur-Mer (Sword Beach). The land operations were commanded by General Sir Bernard Montgomery under the supreme commander of all Allied forces in Europe, General Dwight Eisenhower. Montgomery's plan was, once the perilous landing had been successfully achieved, to hold a bridgehead sufficiently extensive to allow men and material to be built up at a rate appreciably quicker than the Germans could be reinforced. The superiority of German armour and anti-tank guns, 75-mm and 88-mm in calibre, was to be countered by Allied aerial supremacy. The enemy armoured divisions were to be drawn on to the eastern flank, held by British and Canadians, and there weakened by aerial and ground attack, so that a breakout could be effected in the west by General Patton and the American armoured divisions. A wide encircling movement was envisaged, driving deep into France, one arm towards Brittany, the other towards Paris and the Seine. Another prong of Patton's attack would turn north to meet the eastern prong of this pincer movement, advancing via Caen and Falaise. Thus the German forces in Lower Normandy would be encircled and systematically destroyed from the air and ground. From the outset Montgomery wanted to keep the enemy guessing, to have him, as he termed it, continually 'off balance'.

Two crack German armoured divisions, the 12th SS (Hitler Jugend) and the Panzer Lehr, commanded by the experienced Afrika Corps officer Bayerlein, were ordered to advance on 7 June, to co-operate with the 21st Panzer Division near Caen, and in attempting to do so were very badly mauled by Allied aircraft armed with cannon and rockets. German aircraft seldom appeared, save by night. Very soon the panzers found that it was impossible to move by daylight. It was the same with other troop movements. A German war-historian has left it on record: 'Once a tank was spotted it was finished. Mercilessly it would be dive-bombed or attacked, until a bomb or a volley of fire from cannon or rockets had written paid to it.' From D-day + 1, 7 June, the Allies had secured their bridgehead and pushed inland, and the boast of the German armour that it would throw them back into the sea was unfulfilled. Instead of being able to concentrate the 500 vastly superior tanks at his disposal, to effect a crushing defeat on the Allies, Rommel was forced from the beginning to use them in a more or less static role, to employ their splendid guns as artillery to plug the many weak spots in his purely defensive lines. It quickly became obvious that the Allies were winning in the vitally important build-up of men and material. By 18 June (just before the 'Great Storm' of the 19th, the worst experienced for forty years, which did extensive damage to Allied shipping and their artificial 'Mulberry' harbours), Montgomery had some twenty divisions, about half a million men and their equipment, already ashore.

The British on the left had too optimistically thought to capture Caen on D-day, but this was to be denied them for many weeks of costly fighting; yet it proved very costly for the Germans also; and they could not afford such losses. However, in the west the Americans, pushing on from Utah Beach, had captured Carentan on 12 June and cut the Cotentin peninsula by reaching the sea at Barneville on the 17th. On 29 June Cherbourg fell, and, despite the most devastating demolitions carried out by the Germans, the Allies now had a first-class port at their disposal, which could be linked direct with England by the underwater fuel pipeline known as 'Pluto'.

The Allies had been surprised and hurt by the reception of the Normans; they imagined that they would be recognised as liberators, and treated as such. Instead they were looked on sullenly by the local population, even by some with suspicion. The Normans had seen their towns, farms, fields and livestock bombed by the Allies; and the Germans had impressed on them that this was a mere diversion; the Allies would be driven off, and the Germans remain. Attempts made by Allied troops to fraternise were not very successful; nor were attempts to do business much better; the farmers and their wives drove hard bargains for fresh foodstuffs, when they would sell at all. On the entry of the troops of the British 2nd Army into untouched Bayeux on the afternoon of D-day, they were astonished to find mounds of unrationed butter, and plenty of cheeses, cream and eggs. This was not the starving population of Europe they had been told of. Nor did the able-bodied men whom they saw about have the appearance of freedom-fighters, members of the French resistance. The troops were deeply shocked, and not a little disenchanted with the Normans. The traditional characteristics attributed to the Norman peasantry of unrelenting suspicion and relentless money-grubbing seemed only too well-founded. At first. It was only when it was apparent that the Allies were there to stay, that the Germans might be losing, and ultimately when the tide of the battle passed rapidly on, that the Normans softened in their attitude, saw that others also were cruelly suffering (and for them), and finally welcomed their liberators. Typical of this changed sentiment was the grave of a Canadian soldier on the outskirts of ruined Caen, on which every day was placed a bunch of fresh flowers.

By 10 July, when the Allies had more than a million men in Normandy, Montgomery considered that the time was ripe to launch two great offensives. Firstly, in the east by the British and Canadians, to clear the Caen area and drive south for Falaise, and at the same time holding and 'writing down' (that is, destroying) the mass of German armour opposed to them. Rommel had at his command in this region of defensive depth some hundreds of Tiger and other tanks, 100 long-range 88-mm anti-tank guns, 200 pieces of artillery and 272 six-barrelled mortars (*nebelwerfers*, 'Moaning Minnies'). The attack, code-named 'Goodwood', opened on 18 July (the day after Rommel had been put out of action, when his car was shot up from the air), Caen was successfully cleared of Germans, and a severe dent had been made in the carefully planned German defensive positions, but the impetus of the attack was slowed down and halted only a few miles south of the city. Nevertheless, von Kluge, the new German commander, had immediately to withdraw another armed division from the western field of operations to reinforce his depleted armour in the east. This was very much what Montgomery had intended should occur. Some 654 German tanks were massed against the British and Canadians, as well as most of the formidable 88-mm anti-tank guns; opposite General Patton in the west were only about 190 tanks.

The second phase of Montgomery's 'master plan' was now set in train, that known as 'Cobra', which was to prove decisive in the battle of Normandy. On 24 July General Bradley began a 'saturation' aerial bombing over a limited area to the south of the St-Lô–Périers road, and he followed this up with an even heavier bombardment from both air and ground on the following day. This bombardment almost obliterated the excellent Panzer Lehr Division; the effects were terrifying, men went mad and ran about in the open, until splinters cut them down. Patton, with his seven highly-trained armoured divisions, the American 3rd Army, was poised to go. On 28 July Coutances was captured; two days later the Americans were in Avranches and heading south over the one road open to them, pouring into the heart of France. In three days the incredible Patton pushed 100,000 men and 15,000 vehicles through this narrow outlet. Immediately the American 1st Army and the British 2nd Army began to widen the gap open on the western flank of the Germans, the British directed towards Caumont. Meanwhile, in the west the Canadians attempted to thrust towards Falaise. On 7 August Hitler personally ordered the German armour to attack westerly from Mortain, to cut off Patton and his Americans. It failed; and Patton fanned out into Brittany, south towards the Loire and east towards Paris and the Seine. On 15 August the Allies landed in the South of France. The American 3rd Army with its abundance of armour could now turn north and hammer the Germans' southern flank around Argentan and elsewhere. On 14 August the Germans began what was first an orderly withdrawal; but as the threat of being cut off by the closing of the pincer movement at the narrow 'Falaise gap' became imminent, and the Allied air attacks on the crowded roads increased in ferocity, the withdrawal became a rout. The Canadians took Falaise on 17 August, and finally the neck of the pocket was sealed by the meeting of American and Canadian troops at Chambois on 19 August. On 22 August the battle of Normandy was won; the German army, save for those in High Normandy and those fleeing towards the remaining Seine bridges, no longer existed. The German casualties have never been accurately calculated, but must have been in the region of 500,000 men. The Allied ground forces lost 210,000, which included 37,000 killed; and high as the cost of victory was, it will be remembered that in the unsuccessful Dardanelles campaign of the First World War the Allies' losses were some 250,000. The damage to the towns and villages of Normandy through which the battle raged was enormous. The Normans paid a great price for the liberation of France. Today, nearly thirty years afterwards, the scars have long been healed; but when, motoring through the tranquil Norman landscapes, we enter remote villages or small market towns (to say nothing of Caen, St-Lô, Valognes or Argentan), the beautifully rebuilt houses and churches bear witness in their striking modernity, their very newness, to the ancient, destroyed buildings they replace.

It was a Norman, M. E. Lemaigre, a French army officer held prisoner of war in Germany while his country was being liberated, who in a book written by Normans, on their native country (*La Normandie*, edited by M. Adrien Pommier), has furnished an eloquent epilogue to those fierce contests, this expense of life and treasure, which may serve equally as an epitaph on those who died:

> All of you, you citizens of free America, children of Texas or of Missouri; you Canadians from the Great Lakes, the descendants from our old Dieppe families; you British, who share with us a common ancestor in William; and all of you, our friends under whatever flag you be; all you, who have fallen on our soil, sleep in peace. Sleep in peace in our rich Norman earth, under the shadow of your white crosses. Sleep in peace under our apple-trees, you are here at home. . . .

CHAPTER XV

Mont-St-Michel

ST MICHAEL'S MOUNT has been, and is, known under so many different names: Mont-Tombe, St-Michel-en-Tombe, St-Michel-en-Mer, St-Michel-au-Péril-de-la-Mer (by reason of the danger to unwary pilgrims from its treacherous quicksands and the rapidity of the incoming tides), St-Michel-du-Mont, Mont-St-Michel; to local inhabitants it is simply *Le Mont*, but to those who favour superlatives it is La Merveille de l'Occident, The Marvel of the West, which is often shortened to The Marvel *tout court*—unfortunate this last, since a particularly beautiful group of gothic buildings on the Mount is also, and perhaps more appropriately, known as La Merveille. This is not to suggest that Mont-St-Michel is not marvellous; it *is* marvellous (the word is inescapable); marvellous in its situation, this mountain-isle rising warm-pink out of the pearl-grey sea or of the grey-brown sea of sand; marvellous in its construction of superimposed vaulting and sheer granite-faced walls, on which rise the abbey church and monastic buildings; in its beauty, the perfection of the gothic architecture of the thirteenth and fifteenth centuries; and, perhaps above all, in its conception, in this magnificent gesture of faith. But it is not always easy for the casual visitor to see it in those conditions when its uniqueness is most discernible or palpable. One reason for this is demographic: Mont-St-Michel is one of the greatest historical monuments of France, ranking only after those of Paris and Versailles in its attraction of tourists; and it is a centre of pilgrimage, so that unless the visitor is both devout and democratic he should be elsewhere on the first Sunday in May and on 29 September, the festivals of St Michael. It will be remembered that on a day in the summer as many as 6,000 will pay their admission to the abbey. There is a further consideration, an aesthetic one: to see Mont-St-Michel at its most entrancing, it should be seen as an island, and this will require the presence of a spring tide, which happens but twice a month, some thirty-six hours after the new and full moon. Then we may hire a boat, and from the sea, as we pass slowly around its shore, gain some truer comprehension of its isolated majesty. To take in all that there is to see of architectural value on Mont-St-Michel will require more than one escorted visit; it is better, therefore, to stay a night or so, either in the town or the district, which will allow us to see the Mount at sunrise or sunset—and perhaps, if the visit is planned ahead, as it really ought to be, in the radiance and enchantment of moonlight.

The Archangel Michael, the Prince of the Heavenly Armies and the armed Protector of the Church on Earth, is very close to the Normans; the Mount was considered his property, and the saint himself was the patron of the Norman Dukes, and after them the Kings of France. In this they followed Charlemagne, who made St Michael patron of his Empire, with three favoured sanctuaries: Monte Gargano in Italy, Michelsberg in Bavaria (where in a strenuous fight with Satan the Archangel lost a wing feather), and here on the confines of Normandy with Brittany. The connections of the Normans with Monte Gargano were also close; it was on a visit to the shrine there in 1017 that a party of Normans, returning from the Holy Land, were persuaded to intervene in the warfare between Lombards and Byzantines, and from this small but auspicious beginning sprang the Norman Kingdom of the Two Sicilies under the de Hauteville family. But this is to anticipate. In order to sift some truth from the mass of legends which have grown up around the foundation of a Christian sanctuary on Mont-Tombe, as it was then known, we may accept that it was brought about at the beginning of the eighth century (708 is the usually accepted date) by Aubert, Bishop of Avranches. From his high cathedral town he had looked out over the flat strands, awash at high tide, towards this rocky pinnacle, which perhaps suggested in miniature the mountain in Apulia on which the Archangel had once descended and forcibly erased all trace of earlier Mithraism. On Mont-Tombe there had likewise been a temple dedicated to Mithras, to the *sol invictus*; what could be more fitting than that Aubert should erect on its summit a Christian oratory? To Monte Gargano Aubert dispatched emissaries (it may be he himself went with them), who returned with the blessings of the Apulian monks, and two relics of St Michael—a piece of his mantle and a portion of the marble on which he had stood. The popular legend recounts how St Michael had come to Aubert in a dream and commanded him to raise a sanctuary in his honour on Mont-Tombe; but the bishop on waking wondered whether it was truly a vision of the Archangel or simply a dream of his own. So he waited, and fasted and prayed. Again St Michael appeared and more peremptorily repeated his order; but still Aubert hesitated, and remembering that it was his duty to try spirits whether they be of good or of evil, continued to fast and to pray. Finally the Archangel, losing heavenly patience, appeared again and gave Aubert a thump on his cranium such that the saint's thumb penetrated the bone structure. This time he knew. After St Aubert's death the skull with its tell-tale aperture was preserved as a relic in the abbey, until the Revolution, when a Dr Guérin saved it in the general spoliation of the art treasures, and at the beginning of last century presented it to the basilica of St-Gervais and St-Protais in Avranches, where it may now be seen—an object of some osteological and miraculous perplexity.

Legend and history are again intermingled in tracing the formation of the Bay of Mont-St-Michel itself. In the fifth and sixth centuries all the expanse of what is now sea from Avranches to Cancale, and farther north, from Granville to the Chausey Isles (and perhaps farther north still), was covered with forests and swamps, an area which was referred to by a monkish writer of the thirteenth century as the Forest of Scissy. Through the southernmost district of the forest flowed the Rivers Sée, Sélune and Couesnon. Very early in the Christian era the sea began to encroach on these regions, where three granite 'mounts', Mont-Tombe, Tombelaine (now the islet, shaped like a crouching lion, to the north-east of Mont-St-Michel), and farther west in Brittany, Mont-Dol, alone resisted the press of the waves. A legend tells of the surprise of the emissaries, on their return from Monte Gargano in 709, to find that the woods which (when they left) surrounded Mont-St-Michel had in that short interval entirely disappeared, and that the isle now floated offshore like a tall ship riding at anchor. It does seem likely that the final encroachment from the sea did take place about this time, but whether it was from a sudden subsidence or some other seismical action, or from the particularly high equinoctial tides of September-October 709—or from a combination of these causes—is not known. The Chausey Islands were certainly not severed from the Granville promontory until as late as the eleventh century. The tides here today constitute an impressive phenomenon; the waters of the North Sea, held back by the Cotentin peninsula, meet the waters of the Atlantic Ocean, build up, and then are unleashed right down this coast, until they finish in the concavity of the Bay of Mont-St-Michel. The difference between high and low water can be as much as 46 feet (the greatest in France); and since the sea recedes at low water some nine miles, the speed of the incoming tide is formidable, and most spectacular

—accompanied by flights of gulls it races in, from the distance appearing like a moving ribbon of white lace.

This is no place to relate in detail a history stretching over more than twelve and a half centuries, a history not only ecclesiastical but military, since the rock was early fortified and garrisoned—so well that though often besieged it was never once taken until 18 June 1940. The mediaeval *Roman d'Aquin* tells us that the Emperor Charlemagne, on an expedition against the rebellious Bretons, was a guest of the monastery. Each year the number of pilgrims increased, so that it might have appeared that Mont-St-Michel would rival the celebrated shrine of Santiago de Compostella. And this fact suggests the possibility of a most interesting link between these two centres of mediaeval pilgrimage. The armorial device of the abbey shows the *fleur-de-lys* and rows of cockle-shells, while the iconographical accompaniments of the Apostle St James the Great are the pilgrim's staff, a cockle-shell, a gourd, a scroll (or book) and a horn. From the thirteenth century at least the pilgrim was well known,

> By his cockle hat and staff
> And his sandal shoon.

One the face of it, it does seem more than likely that St James acquired his pictorial attributes not from the pilgrims to inland mountainous Compostella but from those who had visited the shrine of St Michael, where cockle-shells were plentiful, and the horn and staff were highly useful equipment, when crossing from dry land the quicksands which separate it from Mont-St-Michel-au-Péril-de-la-Mer. This stream of pilgrims dwindled, when from the ninth century these coasts became the scene of devastating incursions from Scandinavian pirates; but the security offered by this sanctuary watched over by the Archangel Michael brought a number of refugees from neighbouring districts, who founded the town at the foot of the rock.

The Norman dukes held Mont-St-Michel in high favour, Rollo making generous reparation to the abbey for the Vikings' ravages; and in 966 Richard I replaced the canons, whose rule had become lax with the years, by members of the Benedictine Order from Fontenelle-St-Wandrille. It was in 1017 that his son Richard II, 'the Good', whose marriage with Judith of Brittany had been celebrated with great pomp on the Mount, helped to defray the expenses required to carry out the immense constructional work which Abbot Hildebert had planned and set in motion. This was nothing less than the building of a great romanesque abbey on the summit of the Mount, raising it on a platform supported at the west end by the crypt formed by the old Carolingian church of Notre-Dame-sous-Terre. The Crypte de l'Aquilon was not built until after a fire of 1112. Under the remarkable Robert de Torigny, who became abbot in 1154, began a cultural renaissance, both intellectual and architectural. In 1203, after the Bretons had burnt the town and that part of the monastery adjoining it, Abbot Jourdain planned new monastic buildings to replace and amplify those that had been destroyed, and started work on the lowest storey (the Cellier and Aumônerie) of what was to be one of the finest examples of thirteenth-century architecture in France, known almost from the out-set as the *Merveille*. Succeeding abbots continued to carry out the original plans, thus preserving its splendid unity: Ranulphe des Isles (1212–18), who built the second storey, the Salle des Hôtes and the Salle des Chevaliers; Thomas des Chambres (1218–25), who worked on the third, the top storey of the Merveille, completing the Refectory and beginning the lovely Cloister. In 1228, the year of the canonisation of St Francis of Assisi, and just a quarter of a century after its inception, the Abbot, Raoul de Villedieu, saw the completion of the cloister, the crowning jewel on a work of masterly construction, which shows a consummate knowledge of the possibilities of masonry, and which is carried out with that architectural purity and delicacy which mark the gothic style of the early thirteenth century.

So rich a foundation demanded military protection; before 1257 Abbot Richard Turstin, the first abbot to be granted episcopal privi-leges by Pope Alexander IV, built the Belle Chaise (which includes the entrance and the Salle des Gardes) and the strong North Tower of the ramparts. At the outbreak of the Hundred Years' War the abbey was provided with a garrison, under a resident military governor. From 1356 the English occupied and fortified the island of Tombelaine; and henceforth, protracted over the course of nearly a century, the Mount was in a state of almost constant siege. In 1386 the Abbot Pierre le Roy built behind the Belle Chaise the tower that is called after him the Tour Perrine and subsequently, to protect further the Belle Chaise, he raised the imposing Châtelet, with its twin cylindrical towers, the entrance by which visitors to the abbey pass today. Finally, Abbot Robert Jolivet, who in 1423 turned traitor to the English, constructed the line of solid curtain walls and bastions which form the ramparts on the east side of the Mount, from the Tour du Nord right round to the Tour du Roi near the entrance to the town. In 1434, only four years after the death of Joan of Arc, the English mounted their greatest, and last, attack, throwing 8,000 men against the town and abbey—all in vain; the glory of the defence lay with the Governor Louis d'Estouteville and his band of 119 knights. Two English culverin, or bombards, trophies of the French victory, remain today to adorn the Cour de l'Avancée.

In 1421, while the English were threatening without, the great romanesque choir of the abbey came crashing down; and then, with the return of peace, the Cardinal-Abbot Guillaume d'Estouteville, Louis' brother, set about building the Crypte des Gros Piliers, that was to serve as foundation for the magnificent flamboyant gothic choir, which was continued and brought to completion under the two brothers, abbots in succession, Guillaume and Jean de Lamps. In 1520 work was finished, and all this building over so many centuries was brought to its triumphant conclusion. The timing was fortunate, since at the advent of François Ier to the French throne—he visited the abbey in 1518—the disastrous practice was introduced of appointing commendatory abbots, who enjoyed the princely revenues of the monastery, but did little or nothing to carry on its religious, intellectual and charitable functions. Decadence was from this time rapid—the town and abbey suffering much during the Wars of Religion, particularly from the Huguenot attack of 1591; and it continued until the coming in 1622 of monks of the reformed Benedictine Order of St-Maur. These monks, although they possessed illustrious theologians and historians among their members (such as Dom Jean Huynes and Dom Thomas Le Roy), were unaware or oblivious of the beauty of the architecture around them, making alterations which were nothing short of acts of vandalism—and neglecting structural repairs. It is strange to think that such a fine architect as Guillaume de la Tremblaye was one of their Order. At the outbreak of the Revolution the commendatory abbot was no less a person than Cardinal Louis-Joseph de Montmorency-Laval, Bishop of Metz and Grand Almoner of France. The revolutionaries had as little regard for the monks as they had for works of art (except that the latter had a realisable monetary value); the name of Mont-St-Michel was changed to that of Mont-Libre, and to inaugurate this new reign of liberty on the free mount, they cast out the monks and imprisoned there three hundred priests from neighbouring parishes. Prisoners had already been housed in the abbey's dungeons under *lettres de cachet* during the reigns of Louis XIV and XV; and these included the over-loquacious publicist Dubourg, who was brought to the Mount in 1745, and there locked in a narrowly constricting cage, where, despite the kindly attentions of the monks, he lost his reason, and died after a year of incarceration—as we are told, 'without repentance, and in despair, after having torn all his clothes'. Mont-St-Michel became a state prison, especially for political offenders, among them being Armand Barbès, the communistic revolutionary, who was injured and recaptured when in 1842 he let himself down from the terrace of the Saut-Gautier—the rope was too short and he fell to the rocks below.

In 1863 the prison was suppressed, largely from the insistence of Viollet-le-Duc and Mgr Dupanloup; but by this time decay and neglect had brought the abbey to a sadly ruinous condition. Two years later the monastery was rented by the Bishop of Coutances, first to house diocesan missionaries and later the Fathers of St Edmund of Pontigny. Then in 1874 the abbey and the ramparts of Mont-St-Michel were scheduled as *monuments historiques* and placed under the Ministry of Public Instruction and Fine Arts. Public opinion was roused not only to preserve this priceless heritage but to prevent the land-reclamation by speculators, who would have extended the *polders* right up to the island itself. In 1884, the year before his death, Victor Hugo appealed to his countrymen: 'Mont-St-Michel is for France what the Great Pyramid is for Egypt. It must be guarded from mutilation. It must remain an island. At whatever cost this double work of Nature and Art must be preserved.' A society was formed of well-wishers, the Association des Amis du Mont-St-Michel, which has done invaluable work in drawing official and public attention to what needed to be done, and what on no account was to be allowed in future—the erection, for example, of hideous modern buildings. Mont-St-Michel has been most fortunate in the succession of eminent architect-conservators—MM. Corroyer, Petigrand (who rebuilt in 1897 the steeple, and capped it with Frémiet's golden, perhaps a little florid, statue of the Archangel, which usefully serves also as a lightning-conductor), Paul Goût (the authority on the abbey's history), Pierre Paquet, Ernest Herpe. In 1931 the landscape architect M. Lotin laid out the abbey gardens above the monks' wood in a series of pleasant terraces and pathways from which the view over sea and coastlines is quite magnificent. In the Second World War Mont-St-Michel happily sustained no damage. From the 1870s the Benedictine Order has been represented on the Mount by the monks of Farnborough Abbey in Surrey.

From Pontorson the visitor approaches Mont-St-Michel by a cause-
way (*digue*), built in 1880 to the accompaniment of outraged protests
—a rather unworthy, if convenient, means of access—which finishes
between two towers in the ramparts, the Tour du Roi and the Tour de
l'Arcade. On the left, reached by a wooden footbridge, is the main
entrance to the town, the Porte de l'Avancée, which opens on to a small
court of the same name. At high tide boats can land their passengers
here, right in the court, which contains the sixteenth-century guard
room, the Corps de Garde des Bourgeois, and the captured English
culverin, known familiarly as the 'Michelettes'. A second opening leads
to the Barbican, and a further gateway, the machicolated Porte du
Roi, which, built in the fifteenth century, still retains its portcullis.
And here is the celebrated restaurant of Mère Poulard. The Poulards
are an old Montois family who for generations have had restaurants and
hotels at Mont-St-Michel.

From the Porte du Roi the narrow Grande Rue, lined with fifteenth-
and sixteenth-century houses, leads up, past the Maison de l'Arcade,
the parish church (its eleventh-century, but much restored, interior,
tenebrous and lit only by votive candles) and the so-called House of
Du Guesclin, to the entrance of the abbey. In spite of the tourists'
shops, this cobbled, slippery street, relieved at intervals by steps, can
recall, with some effort of the imagination, its mediaeval aspect, when
it was crowded with jostling pilgrims, who put up at inns with such
charming names as the Auberge de St-Michel, the Tête d'Or (now
Hotel Poulard), the Lycorne, the Pot de Cuivre, La Syrène, the
Quatre-Fils-Amyon, and (still existing, up by the abbey entrance) La
Truie qui File (The Spinning Sow), where the soldiers of the garrison
used to sit and drink. By a long flight of steps, the Grand Degré, we
reach the Châtelet, through which we enter the abbey buildings, and
from there an internal stairway, the Gouffre, brings us to the Salle des
Gardes. The escorted tour takes the visitors through such a maze of
apartments, stairs and conventual offices, at different levels and of
diverse periods of architecture, that it is advisable to take with one a
personal guide-book, such as the excellent Michelin *Guide Vert*. The
great abbey staircase, ascending between the abbey church on the
right and the abbot's buildings on the left, which are not yet restored
and open to the public, comes out on the platform known as the 'Saut-
Gautier'. The legend is that in the Middle Ages one Gaultier, to show
how much he cherished his beloved, cast himself from this spot and
was killed on the rocks below—one would imagine that he could

Mont-St-Michel

The front with the Grand Hotel, Cabourg (Proust's Balbec)

Mme Camembert

have thought up an equally convincing and less damaging proof of his love.

From here it is a short way to the Great West Platform, built above the dungeons and the Church of Notre-Dame-sous-Terre, the area being once partly covered by the western three bays of the romanesque church, which (become dangerous) was demolished in 1780 and the present unfortunate façade erected. It is but a step from here to the cloister, one of the most beautiful of its kind in existence, a hanging garden hung between blue sky and sea, surrounded by slender double arcading in quincunx, which is decorated in the spandrels and under the cornice with exquisite carving of fruit and foliage—all a jewel of early French gothic. In considering the constructional problems presented to the architects of the Merveille and their magnificently successful solutions, it must be remembered that we are standing here on the covering of the vast Salle des Chevaliers, which itself is built over the vaults of the Cellier. This Hall of the Knights is also regarded as one of the best examples of large room of its period—'perhaps the finest gothic chamber in the world', it has been called. There in 1469 King Louis XI assembled a chapter of his knights of the Order of St Michael, which he had founded. When we pass into the beautifully austere refectory, with its barrel-vaulted ceiling of wood and the bright illumination proceeding from its high, narrow lancet windows, we will also recall that this is built on the vaulting of the majestic Salle de Hôtes, which in turn rests on the Aumônerie, the offices of the monk-almoner, who in the middle ages dispensed here the abbey's charity to the travel-worn pilgrims.

Mont-St-Michel is a splendid repository of architectural styles from the tenth to the fifteenth centuries, placed in a setting of great natural beauty, and enhanced by our knowledge of its history, where the events which have made most noise are not those of most significance; the roar of the 'Michelettes' and the clamour of revolutionaries are valued less than the patient chipping of masons' mallets, or the tinkling of altar bells. Count Jean de La Varende has expressed the effect which it produces in the visitor: 'the eyes, the mind, the heart belong to the architecture, the constructions seize you and hold you, and will not let you go'. And if we think of this architecture in its entirety—the massive masonry of the period of Norman romanesque (like the nave and transepts), or of the gothic of all periods, with their flying buttresses, ogival arches, arcades and stairways, all carved in a delicate, sharp-cut efflorescence of stone—then Mont-St-Michel gives us a double

H

pleasure, which derives from the perfect fusion here of the utilitarian, the functional, with the freest expression of the aesthetic imagination. In speaking of the fifteenth-century choir, Paul Goût, that most erudite of the abbey's architect-conservators, voices the view that its real interest and value lie not so much in its decorative excellence but 'in the impression of power and the expressive clarity of the general conception'. By the time that the Norman builders of the romanesque church had advanced in their knowledge of the methods necessary to meet the thrusts and pressures of the developing gothic of the Ile-de-France, they were acquiring, had already acquired (in Goût's words), '*une impeccable prévoyance*', so that they worked with 'clear thought, a sure hand, a perfected experience'; and, one may add, with a consummate sense of balance, of form and proportion, and of exquisite decorative relief. These are qualities which, like Mont-St-Michel itself, are not the possessions of just Normandy alone, but of all France.

BIBLIOGRAPHY

BARBEY D'AUREVILLY, A.-J., *Œuvres*, Paris
BELLFIELD, E. and ESSAME, H., *The Battle for Normandy*, London, 1965
BLANCHE, J.-E., *More Portraits of a Lifetime*, London, 1939
BOSQUET, A., *La Normandie romanesque et merveilleuse*, Paris, 1844
BRODERICK, A. H., *Normandy*, London, 1947
BROUARD, M. de (editor), *Histoire de la Normandie*, Toulouse, 1970
CANU, J., *Barbey d'Aurevilly*, Paris, 1945
CHIROL, P., *Cathédrales et Eglises Normandes*, Rouen, 1936
DAVID, E., *French Provincial Cooking*, London, 1960
FLAUBERT, G., *Works*
GOÛT, P., *Tourist's Guide to Mont-St-Michel*, Paris, 1926
HASKINS, C. H., *The Normans in European History*, Boston and New York, 1915
HAYDON, B. R., *Autobiography and Journals*, London, 1950
HERRIOT, E., *Amid the Forests of Normandy*, London, 1926
HÉRUBEL and OTHERS, *Visages de Normandie*, Paris, 1949
HERVAL, R., *Les Veritables Origines de 'Madame Bovary'*, Paris, 1957
— *Normandie*, Paris, 1971
IGNOTUS, P., *The Paradox of Maupassant*, London
JACKSON, S., *Guy de Maupassant*, London, 1938
LA VARENDE, COMTE DE, J. B. M. M., *Flaubert par lui-même*, Paris, 1961
— *Grands Normands*, Rouen, 1939
— *Nez-de-Cuir*, Paris
— *Pays d'Ouche*, 1936
MAUPASSANT, G. DE, *Works*
MUSGROVE, G. M., *A Ramble through Normandy*, London, 1855
MUSSET, L., *Normandie Romane, Basse-Normandie*, 1967
NEWNHAM-DAVIES, LT-COL., *The Gourmet's Guide to Europe*, London, 1911
PERKINS, J., *The Cathedrals of Normandy*, London, 1935
POMMIER, A., and OTHERS, *Normandie*, Paris, 1946
PROUST, M., *Remembrance of Things Past*, trans. C. K. Scott-Moncrieff, London, 1960
ROGERS, B. G., *Barbey d'Aurevilly*, Geneva, 1967
SAINTE-BEUVE, C.-A., *Œuvres*, Paris
SAINTE-PIERRE, M. DE, preface to *Merveilles des châteaux de Normandie*, Paris, 1966
SPENCER, P., *Flaubert*, London, 1952
TURNER, J. F., *Invasion '44*, London, 1959

Index

Compiled by Valerie Lewis Chandler, B.A., A.L.A.A.